T0345057

The Roles of Immigrants and Foreign Students in US Science, Innovation, and Entrepreneurship

A National Bureau of
Economic Research
Conference Report

The Roles of Immigrants and Foreign Students in US Science, Innovation, and Entrepreneurship

Edited by **Ina Ganguli, Shulamit Kahn, and Megan MacGarvie**

The University of Chicago Press

Chicago and London

The University of Chicago Press, Chicago 60637
The University of Chicago Press, Ltd., London
© 2020 by the National Bureau of Economic Research, Inc.
Published 2020
Printed in the United States of America

29 28 27 26 25 24 23 22 21 20   1 2 3 4 5

ISBN-13: 978-0-226-69562-4   (cloth)
ISBN-13: 978-0-226-69576-1   (e-book)
DOI: https://doi.org/10.7208/chicago/9780226695761.001.0001

Library of Congress Cataloging-in-Publication Data
Names: Ganguli, Ina, editor. | Kahn, Shulamit Beth, editor. |
    MacGarvie, Megan, editor.
Title: The roles of immigrants and foreign students in US science,
    innovation, and entrepreneurship / [edited by] Ina Ganguli, Shulamit
    Kahn, Megan MacGarvie.
Other titles: NBER conference report.
Description: Chicago ; London : University of Chicago Press, 2020. |
    Series: A National Bureau of Economic Research conference report |
    Includes bibliographical references and index.
Identifiers: LCCN 2019029999 | ISBN 9780226695624 (cloth) |
    ISBN 9780226695761 (ebook)
Subjects: LCSH: Skilled labor—Economic aspects—United States—
    Congresses. | Students, Foreign—United States—Congresses. |
    Foreign workers—United States—Congresses. | Immigrants—
    United States—Congresses. | Technological innovations—
    Demographic aspects—United States—Congresses. | Science
    and industry—United States—Congresses. | Entrepreneurship—
    United States—Congresses. | United States—Emigration and
    immigration—Economic aspects—Congresses. | United States—
    Emigration and immigration—Government policy—Congresses. |
    LCGFT: Conference papers and proceedings.
Classification: LCC JV6471 .R65 2020 | DDC 331.6/20973—dc23
LC record available at https://lccn.loc.gov/2019029999

♾ This paper meets the requirements of ANSI/NISO Z39.48-1992
(Permanence of Paper).

Relation of the Directors to the
Work and Publications of the
National Bureau of Economic Research

1. The object of the NBER is to ascertain and present to the economics profession, and to the public more generally, important economic facts and their interpretation in a scientific manner without policy recommendations. The Board of Directors is charged with the responsibility of ensuring that the work of the NBER is carried on in strict conformity with this object.

2. The President shall establish an internal review process to ensure that book manuscripts proposed for publication DO NOT contain policy recommendations. This shall apply both to the proceedings of conferences and to manuscripts by a single author or by one or more co-authors but shall not apply to authors of comments at NBER conferences who are not NBER affiliates.

3. No book manuscript reporting research shall be published by the NBER until the President has sent to each member of the Board a notice that a manuscript is recommended for publication and that in the President's opinion it is suitable for publication in accordance with the above principles of the NBER. Such notification will include a table of contents and an abstract or summary of the manuscript's content, a list of contributors if applicable, and a response form for use by Directors who desire a copy of the manuscript for review. Each manuscript shall contain a summary drawing attention to the nature and treatment of the problem studied and the main conclusions reached.

4. No volume shall be published until forty-five days have elapsed from the above notification of intention to publish it. During this period a copy shall be sent to any Director requesting it, and if any Director objects to publication on the grounds that the manuscript contains policy recommendations, the objection will be presented to the author(s) or editor(s). In case of dispute, all members of the Board shall be notified, and the President shall appoint an ad hoc committee of the Board to decide the matter; thirty days additional shall be granted for this purpose.

5. The President shall present annually to the Board a report describing the internal manuscript review process, any objections made by Directors before publication or by anyone after publication, any disputes about such matters, and how they were handled.

6. Publications of the NBER issued for informational purposes concerning the work of the Bureau, or issued to inform the public of the activities at the Bureau, including but not limited to the NBER Digest and Reporter, shall be consistent with the object stated in paragraph 1. They shall contain a specific disclaimer noting that they have not passed through the review procedures required in this resolution. The Executive Committee of the Board is charged with the review of all such publications from time to time.

7. NBER working papers and manuscripts distributed on the Bureau's web site are not deemed to be publications for the purpose of this resolution, but they shall be consistent with the object stated in paragraph 1. Working papers shall contain a specific disclaimer noting that they have not passed through the review procedures required in this resolution. The NBER's web site shall contain a similar disclaimer. The President shall establish an internal review process to ensure that the working papers and the web site do not contain policy recommendations, and shall report annually to the Board on this process and any concerns raised in connection with it.

8. Unless otherwise determined by the Board or exempted by the terms of paragraphs 6 and 7, a copy of this resolution shall be printed in each NBER publication as described in paragraph 2 above.

Contents

Acknowledgments

This volume emerged from a workshop held in Cambridge, Massachusetts, organized by the National Bureau of Economic Research (NBER) on April 27, 2018. Funding for the workshop was provided by the National Science Foundation Science of Science and Innovation Policy Program (award #1745164). Funding for a preconference and the conference volume was provided by the Ewing Marion Kauffman Foundation through its support of entrepreneurship research at the NBER. The conference and volume would not have been possible without the support of Maryann Feldman, Josh Lerner, and Jim Poterba. Richard Freeman and William Kerr were invaluable in helping select the papers for the conference and providing helpful feedback to authors. We are also grateful to Helena Fitz-Patrick, Denis Healy, Alison Oaxaca, Rob Shannon, and especially Carl Beck for administrative and organizational support. We thank discussants Thomas Åstebro, Prithwiraj Choudhury, Patricia Cortes, Delia Furtado, Jennifer Hunt, Anne Le Brun, Sarah Turner, and Bruce Weinberg, as well as panelists Aman Verjee, Ben Waber, and David Weil, for insightful and provocative discussions and comments.

Introduction

Ina Ganguli, Shulamit Kahn, and Megan MacGarvie

Understanding labor markets for workers with specialized training in science, technology, engineering, and mathematics (STEM) is essential for learning about the drivers of innovation and economic growth, yet these labor markets are complex, and their dynamics are not fully understood by economists. Recent decades have seen increasingly important roles for the foreign-born in the US STEM workforce and among recipients of advanced degrees at US universities. Given the potential for STEM workers to contribute to the economic growth and continued prosperity of the United States and in the context of the current public debate about immigration, it is important that policies affecting the supply of these workers be based on careful analysis. There is a pressing need for evidence and consensus-building on the economic impacts of immigration on the STEM workforce and innovation, and this volume aims to contribute to this evidence by highlighting recent research.

The chapters in this volume address three main themes related to the overarching question of how immigrants affect innovation in the US. The first theme focuses on the location choices of innovative workers, specifically inventors and foreign-born STEM doctoral recipients. Return migration of innovative workers is a subject on which there has been relatively little

Ina Ganguli is an associate professor of economics at the University of Massachusetts, Amherst.

Shulamit Kahn is an associate professor of markets, public policy, and law at the Questrom School of Business at Boston University.

Megan MacGarvie is an associate professor of markets, public policy, and law at the Questrom School of Business at Boston University and a research associate of the National Bureau of Economic Research.

For acknowledgments, sources of research support, and disclosure of the authors' material financial relationships, if any, please see https://www.nber.org/chapters/c14100.ack.

research to date but is increasingly important as the countries that have historically sent large numbers of STEM students and workers to the US become more attractive destinations for STEM careers. The chapters on this theme help us understand the implications of increases in return migration for innovation in the US.

The second theme is the relationship between immigration and innovation with regard to initial inflows of migrants rather than their return decisions. These chapters focus on how differences in the number of immigrants— driven by immigration policy—affect the rate of innovation among immigrants as well as natives and how this depends on the skill composition of immigrant flows.

Innovation often requires the inventors or their agents to become entrepreneurs in order to commercialize the innovation. Thus the third theme in this volume is the relationship between high-skilled immigration and entrepreneurship and contributions related to immigrant entrepreneur networks and contrasting immigrant and native PhDs' entrepreneurship.

The chapters on all three of these themes not only share a single focus— immigration and innovation—but also share a methodological commonality: the use of novel data sets and creative approaches to answering important questions. Research in this area has been limited by the fact that immigration, innovation, and entrepreneurship can all be difficult to measure using conventional data sources. The authors of chapters in this volume have all collected new data or are exploiting existing data in creative ways.

The following chapters collectively represent a significant advance in our understanding of immigration and innovation and contain provocative results that raise a new set of questions and point to directions for future research. Below we describe the findings of the chapters and the relationships between them and briefly discuss some of the open questions and fruitful areas for further research.

Location Choices of International Students and Return Migration

In several STEM fields, students of foreign origin represent the majority of PhD recipients in the US, and those who remain in the US after completing their studies make important contributions to US universities and firms. However, there is some indication that stay rates of PhD students from certain key countries may be falling. China and India are especially important as the first and second most common country of origin among STEM doctoral recipients in the US (representing 17.7 percent of all STEM PhD recipients in the 2016 National Science Foundation [NSF] Survey of Earned Doctorates), and the fraction of both Indian and Chinese STEM doctoral recipients reporting definite plans to stay in the US has fallen steadily since 2004 (NSF *Science and Engineering Indicators* 2018 appendix table 3-21). This raises several questions. One is whether the US can expect to continue to retain large numbers of graduates of foreign origin as the conditions for science in students' home countries improve. Another is whether those students leaving the US are positively or negatively selected on ability.

Prior research on return migration has been hampered by a lack of data, as data sets that track individuals across countries are rare and typically based on small samples.[1] Moreover, much of the prior research has focused on PhD scientists[2] and/or on scientists trained in the US despite the fact that there are many more highly skilled immigrant STEM workers with degrees below the PhD level and also many with degrees from outside the US. Chapter 1, by Breschi, Lissoni, and Miguelez, extends our understanding of stay rates for foreigners working in the US who hold degrees at any level of higher education, some of whom came to the US for education and others who came on employment-based visas. These authors have created a new data set of Indian inventors in the information, communications, and technology (ICT) sector compiled from the US Patent and Trademark Office (USPTO) PatentsView data repository matched to public LinkedIn profiles. Breschi et al. construct a panel of location information from the employment histories provided by the LinkedIn profiles. They find that employment-based immigrants have higher return rates than those who arrive to seek higher education and that there has been little change since 1990 in the percentage of employment-based migrants who return to India. However, they document an increase in recent decades in the propensity to return to India across cohorts of Indians who came to the US to study, increasing from 22 percent in 1990 to 24.7 percent in 2000.[3]

Breschi et al. also find evidence of negative selection of foreign students with US degrees returning to India based on the fact that Indians who have obtained master's or PhD degrees in the US are less likely to return home than those who have merely obtained bachelor's degrees in the US. Somewhat surprisingly, there is a slight positive association between the return hazard and the number of patents filed while in the US for work-based migrants. These results suggest the need for further research on selection and return migration, as prior studies have also found mixed results on the relationship between ability and return migration.[4]

1. E.g., Gaulé (2014), Gibson and McKenzie (2014), Kahn and MacGarvie (2016). The International Survey of Doctoral Recipients, which tracks doctoral recipients from US STEM programs over time even if they move internationally, has recently become available and will be a valuable resource for analyzing return migration.

2. E.g., Finn (2014), Grogger and Hanson (2015), and Kahn and MacGarvie (2016).

3. A striking increase in the return rate for the 2010 cohort may be unreliable due to the small number of observations (71) in that group but calls for further analysis in a larger sample to establish whether the actual return rate has increased substantially.

4. Borjas and Bratsberg (1996) model the decision to migrate, whether temporarily or permanently, as a function of expected earnings in the source and receiving countries, the potential migrant's skill/ability and returns to skill at home and abroad, and a random parameter. They find that as long as the returns to skill are higher in the receiving country, migrants come from the upper part of the ability distribution, and those who stay permanently in the receiving

An interesting related finding is seen in chapter 8 by Roach, Sauermann, and Skrentny. In their survey of more than 5,600 doctoral students from US STEM programs, Roach et al. find that although 42.2 percent of all respondents of foreign origin plan to remain in the US permanently, this number is only 17.4 percent for Chinese students. This finding, based on a survey sample, deserves further investigation in a larger data set, but it is striking because China is currently the largest sending country of international students to the US—particularly in fields such as computer science and engineering, in which salaries are high and the supply of native graduates is relatively scarce. Moreover, Roach et al. show that Chinese doctorates are more likely than native peers to express interest in founding a start-up and to prefer joining start-up businesses. To the extent that entrepreneurship is an engine of growth, the high percentage of Chinese students planning to eventually return home combined with their high preferences for entrepreneurship warrants further investigation.[5]

A different perspective on rates of return migration is offered in chapter 2 by Ganguli and Gaulé, who survey doctoral students in chemistry from US universities, obtaining data on 1,605 students at the top 54 research universities. Ganguli and Gaulé use a hypothetical choice method to determine preferences over different attributes of postdoctoral positions and find that international students have *stronger* preferences for remaining in the US for postdoctoral training than do domestic students. This difference persists after controlling for test scores and career preferences as well as the ranking of hypothetical postdoc institutions in the US and abroad. The survey, which was conducted in the fall of 2017, is one of the most recent estimates of the stay rate intentions of international students in the US since Roach et al.'s student survey was conducted in 2010. Their survey results seem to suggest that concerns about declining stay rates of foreign students may be misplaced (at least for the postdoctoral period).

Ganguli and Gaulé also find that international students have stronger preferences for academia (with an 11 percentage point higher probability of accepting a postdoc at a top university when compared to native students) and that this is true even after controlling for ability via GRE score and publications while in graduate school. This stands in contrast to Roach et al., who find no difference between native and foreign students in the tendency to prefer academia but a stronger preference for entrepreneurship among

country will be those with the highest ability. Using the admittedly imperfect proxy for ability of rank of a student's graduate program, Grogger and Hanson (2015) find that doctoral recipients from the top graduate programs are less likely to have plans to leave the US at graduation, but Brentschneider and Dai (2017) and Kahn and MacGarvie (2018) find no relationship between the rank of the graduate program and actual propensity to remain in the US.

5. In a related study focused specifically on the return intentions of Chinese students abroad, Zeithammer and Kellogg (2013) find that approximately 70 percent of Chinese STEM PhDs would prefer to return to China if offered a salary equal to what they expect to receive in the US but that salary differentials between the US and China keep the majority in the US.

international students. The difference may be related to the fact that Ganguli and Gaulé survey recent doctorates about their plans for postdoctoral study, while Roach et al. survey PhDs about career plans over a longer time horizon. The differences between preferred stay rates from these two chapters call for more research into the career trajectories of US-trained STEM PhDs of foreign origin.

The chapters on this theme raise new questions that may be fruitful topics for ongoing research. One of these is if the stay rates of Chinese and Indian graduates fall, which other countries will take their places as the main sending countries of PhD students who remain in the US to work after graduation? Or will wages rise and draw more native students into STEM fields?

Additionally, if international students stay for postdocs and then go back to their home countries, what are the impacts on US researchers with whom they formed connections during their stay in the US? Will these networks persist over time and give US scientists access to collaborations and new knowledge and innovations being developed abroad?

Finally, given the variety of results about selection and return rates in the prior literature, how can we better measure the ability of students, inventors, and entrepreneurs in order to understand selection effects, as existing data can be coarse (education levels) or may be unreliable if self-reported through surveys?

The next section of this volume addresses the relationship between overall immigration *policy* and innovation. However, a question left unanswered relates policies to the location decisions. How does immigration *policy* affect the stay versus return location decisions of the highly skilled foreign-born who enter the US either as PhD students or on employment-based visas? Also, how do policies that affect the stay versus return decisions of the highly skilled in turn affect future entrepreneurship in the US and in home countries (see the final section of this volume)? All of these relationships remain to be established.

Immigration Policy and Innovation

Immigration and visa policies can have wide-ranging and complex impacts, including effects on innovation. Three chapters in this volume discuss impacts of two immigration policies—one current and one historical—that targeted specific subgroups of immigrants: (1) H-1B visa programs intended to use noncitizens to fill a temporary need for skilled employees and (2) historical quotas aimed at limiting the number of immigrants from particular less-industrialized countries. The main thrust of these chapters is not to comment on the policies themselves but to use them to trace the impact of different kinds of immigration on US innovation.

Prior research (e.g., Hunt and Gauthier-Loiselle 2010; Kerr and Lincoln 2010) has looked at the relationship between immigration and patenting, but a common critique of such research is that patents only capture the tip of the iceberg, since many innovations are not patented. Khanna and Lee's contribution to this volume (chapter 3) begins to address this lacuna. Khanna and Lee ask how employees on (temporary) H-1B visas contribute to consumer product innovations, measuring innovations as whether a company introduces a new retail product and/or takes an existing product off the market. This kind of product innovation—which they call product reallocation—is typically not related to a patent. Instead, Khanna and Lee's measure is more likely to pick up small, incremental innovations being put to commercial use. It is also one of the only analyses of the impact of skilled immigration on consumer markets.[6]

Since the innovations can be as small as a change in packaging size, one might think that these product reallocations are unlikely to be correlated with the firm's profitability. However, Khanna and Lee show otherwise: these reallocations are highly correlated with revenue growth in the following year. Khanna and Lee then link these innovations to measures of the company's propensity to employ H-1B immigrants, which they measure using the Department of Labor's labor condition applications (LCAs) for H-1B visas, which have been used by others as a proxy for H-1Bs.[7] Khanna and Lee acknowledge that LCAs are more likely to be measuring a *tendency* to use H-1Bs rather than actual H-1Bs employees, since not all Department of Labor–certified H-1B requests are granted by the US Citizenship and Immigration Services Bureau (USCIS; Mayda et al. [chapter 4 in this volume] have obtained data on H-1Bs actually granted). Nevertheless, the relationship between H-1B certifications and product innovation is substantial.[8] This association may not be a causal effect of H-1Bs. For instance, firms wanting to hire H-1Bs may be particularly proactive in pursuing continual change and/or cutting-edge data analytics. However, results on the timing of the effect are at least highly suggestive of a causal effect of H-1Bs on innovation and thus of a possible role that highly skilled temporary immigrants may have in the retail product market.

In chapter 4 in this volume, about H-1B workers, Mayda, Ortega, Peri, Shih, and Sparber have obtained—via Freedom of Information Act (FOIA) requests—data on actual approved H-1Bs instead of using more easily available LCA data. Thus their data represent actual temporary residents rather than temporary visas applied for. This alone is a substantial advance.

Although using quite different data, some of the Mayda et al. results on H-1Bs—while not related to consumer product markets or innovations—

---

6. One other is Cortes (2008) on the effect of low-skilled immigrants on the prices of household services.

7. For instance, see Kerr and Lincoln (2010) and Ghosh et al. (2014).

8. For instance, controlling for firm and year, using their results, we calculate that a one percentage point increase in the share of certifications (as a percent of employment) is associated with a 22 percent increase in the reallocation rate.

confirm some of Khanna and Lee's findings. Similarities between Mayda et al. and Khanna and Lee include (1) their near-identical estimates that 42 percent to 44 percent of publicly traded companies have at least one H-1B employee; (2) that—among publicly traded firms—higher-revenue firms and larger firms were more likely to utilize H-1Bs; and (3) that there is greater revenue growth in firms with more (new) H-1Bs. They also agree on the prevalent occupational categories of H-1Bs.

Mayda et al. advance what we know about H-1B employees in other ways as well. In their analysis not limited to publicly traded companies, Mayda et al. find increasing concentrations of H-1Bs in a few companies and a few metropolitan areas, which they attribute to the rise of business, IT, and scientific services firms. Their findings on the growth and patterns of H-1B use in these services firms over 13 years are an important contribution to our understanding of how highly skilled temporary immigrants are used in our economy. An important focus of future research should be whether the growth of business, IT, and scientific services firms partially enabled by H-1Bs fundamentally changes US economic innovation and growth and the careers of highly skilled natives.

A final chapter related to immigration policy—chapter 5 by Doran and Yoon—addresses the impacts of the immigration quotas of 1924. This law radically decreased immigration, particularly of low-skilled immigrants from Southern Europe. There are several other contemporaneous articles (mostly working papers) on these quotas, each concentrating on different aspects of possible impacts. Doran and Yoon's chapter starts with a detailed synthesis of this mostly unpublished work. It then applies this quota change to understand how immigration's impact on innovation depends on language commonalities between immigrants and people currently living in a given city. Language commonalities are differentiated from ethnic similarities insofar as foreign-language persistence across generations differed from city to city.

Doran and Yoon find a U-shaped pattern. Innovation is most stimulated by (low-skilled) immigrants arriving in a city if the existing population and the immigrants are somewhat close linguistically (i.e., the distributions of languages in the two populations are not too dissimilar). However, innovation is not stimulated at the extremes, among those who are either linguistically far or linguistically close, and in fact there might be a negative impact on innovation when new immigrants are linguistically far. Note that this innovation is not innovation by the new immigrants but rather innovation by residents of the city who had already been inventors before the quota policy change. The mechanism behind these results is uncertain. The authors argue that perhaps linguistic diversity increases the diversity of ideas and experiences that people communicate to each other, but only if people are still able to somehow communicate with each other. So the optimal amount of linguistic diversity is at neither extreme.

Overall, both policies allowing increased temporary immigration of highly skilled workers through H-1Bs and those decreasing unskilled immigration to particular cities provided the authors with exogenous variation to address the complex interactions between innovation and immigration. In all three chapters, immigrants (at different skill levels and in different historical eras) increased innovation within existing firms and innovations by natives. They also may have contributed to the growth of business and scientific services firms that provide a flexible scientific workforce that can be deployed where needed.

Doran and Yoon provide an intriguing historical study that points toward the need for more research on whether and how inflows of unskilled immigrants may affect innovation in the present day. For example, Cortes and Tessada (2011) show that increases in unskilled immigration increase the labor supply of highly skilled women. Peri and Sparber (2009) demonstrate that unskilled immigration causes natives to specialize in more communication-intensive tasks. Do Doran and Yoon's findings extend to innovation and/or entrepreneurship today? Or are the results in their chapter specific to the historical context? Moreover, is the complementarity between skilled natives and unskilled immigrants documented by Doran and Yoon also a relevant phenomenon for more-skilled immigrants (e.g., H-1B recipients)?

A similar question relates to the other two chapters on immigration policy. To what extent was the growth in business/scientific/IT services firms in recent decades a direct result of the hiring of larger numbers of temporary workers documented by Mayda et al.? And does this joint growth in business services and temporary residents enable companies that hire IT outsourcing firms to be more innovative and/or enable the creation of new STEM entrepreneurial ventures? Khanna and Lee's findings suggest that this may be the case, but additional research is needed to document this more comprehensively.

Immigration and Entrepreneurship

Our understanding of immigration's relationship to entrepreneurship is hampered by a lack of entrepreneurship data. Immigrants have been shown to be disproportionately represented among entrepreneurs, especially in the high-tech sector, thus making important contributions to innovation and economic growth. Fairlie and Lofstrom (2015) and others have documented that immigrant and foreign workers are more likely than US natives to become entrepreneurs in technology and science-based businesses. Kahn, La Mattina, and MacGarvie (2017) found using the Scientists and Engineers Statistical Data System (SESTAT) data that the foreign-born are about twice as likely as nonimmigrants to be engaged in science-based entrepreneurship. Immigrant-founded businesses also appear to be more successful than native-founded ones: Kerr and Kerr (2016) use the Longitudinal Employer-Household Dynamics (LEHD) database to show that immigrant-founded new businesses grow faster than those founded by natives. However, many of these studies lack complete data on immigrant characteristics, so the question remains: Are immigrants really more entrepreneurial and innovative? If so, is this because they differ from natives in terms of previously unobservable characteristics positively correlated with entrepreneurship? Which characteristics matter most for explaining the immigrant entrepreneurship premium?

Several chapters in this volume seek to address the ways that immigrants and native entrepreneurs differ in the high-tech and science-based business sectors, providing important new insights by documenting significant differences on several dimensions between immigrant and native entrepreneurs. The chapters in this volume significantly contribute to this literature by analyzing rich new data sets on immigrant entrepreneurship.

Chapter 6 by Brown et al. links entrepreneurship to innovation by asking whether there is an immigrant "advantage" among entrepreneurs and business owners in terms of innovation performance measures, particularly in the key area for economic growth of the high-tech sector. This chapter sheds new light on the differences in innovation performance between immigrant- and native-owned firms in the high-tech sector with a much larger database of businesses than has been used in the past. Using the Annual Survey of Entrepreneurs (ASE), a new database from the US Census Bureau, Brown et al. are able to access data on 11,000 owners of 7,400 high-tech employer businesses based on a random sample of all nonfarm businesses. Importantly, these data allow the authors to draw on rich measures of innovation activities in the firms, which make up the main outcomes of interest. While previous research has studied the role of immigrants in the high-tech sector as inventors, employees, or individual entrepreneurs, less attention has been focused on immigrant-owned firms in this sector.

A key contribution of this chapter is using multiple measures of innovation performance by firms, including measures related to product and process innovation, research and development (R&D), and intellectual property. Among their main findings are that—across the board—there are higher rates of innovation in immigrant-owned firms than in native-owned firms in all of these measures. However, in many cases, some of these differences are no longer significant after including controls, especially when accounting for differences between immigrant and native owners in terms of motivation for entrepreneurship, levels of start-up capital, and choices of industry. Higher immigrant motivation for entrepreneurship has been documented by others (including Roach et al., chapter 8 in this volume, discussed below), as have differences in field of study (e.g., see Hunt 2011), and this confirmation of their direct impact on immigrant entrepreneurship is extremely valuable.

The identification of higher levels of start-up capital of immigrant high-tech entrepreneurs as important is both novel and intriguing. This suggests that research into this difference may be a fruitful area for further investigation.

Brown et al. also examine whether the immigrant advantage in innovation varies by education, firm age, and race/ethnicity. While they do not find that this advantage varies by firm age or race/ethnicity, they do find that across the measures, immigrants tend to be more innovative than natives, particularly among owners with less than a bachelor's degree, although even this immigrant-native difference is not significant at standard levels.

Brown et al.'s findings point to important dimensions along which immigrant and native business owners differ and suggest that immigrants may be contributing disproportionately to innovation activities in the US economy. The chapter also raises a set of questions for further research. For example, given the interest in the impact of diversity on innovation (see, e.g., Doran and Yoon, chapter 5 in this volume), do firms with both an immigrant and a native owner have different innovation performance relative to only-immigrant-owned or only-native-owned firms? Also, since the innovation measures are self-reported by firms, are there differences in the accuracy of responses among immigrant and native firms?

Many entrepreneurship scholars have documented the importance of networks for firm performance, yet few papers differentiate between immigrant and native entrepreneurs and ask how their networking behaviors may differ. Chapter 7 by Kerr and Kerr contributes to this literature by examining the networking of immigrant versus native entrepreneurs in a particularly active entrepreneurial context—the CIC (formerly the Cambridge Innovation Center), a technology coworking space that has become the de facto epicenter of the Boston entrepreneurial and innovation ecosystem.

Kerr and Kerr use unique survey data for 1,222 entrepreneurs collected in CIC's three locations in the Boston area and in the first expansion location in St. Louis. They examine three types of questions about networking opportunities asked in the survey: (1) about self-reported perceptions of CIC networking benefits, (2) about the types of networks—including where they networked at CIC—and finally (3) about how often they asked for or received advice external to the firm.

They find that immigrants report higher perceptions of CIC helping their business via networking than natives and also find that immigrants report higher rates of exchanging advice. These results are robust to including many controls. While the size of the immigrants' networks is slightly larger than natives', the difference is not statistically significant.

This chapter opens up a range of further questions and points to the need to collect new sources of data related to the networking behavior of immigrant entrepreneurs. Further data could answer questions such as the following: Do similar patterns hold outside of the CIC setting? How do these differences in networking affect the longer-run performance of the firms, which might be addressed by linking survey data on networking and/ or networking data from sources such as LinkedIn to the actual performance outcomes of the firms?

The final chapter, by Roach et al., examines differences in the extent to which immigrants join start-ups as employees rather than as founders. Examining differences among immigrants and natives in their preferences and actual employment to become entrepreneurial "joiners" has been understudied in the entrepreneurship literature despite their important role—especially in the high-tech sector. As discussed previously, Roach et al. provide evidence on the entrepreneurial preferences and outcomes of natives and immigrants using a unique survey data set of 5,600 STEM doctoral students at US research universities. They then resurvey these students after graduation, which allows them to observe ex-ante preferences typically unobserved by the econometrician. Strikingly, Roach et al. find that while foreign PhD students were more likely than natives to intend to become founders or join a start-up during graduate school, after graduation, of the more than 2,300 working in their first jobs in a US industry in an R&D position, foreign PhDs are *less* likely than natives to either become founders or join start-ups as employees and instead are more likely to work in established firms.

This evidence is important in showing that foreign PhD students have entrepreneurial preferences different from those of native students while in graduate school, which suggests that some of the differences between immigrant and native entrepreneurs in the high-tech sector documented by other scholars—including Brown et al. (chapter 6) and Kerr and Kerr (chapter 7) in this volume—may be related to differences in preferences and intentions observed even earlier during graduate studies. The findings also underscore the important point related to many of the chapters in this volume—that some of the differences observed between immigrant and native students in terms of career preferences and outcomes may be driven by the nature of the selection into immigration and into doing a PhD. In this case, the differences between foreign versus native students in characteristics and preferences documented by Roach et al., such as differences in the tolerance for risk and subjective ability, may explain some of the differences in entrepreneurial preferences. For example, as they note, it may be that the foreign-born who come to the US are less risk averse and are of higher ability than other individuals who do not immigrate, resulting in higher-than-average levels of risk tolerance and ability levels among foreign PhDs. On the other hand, there could also be a different kind of selection among *natives* who decide to do a PhD if those who are more interested in entrepreneurship do not decide to do a PhD. These selection effects could explain part of the observed differences in preferences for being a founder or start-up employee among foreign and native students while they are still in school.

However, Roach et al.'s striking finding that the foreign PhDs are subsequently less likely to pursue their preferred career paths suggests that there are other factors, such as visa policies or economic conditions, that may be differentially impacting the career choices of foreign and US students. As the authors note, foreign PhDs with founder intentions may be required to seek employment in an established firm rather than start their own company in order to obtain a work visa first. An important caveat is that the Roach et al. sample surveyed in the follow-up survey only includes those individuals who stayed in the US and those individuals whose first position was in industry, so we do not know from these results how *ex-ante* preferences are related to career paths not included in their analysis (in academia or in industry positions abroad).

Thus an open question stimulated by both Roach et al. (chapter 8) and Ganguli and Gaulé (chapter 2) is whether visa policies influence preferences during the PhD as well as postgraduation innovation and entrepreneurship outcomes.

Another open question relates to chapter 6 by Brown et al. and chapter 7 by Kerr and Kerr, as well as chapter 5 by Doran and Yoon regarding interactions between foreign-born and native entrepreneurs. That is, how do collaboration and connections among the foreign-born and natives influence entrepreneurship and innovation activities?

Conclusion

This book offers new information about the many linkages among highly skilled immigrants, innovation, and entrepreneurship. The chapters are grouped according to the themes of return migration, immigration policy, and entrepreneurship. Several links among these themes are apparent. First, several of the chapters have developed new, detailed measures—quite different from those typically used—of both innovation and entrepreneurship and have studied how immigrants and natives differ along these measures. Second, many of the chapters also address *why* rates of innovation and entrepreneurship are different for immigrants and natives—due to preferences and motivations, fields of study or employment, selection of who comes and who remains in the US, and perhaps the increased nimbleness of an enlarged business/IT services sector flexibly staffed by temporary residents. Also, two chapters (3 by Khanna and Lee and 4 by Mayda et al.) suggest that the innovation of immigrants translates into revenue growth.

This volume also shows the key role played by immigrants' networks—from today's high-tech entrepreneurs to the historical importance of language similarities in the context of early 20th-century immigration quotas. Finally, we learn about the important and interrelated roles of the US higher education system and visa policy for attracting and retaining highly skilled foreigners and making it possible for them to engage in entrepreneurial activities. Perhaps the single most important commonality across the three themes of the volume—even when it is not always the explicit focus of the chapter—is the crucial role of immigration policy in shaping innovation in the US. The ease of obtaining work visas after graduation for highly skilled STEM PhDs may affect their location choices as well as what type of job to accept if they stay, and the number and composition of immigrants admitted shapes the direction of innovation and entrepreneurship in the US.

Together, the chapters in this volume make important contributions to our understanding of immigration, innovation, and entrepreneurship. Of course, many questions remain unanswered, and in this introduction we have tried to highlight some of the new questions provoked by the findings contained in this volume. We hope that researchers will be stimulated to seek answers to these questions.

References

Borjas, George, and Bernt Bratsberg. 1996. "The Outmigration of the Foreign-Born." *Review of Economics and Statistics* 78 (1): 165–75.

Brentschneider, Stuart, and Yiqun Dai. 2017. "Why Do Foreign Citizens with US Ph.D. Degrees Return Home?" Working Paper.

Cortes, Patricia. 2008. "The Effect of Low-Skilled Immigration on U.S. Prices: Evidence from CPI Data." *Journal of Political Economy* 116 (3): 381–422.

Cortes, Patricia, and José Tessada. 2011. "Low-Skilled Immigration and the Labor Supply of Highly Skilled Women." *American Economic Journal: Applied Economics* 3 (3): 88–123.

Fairlie, Robert W., and Magnus Lofstrom. 2015. "Immigration and Entrepreneurship." CESIFO Working Paper no. 5298.

Finn, Michael. 2014. "Stay Rates of Foreign Doctorate Recipients from U.S. Universities, 2011." Oak Ridge Institute for Science and Education Working Paper. Accessed December 30, 2017. https://pdfs.semanticscholar.org/7a4c/49e7878730b587201548338aa6052e2401b7.pdf.

Gaulé, Patrick. 2014. "Who Comes Back and When? Return Migration Decisions of Academic Scientists." *Economics Letters* 124 (3): 461–64.

Ghosh, Anirban, Anna Maria Mayda, and Francesc Ortega. 2014. "The Impact of Skilled Foreign Workers on Firms: An Investigation of Publicly Traded U.S. Firms." IZA Discussion Papers 8684, November. Institute for the Study of Labor (IZA).

Gibson, John, and David McKenzie. 2014. "Scientific Mobility and Knowledge Networks in High Emigration Countries: Evidence from the Pacific." *Research Policy* 43 (9): 1486–95.

Grogger, Jeffrey, and Gordon H. Hanson. 2015. "Attracting Talent: Location Choices of Foreign-Born PhDs in the United States." *Journal of Labor Economics* 33 (S1): S5–S38.

Hunt, Jennifer. 2011. "Which Immigrants Are Most Innovative and Entrepreneurial? Distinctions by Entry Visa." *Journal of Labor Economics* 29 (3): 417–57.

Hunt, Jennifer, and Marjolaine Gauthier-Loiselle. 2010. "How Much Does Immigration Boost Innovation?" *American Economic Journal: Macroeconomics* 2 (2): 31–56.

Kahn, Shulamit, Giulia La Mattina, and Megan J. MacGarvie. 2017. "'Misfits,'

'Stars,' and Immigrant Entrepreneurship." *Small Business Economics* 49 (3): 533–57.

Kahn, Shulamit, and Megan J. MacGarvie. 2016. "How Important Is U.S. Location for Research in Science?" *Review of Economics and Statistics* 98 (2): 397–414.

Kahn, Shulamit, and Megan J. MacGarvie. 2018. "The Impact of Permanent Residency Delays for STEM PhDs: Who Leaves and Why." NBER Working Paper no. 25175. Cambridge, MA: National Bureau of Economic Research.

Kerr, William R., and Sari Kerr. 2016. "Immigrant Entrepreneurship." NBER Working Paper no. 22385. Cambridge, MA: National Bureau of Economic Research.

Kerr, William R., and William F. Lincoln. 2010. "The Supply Side of Innovation: H-1B Visa Reforms and U.S. Ethnic Invention." *Journal of Labor Economics* 28 (3): 473–508.

Peri, Giovanni, and Chad Sparber. 2009. "Task Specialization, Immigration, and Wages." *American Economic Journal: Applied Economics* 1 (3): 135–69.

Zeithammer, Robert, and Ryan P. Kellogg. 2013. "The Hesitant Hai Gui: Return-Migration Preferences of U.S.-Educated Chinese Scientists and Engineers." *Journal of Marketing Research* 50 (5): 644–63.

I

Location Choices of International Students and Return Migration

Return Migrants' Self-Selection
Evidence for Indian Inventors

Stefano Breschi, Francesco Lissoni, and Ernest Miguelez

1.1 Introduction

Return migration represents an important share of present-day total cross-border population flows. In 2008, the International Migration Outlook of the Organisation for Economic Co-operation and Development (OECD), based on indirect estimation methods, suggested that 20 percent to 50 percent of adult immigrants to advanced countries might leave within five years after their arrival, albeit with much variation due to heterogeneity of sending-receiving country pairs, years of entry, and the definition of "return migrant" itself (OECD 2008).[1]

Stefano Breschi is professor of applied economics at Bocconi University in Milan and director of the Invernizzi Center for Research on Innovation, Organization, Strategy and Entrepreneurship (ICRIOS).

Francesco Lissoni is professor of economics at GREThA, University of Bordeaux, and an affiliate of the Invernizzi Center for Research on Innovation, Organization, Strategy and Entrepreneurship (ICRIOS) at Bocconi University in Milan.

Ernest Miguelez is a research fellow at the French National Centre for Scientific Research (CNRS) attached to GREThA, University of Bordeaux, and a research affiliate at the Regional Quantitative Analysis Research Group (AQR-IREA) at Univeristat de Barcelona.

We gratefully acknowledge financial support from NBER and the French National Research Agency (TKC project—reference: ANR-17-CE26-0016). For acknowledgments, sources of research support, and disclosure of the authors' material financial relationships, if any, please see https://www.nber.org/chapters/c14104.ack.

1. In what follows, unless otherwise stated, we will adopt Dustmann and Weiss's (2007) definition of return migrants as those who settle back in their home country by their own choice after having spent several years abroad. This echoes the definition provided for statistical purposes by the United States Statistical Division of "persons returning to their country of citizenship after having been international migrants (whether short-term or long-term) in another country and who are intending to stay in their own country for at least a year" (UN 1998; as quoted by OECD 2008) but hides more complex migration patterns, such as circular and repeat migration (Constant and Zimmermann 2016).

Such high rates also affect high-skilled (highly educated) migrants. Based on a large sample of foreign recipients of a US doctorate in science and engineering, Finn (2014) calculates an average return rate—five years after graduation—of about 30 percent, with country-specific figures ranging from less than 10 percent for India and China to over 40 percent for Western European countries. In addition, evidence from questionnaires on return intentions suggests, for migrants to the United States and Germany, a U-shaped relationship between years of schooling and return rates (Dustmann and Görlach 2016)—that is, a self-selection of return migrants with respect to very low and very high educational levels. OECD (2008) estimates on actual returns conform to this pattern, especially for the United States.

High-skilled return migration is especially relevant for innovation studies. From the viewpoint of migrants' home countries, returnee scientists, engineers, and other professionals can play a role in knowledge diffusion and new business creation.[2] In this respect, high-skill return migration can act as a potential compensating mechanism for the "brain drain" suffered by sending countries (Dustmann, Fadlon, and Weiss 2011; Gibson and McKenzie 2011).

As for host countries, their policy-makers, higher education institutions, and knowledge-intensive firms fret not only about attracting but also about retaining the "best and brightest" among foreign workers and students (Hawthorne 2018; Teitelbaum 2014; Wadhwa et al. 2009). This begs the question of whether returnees self-select positively not only with respect to their immediately observable skills, such as educational level, but also with respect to harder-to-observe skills, such as inventiveness, creativity, or entrepreneurial propensity, conditional on education.

More generally, the issue of skill-based self-selection of return migrants plays a crucial role in economic theories of migration as a lifetime investment with important implications for the expected economic and social assimilation of both permanent and temporary migrants (Borjas and Bratsberg 1996; Dustmann and Görlach 2016).

Despite its relevance, return migration is an understudied topic due to a lack of data. National authorities commonly register the inflows of foreign-born and foreign nationals but not their outflows, which makes it nearly impossible to know precisely how many immigrants later leave the country and when, let alone their individual characteristics. Quantitative research then relies on longitudinal surveys or on complex manipulation of administrative panel data (Dustmann and Görlach 2016).

Most surveys, however, concern specific, often low-skilled migrant groups

---

2. On entrepreneurs, see Nanda and Khanna (2010), Filatotchev et al. (2011), and Luo, Lovely, and Popp (2013). On scientists, see Kahn and MacGarvie (2016), Jonkers and Cruz-Castro (2013), Trippl (2013), and Gibson and McKenzie (2014). On managers, see Nanda and Khanna (2010) and Choudhury (2016).

(such as the *gastarbaiters* of the 1960s and 1970s in the much-used German Socio-economic Panel) and/or focus on labor market determinants of return migration, such as unemployment (Bijwaard, Schluter, and Wahba 2014). Notable but rare exceptions concern academic scientists, whose return rates and individual characteristics can be obtained by combining archival and bibliometric data sources, as in Gaulé (2014) and Kahn and MacGarvie (2016).

In a recent assessment of the emerging literature on migration and innovation, Kerr (2017) states that we know very little about return migration of workers engaged in innovation and entrepreneurship except that it is rapidly growing in importance and that "clever data work to . . . quantify [it] would be most welcome" (Kerr 2017, 212). This chapter answers the call. Based on an ambitious data-linkage project joining patent data and inventors' biographical information from a web-based, professionally oriented social network, we build a large sample of US immigrant inventors of Indian origin specializing in the information and communication technologies (ICT) sector. This is a social group that both figures prominently in the recent debate on temporary work migration to the United States (most notably on the use of H-1B visas; Kerr and Lincoln 2010) and contributes significantly to international student mobility (OECD 2017).

Our data-mining strategy allows us to identify only migrants entering the United States via work and education channels, most likely associated with temporary visas. Yet we do not consider it a weak point due to two well-established stylized facts:

1. The overwhelming importance of temporary channels as a source for high-skilled immigration into the United States via the transformation of both temporary work and student visas into permanent ones (in contrast with countries such as Australia and Canada, where permanent visas for the highly skilled are more easily obtained upon entry; Koslowski 2018)

2. The remarkable innovation impact of migrant scientists and engineers entering the United States with work and student visas, as opposed to those entering through the channel of family reunions, as documented by Hunt (2013)

While subject to a number of limitations, our data set allows us to trace return migration from the United States with a degree of precision comparable to survey data, but on a much larger scale and with original information on its possible determinants. For each individual in the data set, we estimate the year of entry, the likely entry channel (work or education), and the permanence spell up to either the return to India or 2016 (right-censoring year). By means of survival analysis, we provide estimates of the probability of return migration as a function of the conditions at migration (age, education, patenting record, migration motives, and migration cohort) as well as some activities undertaken while abroad (education and patenting).

Our results, albeit exploratory, find rather different patterns for work and education migrants. Considering the former, we find that Indian inventors' return risk is positively associated with their age and education at migration, as well as their propensity to patent while in the US. As for education migrants, the return risk correlates negatively with the education level they attain. We also find some evidence of negative (positive) time-dependence for work (education) return migrants, which we interpret as indicative of negative (positive) self-selection with respect to unobservable skills acquired in the host country.

We proceed as follows. In section 1.2, we present in a rather succinct way our database-building strategy (more details in the appendix: http://www .nber.org/data-appendix/c14104/appendix.pdf), introduce our own definitions of *migrant* and *return migrant*, and propose some descriptive evidence. When necessary, we discuss some conceptual and methodological issues concerning the definition of *return migrant*. In section 1.3, we present our model specification and discuss how it serves the purpose of investigating skill-based self-selection in return migration. In section 1.4, we perform the related econometric exercise and comment on the results. Section 1.5 concludes with a special focus on further research plans and some tentative policy implications.

1.2   Data: Methodology and Descriptive Statistics

1.2.1   Methodology

Our data set originates from an ambitious data-linkage project between patent and inventor data gathered from PatentsView (http://www.patentsview .org/web/) and biographical information extracted from a large number of LinkedIn profiles. PatentsView is a data repository recently made available by the United States Patent and Trademark Office (USPTO), which provides, among other things, disambiguated data on all the inventors of patents granted by the USPTO from 1975 onward, irrespective of their country of residence. LinkedIn, a well-known professional-oriented social network, represents an unparalleled source of information on the international mobility of individuals, as the members' public profiles include information on names and (possibly) locations of their educational institutions and employers, along with graduation and recruitment years (Ge, Huang, and Png 2016; Zagheni and Weber 2015).

As a pilot project, we focus on a subset of high-skilled migrants in the United States—namely, Indian inventors with ICT patents. This is a distinctive social group due to both its inventive contribution (Kerr and Lincoln 2010; Breschi, Lissoni, and Miguelez 2017) and its implication in two important temporary migration channels—namely, highly qualified temporary work (most notably through the H-1B visa system; Kerr et al. 2015; Kapur and McHale 2005) and education (Finn 2014; Kapur and McHale 2005). It is also a highly represented group on LinkedIn, which in 2016 registered well over 100 million members in the US and over 30 million in India, with the two countries standing at the top of LinkedIn world rankings for both membership and traffic.[3]

We extracted from PatentsView all the patents granted to the 179 largest US public firms in the ICT industry from 1975 to 2016 and the relative inventors for a total of 262,847 distinct individuals.[4] We then proceeded to the ethnic analysis of such inventors' names and surnames based on Global Name Recognition, a name search technology produced by IBM (from now on, IBM-GNR) and adapted to our purposes by Breschi et al. (2017). This allowed us to identify inventors of presumed Indian origin (from now on, Indian inventors) for a total of 24,017 individuals representing 9.1 percent of all inventors employed by the companies in our sample. Each Indian-named inventor was then matched to one LinkedIn profile based on name and company matching with extensive manual checking. This exercise yielded 10,839 inventors with valid LinkedIn accounts (around 45 percent of the original sample). For details, see sections C and D of the appendix.

We then proceeded to codify three major sets of variables, concerning education, employment, and patent records. On that basis, we also estimated the inventors' years of birth as well as their migrant, nonmigrant, and return migrant status.

We coded information on education according to the 2011 version of UNESCO's International Standard Classification of Education (ISCED) for educational levels from 3 (upper secondary) to 8 (doctoral or equivalent).[5] After jointly treating ISCED levels 5 and 6 (respectively, short-cycle tertiary and bachelor's) and distinguishing between master's of arts and/or science and MBAs, we ended up with the following classification: upper secondary education, bachelor's, master's, MBA, and PhD, plus a residual unclassified category. We then geolocalized as many education institutions as possible at the country level by means of Google Maps and obtained at least one geolocalization per inventor. (For full details, see section E of the appendix.)

As for employment, we recorded the start and end years of each related employment spell as well as the employer's name. We geolocalized the latter, at the country level, only on the basis of the information provided by the

---

3. Unofficial statistics are from https://www.statista.com/statistics/272783/linkedins-membership-worldwide-by-country/ (last visited April 2018).

4. The definition of an ICT industry follows the one provided by the OECD (https://www.oecd.org/sti/ieconomy/1835738.pdf). More details in section B of the appendix: https://www.nber.org/data-appendix/c14104/appendix.pdf.

5. See http://ec.europa.eu/eurostat/statistics-explained/index.php/International_Standard_Classification_of_Education_(ISCED) (last visited March 2018).

LinkedIn profile, with no further attempt to use GoogleMaps, which would prove useless for multinationals with several branches and affiliates in multiple countries. Thus our estimates on migration and return migration for work reasons have to be considered extremely conservative. In section F of the appendix, we discuss some possible ways to improve them by capturing more return moves based on a more sophisticated treatment of LinkedIn information.

As for the inventive activities of each inventor, we geolocalized them at the country level on the basis of the inventor's address as reported on his or her various patents and dated them on the basis of the patent's priority year (De Rassenfosse et al. 2013).[6] Based on the unique inventor ID provided by PatentsView, we could then calculate the number of patents signed by each inventor each year either in India or abroad.

Coming to the inventor's year of birth, our preferred option was to estimate it on the basis of education information, with reference to the lowest-level education achievement among those reported in the LinkedIn profile, the year of completion, and the presumed age at start (see section G in the appendix; see also Gaulé 2014). For the inventors whose profiles did not report any information on the timing or level of education, we estimated the year of birth based on the average age of the other inventors in the same patent cohort (i.e., the inventors who filed their first patents in the same year). In most cases, the age so calculated is around 32, which is close to general estimates by Jones (2009).

After dropping the inventors whose LinkedIn profiles did not provide sufficient information for estimating either the educational level or the year of birth, 8,982 observations remained (see table 1A.5 in the appendix). For these, we estimated the accuracy of our PatentsView-LinkedIn match based on around 1,000 LinkedIn profiles of Indian ICT professionals that report patent information. Based on around 800 "true positives" (successful matches of a LinkedIn profile to an inventor in PatentsView with coherent patent information) and 30 "false positives" (successful matches, but with discordant patent information), we calculated a 96.4 percent precision rate and a 77 percent recall rate. The high precision rate suggests that the education, employment, and age information in our data set are rather accurate (i.e., it is unlikely that they refer to the wrong inventor). However, the low recall rate suggests that our sample possibly suffers from truncation problems, to the extent that the excluded inventors may share some characteristics associated with the phenomenon of our interest (return migration).[7]

---

6. We obtain the priority year of the patent from its priority date—namely, the date of filing of the first USPTO application or, in case of patents extended to the United States but first filed abroad, the first application worldwide.

7. In section 1 of the appendix, we further investigate the properties of our sample of 8,982 inventors. We first compare their patent records to those of other Indian-named inventors in

We finally proceeded to identify migrant and return migrant inventors to/from the United States, as described in detail by figures 1A.6 and 1A.7 in the appendix. We proceeded by elimination, first dropping from our sample all the inventors without any education, employment, or patenting records within India, who may include second-generation migrants or members of the historical Indian diaspora in the former British Commonwealth. Second, we dropped all those we consider nonmigrants—namely, the inventors without any education, employment, or patenting records outside India. Among the remaining inventors, we considered as "education migrants" all the inventors whose LinkedIn profiles report enrolment in foreign higher education institutions as the first events in their lives taking place outside India and occurring earlier than any patenting activity abroad. Similarly, we considered as "work migrants" all the inventors whose LinkedIn profiles report recruitment by foreign-based companies as the first events taking place outside India and/or who have at least one patent abroad dating to before any enrolment in foreign higher education institutions.

Finally, we restricted our attention to migrants whose first moves outside India occurred in the United States. This left us with 3,943 "education migrants" and 1,589 "work migrants" from India to the United States for a total of 5,532 individuals. For the former, we considered as the migration year the starting year of the first education program undertaken in the United States. For the latter, we similarly defined the migration year as the beginning year of the first working spell in the United States or, alternatively, the priority year of the first patent. When distinguishing between "work" and "education" migrant inventors, it is important to keep in mind that the distinction refers only to the individuals' condition at migration time. Nothing impedes a work migrant from entering a master's or PhD program in the United States or impedes an education migrant from starting to work there. Indeed, the first case is rather frequent, and the second is very frequent.

Coming to return migration, we record as a returnee every migrant report-

---

our initial data set and find no significant differences for what concerns the average number of patents granted, conditional on the year of the first patent. However, based on the year of the first patent, inventors with a LinkedIn profile appear to be younger than those without one. Second, we compare the inventors for whom we found a LinkedIn profile (whether complete or not) to all others and find that inventors who patent exclusively in India have a significantly higher probability of being matched with a LinkedIn profile than inventors who patent exclusively in the US or both in India and in the US. These diagnostics suggest that, based on our data, we may underestimate migration from India, especially for more recent calendar years, due to the relative overrepresentation of India-based inventors versus US-only- and US-plus-India-based ones, the former group being more likely to contain nonmigrants and the latter more likely to contain migrants. Reasoning along similar lines, we may risk overestimating return migration, since the propensity to have a LinkedIn profile is higher for US-plus-India-based inventors than for US-only-based inventors. More generally, the younger the inventors, the more representative our sample.

ing an employment or a patent in India after having moved to the United States. We do not record return events related to further education in India, but we suspect these to be very few. However, we record employment in higher education. As for the return year, this coincides with either the start of the relevant employment spell or the priority year of the relevant patent. All migrants for whom we do not observe any return event are considered as still living in the United States in 2016, our final year of observation. For the sake of simplicity, at this stage of our research, we do not code any event following the first return to India. Similarly, we ignore any move from the United States to a country other than India. For example, we will treat an Indian student in the United States who leaves for the United Kingdom after graduation as if he or she was staying in the United States. This implies that we ignore circular migration. A cursory look at our data, however, reveals very few instances of this type.

Albeit imperfect, our coding of return events (and, in consequence, permanence abroad) does not compare unfavorably with similar coding one can find in the literature. Borjas's (1989) classic study based on the 1972–1978 Survey of Scientists and Engineers simply recorded as returnees all foreign respondents to the 1972 questionnaire who had left the sample by 1978. Gaulé (2014), who relied on several editions of the Directory of Graduate Research of the American Chemical Society from 1993 to 2007, first identified as potential returnees all foreign faculty and postdocs who appear at least once in the directory and then disappear. He then looked manually in bibliographic and web resources for information on the likely motives for the disappearance (to distinguish between return to the home country while not ceasing the academic career and moves to industry or third countries, and deaths). To our knowledge, the only accurate survey of return moves is provided by Gibson and McKenzie (2014), but for a very small sample.[8]

Even much-used resources for studying low-skill return emigration, such as the German Socio-economic Panel (GSOEP), are far from faultless. In some cases, they resort to measuring return intentions rather than actual moves.[9]

8. Gibson and McKenzie (2014) survey around 800 high-achieving secondary school graduates from New Zealand, Tonga, and Papua New Guinea, 200 of whom undertook academic careers. In this subgroup, 78 percent moved abroad, with a 25 to 30 percent return rate.

9. As explained by Bönisch, Gaffert, and Wilde (2013), the basic information on return migration provided by GSOEP consists of nonresponse items accompanied by the "moved abroad" motivation. This amounts to underreporting, as observed by Constant and Massey (2002), who find that a much larger number of individuals in the panel leave for one or more years without providing a motivation explicitly related to a move back home and hence resort to code as returnees all absentees for three or more years. Kirdar (2009) reports similar problems for more recent issues of the survey. As in many surveys of low-skilled migrants, the GSOEP collects information on return intentions. Similar information for the highly skilled is collected by Baruffaldi and Landoni (2012). While useful for testing theoretical models of temporary migration, return intentions may be different from de facto choices. For example, the 2000–2013

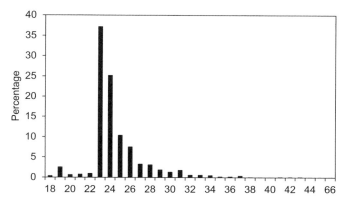

Fig. 1.1a   Estimated age at migration, education channel (percentage distribution of all education migrants to the United States)

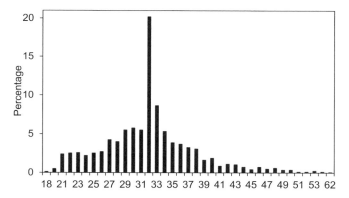

Fig. 1.1b   Estimated age at migration of work migrants (percentage distribution of work migrants to the United States)

1.2.2   Descriptive Statistics

In what follows, we produce a number of descriptive statistics that serve the dual purpose of checking the information contents and quality of our data and providing some basic evidence on the phenomenon under study.

Figures 1.1a and 1.1b report the distribution of the age at migration for education and work education migrants, respectively. We notice that the overwhelming majority of the former move to the US at 23 or 24 years of

trends for return migration and return intentions calculated by Finn (2014) for a longitudinal cross-section of foreign doctoral graduates in the US are markedly different.

age, which is compatible with the age for starting a master's course or possibly a PhD. The very sparse observations for ages less than 19 are due to either errors in our calculation of migrants' years of birth or the very few Indian migrants who move to the US for bachelor's studies. As for the very few apparently moving at older ages, especially over 30, they may be mature postgraduate students or professionals taking MBA courses. Figure 1A.12a in the appendix reports the distribution of age at migration for all Indian immigrants in science, technology, engineering, and mathematics (STEM) occupations for the migration cohorts 1990s and 2000s based on data from the American Community Surveys 2000 and 2010 (pooled samples; IPUMS US). Figure 1A.12b reports the same calculations for the subset of STEM-employed Indian immigrants with education at the college, master's, or PhD level. The modal values are, respectively, 24 and 25, which is slightly higher than for our educational sample. Moreover, the age at migration distribution taken from IPUMS data is flatter. Again, as our sample is composed of educational migrants, this concentration in early ages of migration is expected.

For comparison purposes, we also look at the number of H-1B petition filings by age for the years 2007–2017 from the US Citizenship and Immigration Services (figure 1A.13 in the appendix). The most numerous group is the one at ages 25–34, followed by the 35–44 group. Again, this is slightly different from our education sample. In this regard, figure 1.1b shows the distribution of the age at migration as way more skewed to the right. However, the figure shows a high peak at 32, which also differs from figures 1A.12 and 1A.13 and seems to be a statistical artifact that results from the inclusion in this migrants category of many inventors with two characteristics. First, for want of better information, we estimate their ages based on the priority year of their first patents. Second, they appear on these patents with US addresses, and this is the earliest evidence we have of their migration. Yet we notice that the age distribution is rather symmetric around 32. This is compatible with migrants in this group moving abroad after completing their education in India and starting their careers there, as happens with many H-1B visa holders, as well as being employees of Indian firms temporarily detached to the United States. When excluding from the work migrants all inventors whose ages were determined by the year of the first patent, the shape of the distribution does not change much, since the modal value remains at 32 and the symmetry is preserved (figure 1A.15 in the appendix). However, the percentage of people migrating at 32 goes from 20.2 percent to 13 percent in figure 1A.15, which is significant. In any case, we should be cautious when interpreting the estimates of the effect of age at migration on return decisions (for work migrants).

Table 1.1 provides a breakdown of our data set by migration motives and cohorts (decades during which migration occurred). Two features emerge.

Table 1.1   **Migrants to the United States by cohort and channel**

Channel	1960	1970	1980	1990	2000	2010	Total
Education	19	102	697	1,739	1,315	71	3,943
% column	100	95.3	95.2	85.9	56.3	22.8	71.3
Work	0	5	35	286	1,022	241	1,589
% column	0.0	4.7	4.8	14.1	43.7	77.2	28.7
All channels	19	107	732	2,025	2,337	312	5,532
% column	100	100	100	100	100	100	100
% row	0.3	1.9	13.2	36.6	42.2	5.6	100

First, most migrants in our sample belong to the 1990s and 2000s cohorts. This is broadly compatible with historical records of high-skilled Indian migration to the United States (Desai, Kapur, and McHale 2005) but also possibly emphasized by the characteristics of our LinkedIn records— namely, right truncation at 2016 and underreporting for the earlier cohorts (the older an individual, the less likely he or she is to maintain a LinkedIn profile).

Second, the importance of the education channel relative to the work channel is both evident for early cohorts and declining over time. This trend again is broadly compatible with the history of graduate and postgraduate education in India since the 1960s, whose offer and quality were extremely limited until the 1990s (so an early Indian migrant seeking a job in science or engineering usually obtained a graduate education in the host country; Kapur 2010). But it may be accentuated, once again, by underreporting for early cohorts and its correlation with educational levels (the more likely an individual is to have migrated through the work channel, which is associated with a lower education level, the less likely he or she is to maintain a LinkedIn profile, especially in the case of an older individual). These observations suggest that our data are more reliable for the 1990s and 2000s cohorts, which concern 4,362 individuals—namely, 79 percent of migrants in our database.

Figures 1.2a and 1.2b provide further details on the education levels of both education and work migrants. We first remark on how the overwhelming majority of the former and the relative majority of the latter hold masters' degrees. This suggests that PhD holders and academic scientists, for which Finn (2014), Gaulé (2014), and Kahn and MacGarvie (2016) have provided some evidence, are not a representative sample of migrant inventors in the ICT industry. We also notice that the share of doctorate holders is higher for education-based migrants, while the share of bachelor holders is higher for work-based ones, which is in line with our selection criteria for the two categories.

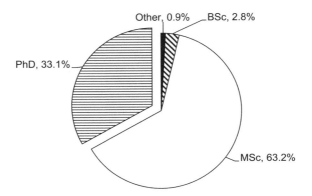

Fig. 1.2a   Highest educational attainment, percentage distribution: education migrants

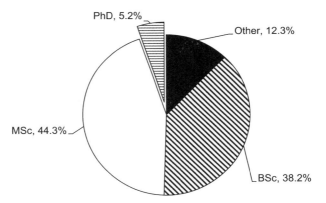

Fig. 1.2b   Highest educational attainment, percentage distribution of work migrants

Figure 1.3 reports the total return rates for all migrants in our sample (irrespective of length of stay) by migration channel. For comparative purposes, the return rates are calculated both according to the definition of returnee we adopted earlier (first job or patent back in India, as per LinkedIn profile) and to a purely patent-based definition (first patent back in India, irrespective of other information). The latter corresponds to that found in most of the available literature on the international mobility of inventors, which relies exclusively on patent data and can observe a cross-border move only for inventors with at least two patents in as many different countries (e.g., Oettl and Agrawal 2008). We notice immediately that this definition severely underestimates return rates (black bars) compared to the one also based on job information (white bars), whatever migration channel we consider. In fact, the latter also includes among the returnees the inventors

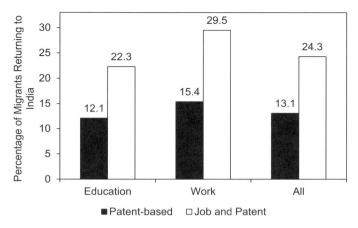

Fig. 1.3   Total return rates by migration channel (irrespective of the length of stay in the United States)

with no more than one patent in their careers (either in the United States or in India) but education or employment in a different country than the one where that only patent was signed. More generally, it also counts as returnees the inventors whose entire patent production occurred in one country but whose education or career took place elsewhere.

When comparing migration channels, figure 1.3 reports a seven-point difference in the return rate of work-migrant inventors compared to education ones. This may be due to the different types of visas used to enter the United States in terms of both initial validity length and renewal ease and also different efforts that work and education migrants may make to convert their temporary visas into permanent ones. Different types of migrants may also be differently exposed to opportunities to establish social ties in the United States, which may influence their propensity to return at each point in time.

Figures 1.4a and 1.4b report the total return rates (based on both patent and job information) for different cohorts of migration to the United States. The return rates for education migrants appear to be increasing, and this is despite the longer observation interval for older cohorts (which intuitively should lead to more accumulated returns). However, for cohorts before 1990, the number of observations is rather limited, and as discussed in the previous subsection, the probability of underreporting by return migrants is rather high. As for the 2010 cohort, once again we are faced with very few observations, which makes the very high return rate figure extremely unreliable. Once again, we can trust only the data for the 1990 and 2000 cohorts, which still exhibit different return rates.

Contrary to education migrants, the return rates of work migrants appear rather stable, especially for recent cohorts.

As discussed in the introductory part of the chapter, the return rates found

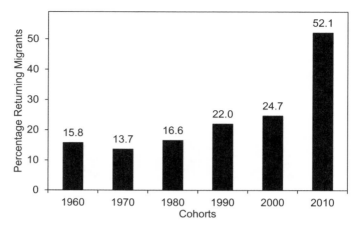

Fig. 1.4a   Percentage of education migrants returning to India by cohort (irrespective of the length of stay)

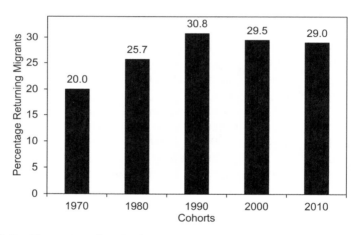

Fig. 1.4b   Percentage of work migrants returning to India by cohort (irrespective of length of stay)

in the literature vary considerably depending on the sample and countries analyzed. While Finn (2014) calculates a return rate just after graduation of about 10 percent for India (up to around 15 percent in more recent estimates; Finn and Pennington 2018), other studies report return rates of around 40 percent both for Indian H-1B visa holders (Lowell 2000) and for Indian PhD or master's students (Wadhwa 2009).

Figure 1.5 reports the Kaplan-Meier estimators for work and education migrants from the 1990 and 2000 cohorts, with time measured yearly. We notice that the survival (stay) rate for work migrants is both lower and more

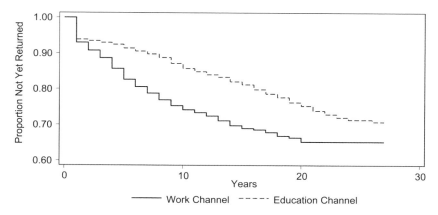

Fig. 1.5   Stay rates over time (years since migration) by migration channels (1990 and 2000 cohorts)

rapidly decreasing over time than for education ones. We also notice that the stay rate after 10 years since migration for education migrants (slightly less than 90 percent) is very close to what is reported by Finn (2014) for Indian PhD graduates in the United States. We take this as a sign of the reliability of our data.

Table 1.2 provides detailed information on the return time for migrant inventors in the 1990 and 2000 cohorts. Returnees in the first cohort leave the United States, on average, 11 years after their arrival. The minimal return time is zero (which implies a return to India less than a year after entry into the United States), and the value of the first quartile is 5.5. This indicates that 25 percent of the returnees in the 1990 cohort go back to India either in the same year of their arrival or not later than 5.5 years afterward. An additional 25 percent leave between 5.5 and 11 years after their arrival, followed by 25 percent more who leave between 11 and 16 years. The maximum stay, for returnees, is 25 years. When splitting the 1990 cohort between work and education returnee migrants, the former exhibit shorter stay periods both on average and according to the quartile distribution. The 2000 cohort exhibits, on average, shorter stays than the 1990 one (which may be due to shorter exposure to the return risk) but also less striking differences between work and education migrants.

1.3   Specification

We exploit our data to explore the extent of skill-based self-selection in return migration of the highly skilled. Skill-based self-selection was first investigated by Borjas (1989) in order to provide an explanation for two common stylized facts concerning the education and income levels of migrants.

Table 1.2   **Average time to return by cohort**

	All channels	Education	Work
Cohort 1990			
# of inventors in cohort	2,025	1,739	286
# of returnees	471	383	88
Mean	10.58811	11.22193	7.829545
Std	6.643841	6.71642	5.560992
Min	0	0	0
25%	5.5	7	3
50%	11	12	8
75%	16	16	13
Max	25	25	19
			t-test 4.952 (*p*-value 0.000)
Cohort 2000			
# of inventors in cohort	2,337	1,315	1,022
# of returnees	626	325	301
Mean	3.889776	4.132308	3.627907
Std	3.897362	4.316674	3.374574
Min	0	0	0
25%	0	0	0
50%	3	3	3
75%	7	8	6
Max	16	16	15
			t-test 1.635 (*p*-value 0.103)

Note: Cohort 1990 includes inventors who migrated to the US between 1990 and 1999; cohort includes inventors who migrated to the US between 2000 and 2009.

First, stock data on foreign-born versus native populations recurrently show that the former are, on average, better educated than the latter for most traditional destination countries. Second, when observing a cohort of foreign-born over time through successive censuses, it is often found that starting from a lower average wage or income level, migrants catch up relatively quickly. Regardless of whether migrants are positively self-selected at entry, with respect to their education and/or unobservable skills, negative self-selection may help explain this evidence to the extent that return migrants escape successive censuses, therefore leaving behind them, in the host country, only the best and brightest of their respective immigration cohorts.

Borjas and Bratsberg (1996) provide a classic treatment of the topic, in which they show that different remuneration levels of skills in the host and home countries jointly determine whether migrants will be positively (negatively) self-selected upon arrival and, conversely, negatively (positively) selected upon return. In other words, return migration is expected to reinforce the sign of skill-based self-selection at entry. Dustmann and Görlach (2016) provide the last in a series of refinements of this basic idea, which describes the migrant's behavior at his or her destination (including his or her investment in the acquisition of education and skills) as resulting from the same lifetime optimization plan that determines the return decision and timing.

Other, less-dominant theories of return migration stress the fact that many migrants neither move permanently to the host country nor return home once and for all after a prolonged spell abroad. Instead, they move back and forth between the home and the host countries (or several host countries), possibly in response to economic shocks (Constant, Nottmeyer, and Zimmermann 2013). In this case, we should not expect any positive or negative self-selection, the economic shocks being orthogonal to skill levels.

Empirical studies on return migration can be categorized according to two criteria: (a) whether they observe and explain the actual duration of migration spells, from entry to return, or simply compare the characteristics of stayers and returnees; and (b) whether they focus on observed return moves or on return intentions.

With respect to (a), empirical studies fall into one or the other category depending on data availability and, to a lesser extent, on their theoretical focus. On the data side, most studies simply do not have longitudinal information on individual migrants—that is, they have no records on entry and return dates. Based on this limited information, they can only apply linear probability or logit/probit models and investigate the determinants of the probability to return, irrespective of when this occurs. When longitudinal data are available, instead, one can apply duration analysis (also known as survival or event history analysis; Allison 2014). This has two advantages over linear probability or logit/probit models. First, it is not inherently static, and therefore it allows one to consider time-varying covariates, so as to study how intervening changes in the migrant's characteristics may affect the return decision. Second, and more importantly, duration analysis allows estimating the propensity to return for those who have not yet returned, at each point in time during their entire permanence abroad, and not just the probability to return after a pre-determined spell abroad (say one, two or five years). By derivation, one can explain or predict the timing of the return decision and not just the probability of its occurrence. This also implies that by means of duration analysis, we can test whether the probability to return is time-dependent, either positively or negatively. According to Constant and Massey (2002), negative time dependence may be indicative of negative skill-based self-selection (where skills are unobservable). The longer a migrant stays in the host country, the more country-specific skills he or she accumulates, which are hard to transfer and/or are less remunerated at home, ceteris paribus. This makes return increasingly less likely. At the same time, to the extent that migrants vary in the speed at which they accumulate local skills, early returnees would necessarily be those who, at a given point in time, have accumulated fewer local skills.

Coming to the distinction between studies based on observed return moves or declared return intentions, this often boils down, once again, to data availability, with survey data being much better at recording the latter than the former (see our earlier discussion on how we record return moves). However, some recent literature suggests that data on return intentions better serve the purpose of testing lifetime income maximization models. This is because, according to such theories, most migrants leave their countries with the intention to return at a date which depends on their investment plans in education and skill acquisition while abroad.

The data structure for our regression exercises is a panel one, with each inventor i being observed repeatedly since his or her immigration year until the minimum between his or her return year (when he or she exits the panel) and 2016, our last observation year. In this way, we have a large number of right-censored observations, but no left-censored ones. In what follows, we exploit this feature of our data and estimate the determinants of actual return decisions by means of discrete time duration analysis. Given the exploratory nature of our exercise, we do not put forward any claim of having established causal links. We care instead for producing much-needed evidence on return frequency and timing and its association to observable and unobservable skills (i.e., self-selection based on education, patenting activity, and time spent in the United States).

Following Jenkins (2005), we assume a proportional hazard function, which, in a discrete time setting such as ours, results in a complementary log-log (cloglog) model, as follows:

$$h(t, x)_i = 1 - \exp[-\exp(c(t) + \beta_i X_i)],$$

where $c(t)$ represents a generic inventor's baseline probability to return home after a migration spell t (duration), conditional on not having yet returned, and $\beta_i X_i$ is a scaling factor depending on specific inventor i's characteristics X_{it} (some of which are time-variant). As for t, we measure it as either the number of years (plus 1) spent in the US since immigration or, for conducting robustness checks on education migrants only, the number of years since the end of their first education spell in the United States.

Concerning the baseline hazard ratio $c(t)$, we adopt two alternative specifications. First, we follow Constant and Massey (2002) and enter t with a quadratic term, as follows:

(1) $c(t) = \alpha_1 t + \alpha_2 t^2.$

This parametric specification may allow us to test for any time dependence of the hazard ratio, and its sign, in a rather immediate and intuitive way, on the basis of estimates for α_1 and α_2. But it comes at the cost of imposing a specific functional form to $c(t)$.

Second, we experiment with a nonparametric specification (as in Gaulé 2014) and make use of fixed effects, as follows:

$$(2) \qquad c(t) = \eta_1 t_1 + \ldots + \eta_N t_N,$$

where $(t_1 \ldots t_n)$ is a set of duration dummies corresponding to migration spells lasting from 1 to N years (and N is the longest spell observed in our data). This model has the advantage of not imposing any functional form to the hazard ratio, but it produces so many estimated coefficients that in order to appreciate any time dependence of the hazard ratio, one needs a graphical representation.

Based on the evidence from figures 1.4 to 1.6, plus table 1.2, in the previous section, we expect time to affect differently the hazard ratio of work- and education-based migrant inventors. Hence we run separate regressions for the two types of migrant inventors. We also restrict our regressions to the two most populated migration cohorts in our sample—namely, the 1990s and the 2000s ones, for which data are more reliable. We also right-censor our data at 2016 as a matter of convenience. This makes the longest possible duration equal to 27 years.

Coming to our choice of regressors X_i, they include both a set of time-invariant variables that describe the migrant's conditions at entry in the United States and a set of time-variant ones that describe his or her activities during his or her permanence there (see table 1.3 for descriptive statistics).

As for conditions at entry, we consider the inventor's age, educational level, migration cohort, and patenting experience at migration, all of which we expect to be positively associated to the return hazard, as they may proxy for the inventor's stronger attachment or professional insertion in India and may negatively affect his or her chance to renew the initial temporary visa. We measure age in years (*Age at migration*) and education with the dummy variable *Master's or more at migration* (the reference case being that of migrants with no more than a bachelor's at migration; as for doctorate holders, they are too few to create a meaningful separate category, so we treat them as master's holders). Due to our restriction of the analysis to just two migration cohorts, we control for them with just a dummy for the 2000s one (1990s as reference). As for patenting experience, we measure it with the cumulative number of patents signed at the time of migration (*Patent stock at migration*).

As for activities in the United States, we consider the following:

- the migrant's student status (*Student*), which is a dummy taking a value of one for all the years between the start and end years of an education spell in the United States, whatever its level, and zero otherwise;

- the migrant's educational attainment while in the United States, as measured by the dummy variables *Master's* and *PhD*, which takes a value of zero before the year of completion of, respectively, the migrant's master's or doctoral studies, and one thereafter;
- the migrant's productivity as an inventor while abroad, which we measure with the *cumulative number of patents* from entry into the United States up to observation time *t*.

We expect the student status to lower return hazard, as it guarantees the migrant the renewal of his or her temporary visas. As for the educational attainment, based on the existing evidence of Indian graduates' low return rates, we also expect a negative impact on the return hazard. In other words, we expect negative self-selection based on education. As for the number of patents filed in the United States, we would expect negative self-selection, but the interpretation of this variable is complicated by the fact that not all migrants in our sample, once in the United States, pursue careers as inventors but may instead move on to management, entrepreneurship, or academia. (We come back to this issue when commenting on the results.)

1.4   Results

Table 1.3 reports separate descriptive statistics for the education and work migration channels. We notice some important differences between education and work migrants besides the age at migration.

First, work migrants are considerably more likely to leave India after graduating at the master's level; most education migrants move to the United States precisely to earn that same degree. As for earning a PhD, this happens almost exclusively to education migrants. In this respect, it is important to remark that this may happen on top of getting a master's but also as an alternative to it, with the latter case being the most frequent.[10]

Both education and work migrants exhibit a rather low average number of patents before moving to the United States, but the figures are higher for the latter. At a closer inspection, our data reveal that most migrants in our sample leave India without having filed any patent there. In fact, only about 1 percent of education migrants and 4 percent of work migrants have a nonnull patent record before migrating. As for the cumulative number of patents filed while in the United States, its average value is higher for work migrants than for education ones (around five against four). When looking at the underlying distribution (unreported in the table), we notice that only 2 percent of work migrants never file any patent while in the United States, while the same figure for education migrants amounts to 14 per-

10. It is very likely, however, that we largely overestimate the number of PhD holders without a master's. This is due to many LinkedIn members reporting only their highest educational achievements (such as a doctorate) and not the previous ones (such as a master's).

Table 1.3   Descriptive statistics by migration channel

	Education channel					Work channel				
	Obs	Mean	Std. dev.	Min	Max	Obs	Mean	Std. dev.	Min	Max
Migration cohort	50,211	1,993.1	4.630	1,990	2,000	15,333	1996.8	4.648	1,990	2,000
Age at migration	50,211	24.32	2.652	18	52	15,333	31.87	5.956	18	62
Master's or more at migration	50,211	0.09	0.283	0	1	15,333	0.34	0.473	0	1
Current student status	50,211	0.20	0.403	0	1	15,333	0.04	0.192	0	1
Master's in the US	50,211	0.66	0.474	0	1	15,333	0.04	0.202	0	1
PhD in the US	50,211	0.20	0.400	0	1	15,333	0.01	0.097	0	1
MBA in the US	50,211	0.08	0.267	0	1	15,333	0.04	0.201	0	1
Patents at migration	50,211	0.01	0.114	0	5	15,333	0.03	0.354	0	12
Cumulative # patents US	50,211	3.83	10.64	0	261	15,333	4.71	9.07	0	162

cent (the overwhelming majority of these individuals patent only when they return to India, while a tiny minority may have patents before migrating). As for those who filed at least one patent in the United States, the differences between work and education migrants are much less striking, albeit education migrants exhibit more variability (witness the standard error reported in table 1.3). In both subsamples, over a third of migrants file just one patent while in the United States and as many file from two to five (followed by a very long tail for values higher than ten), but education migrants are slightly more likely to file just one patent, or two to five, as well as more than one hundred.

We notice an important difference between education and work migrants with respect to the number of patents filed while in the United States, which on average is higher for the latter. As for the very high maxima that we observe for this variable, they correspond to very senior principal scientists in large ICT companies.[11]

Table 1.4 reports the results of our regressions, which we run separately for education and work migrants. The first two columns refer to parametric specification (1) of the baseline hazard ratio $c(t)$, while the other two refer to the nonparametric specification (2). In both cases, we calculate the estimated odds ratios, which we read as the marginal effects of the covariates on the return hazard ratio (Jenkins 2005).

We first ask to what extent return migrants appear to be self-selected with respect to either one of their observable skills, namely, education and patenting activity. We then move on to analyze the sign of time dependence of the hazard ratio.

Concerning education, we first notice that the odds ratio for *Master's or more at migration* is greater than one in all columns of table 1.4, but it is significant in only one case (for education migrants in column 1). Hence there is evidence of return migrants being positively selected with respect to education they obtained in India, but it is rather weak. On the contrary, all return migrants appear to be negatively selected with respect to education obtained in the United States. For education migrants, both *Master's in the US* and *PhD in the US* have estimated odds ratios largely inferior to one (the reference case being migrants obtaining only a bachelor's degree or not completing their graduate studies).

However, the difference between the underlying coefficients is nonsignificant, which suggests that for individuals holding either a master's or a PhD, graduate education is all that matters, and more advanced or research-oriented degrees do not convey any particular advantage to migrants intending to stay in the United States or to those with return intentions. As for

11. These are the cases, respectively, of education migrant Durga Malladi of Qualcomm (261 patents) and work migrant Alok Srivastava, an independent consultant with activities in both India and the United States (162 patents).

Table 1.4   **Event history analysis of return risk, discrete time analysis, by migration channel**

	Education channel (1)	Work channel (2)	Education channel (3)	Work channel (4)
Time from migration	0.881***	0.883***		
	(0.0201)	(0.0307)		
Time from migration^2	1.005***	1.002		
	(0.000830)	(0.00195)		
Migration cohort = 2000	1.779***	1.423***	1.867***	1.424***
	(0.138)	(0.168)	(0.150)	(0.170)
Age at migration	0.872***	0.899***	0.977	0.904***
	(0.00565)	(0.00467)	(0.0159)	(0.0115)
Master's or more at migration	1.623***	1.154	1.180	1.138
	(0.227)	(0.136)	(0.176)	(0.139)
Current student status	0.595***	0.160***	0.459***	0.173***
	(0.0681)	(0.0809)	(0.0908)	(0.0884)
Master's in the US	0.432***	0.724	0.568***	0.719
	(0.0444)	(0.215)	(0.0709)	(0.216)
PhD in the US	0.552***	1.259	0.585***	1.430
	(0.0744)	(0.763)	(0.0805)	(0.835)
MBA in the US	0.866	0.401**	0.711**	0.403**
	(0.148)	(0.169)	(0.124)	(0.171)
Patents at migration	2.525***	1.429***	2.320***	1.431***
	(0.358)	(0.0842)	(0.301)	(0.0822)
Cumulative # patents US	1.001	1.011**	0.999	1.012**
	(0.00429)	(0.00528)	(0.00524)	(0.00528)
Observations	50,211	15,333	50,211	15,094
Times dummies	NO	NO	YES	YES
# unique inventors	3,054	1,308	3,054	1,308
Chi2	11,757	4,625	11,347	4,604
LogL	–3,623	–1,684	–3,442	–1,664

Note: Inventor-level clustered standard errors in parentheses. *** $p < 0.01$, ** $p < 0.05$, * $p < 0.1$.

those holding both a master's and a PhD, however, the two effects may sum up, which reinforces the negative selection effect of education on return migrants.

As for work migrants, neither *Master's in the US* nor *PhD in the US* is significant, and what really seems to count to increase their chances of staying in the United States is getting an MBA, whose coefficient is way less than 1, although significant only at 95 percent. Notice that *MBA in the US* also appears significant in one of the regressions for education migrants, but with an odds ratio closer to one.

Coming to patenting activity, inventors who leave India with substantial patenting experience are definitely those with the higher return hazard: witness the size of the odds ratio of *Patents at migration* for both education and work migrants (respectively, well over 2 and close to 1.5). Whether this result can be interpreted as evidence of positive self-selection (in contradiction with the education-based negative self-selection) is doubtful. The number of individuals in our sample with at least one patent at migration is very limited, and for several of them, we may overestimate the occurrence of return.[12]

As for the patenting activity in the United States (*Cumulative # patents US*), we also find it to be positively related to the return hazard, with odds ratios barely larger than one and not significant for education migrants. However, rather than being related to positive self-selection, this result may be related to specialization. In fact, inventors in our database range from the occasional to the professional ones, the former having signed one or very few patents before or after migration, the latter displaying instead a significant patenting record, one that possibly spans several years. In the absence of information on the migration strategies adopted by individuals in our sample or on the opportunity and constraints that may shape them, we can speculate about what follows. Professional inventors are more likely to move to the United States on a strictly temporary basis and for the specific task of undertaking inventive activities there, possibly on request of their employer in India, which organizes their two-way trip. Occasional inventors instead may be a more heterogeneous group, which includes a large number of individuals moving to the United States on their own initiative, rather than their employer's, and more determined to turn an originally temporary visa into a permanent one. They will be at once more open toward different career options and less bound by the original visa arrangements. For example, they may move out of the research and development (R&D) laboratory and stop producing patents, possibly to undertake managerial functions or an entrepreneurial career, thus getting more chances to stay in the United States. This interpretation fits with the size and significance ratio of the MBA in the US variables, on which we commented above. Notice that this explanation applies better to work migrants than education ones, all of them entering the United States via a higher education program and therefore more likely to be occasional rather than professional inventors. This is coherent with the odds ratios for *Cumulative # patents US* being de facto equal to one in the regressions for education migrants.

Moving to time dependence of the hazard ratio, the estimated odds ratios in columns (1) and (2) suggest it to be negative and monotonic for work

---

12. Many individuals with patents at migration are considered returnees on the basis of their patenting activity, with the patent apparently marking their return ("return patent") to India closely following the event (job, education, or patent) marking their original migration to the United States. For education migrants, it may well be that the "return patent" was actually invented before the migration event but filed afterward, so we are facing a false positive case of return migration. For work migrants, besides false positives, we may face cases of inventors temporarily detached in the United States for very short periods.

migrants (the coefficient for the time-squared is not significant) but possibly nonmonotonic for education ones (the coefficient for the time-squared is significant, and the odds ratio is greater than one).

Following Constant and Massey (2002), we interpret the negative time dependence of the return hazard ratio as indicative of some negative self-selection with respect to unobservable skills the migrant acquires through experience in the host country that are not as well rewarded back at home. Admittedly, Constant and Massey's interpretation of the time-dependence of the hazard ratio is rather speculative, since other factors besides skill accumulation may intervene, such as increasing investments in real estate or social capital, both of which increase the opportunity cost of return. Still, the negative time dependence we find for work migrants is coherent with the possibility that those among them who stay longer in the United States also engage in managerial functions or undertake entrepreneurial careers. Such career moves come with developing skills for which the US-India remuneration gap may be higher than that for the skills exclusively associated with R&D-performing tasks, thus discouraging return. They may also come with job contracts for which it is easier to obtain a permanent visa than a temporary one..

As for the time pattern of education migrants' return hazard ratio, regression in column (1) is not very enlightening. First, it results from imposing a parametric form to $c(t)$; second, it requires one to understand whether opposite signs of the estimated coefficients for α_1 and α_2 imply some nonmonotonicity, which is not immediately clear in the case of nonlinear estimation methods such as cloglog. For this reason, we prefer relying on the results of the nonparametric estimation of column (3). Based on such results, figures 1.6a and 1.6b report the within-sample estimates of the total hazard ratio $h(t)$ as a function of time and for different educational levels by migration cohort.

Both figures suggest that the return hazard follows an inverted U-shaped function of time over the first 13 years of permanence in the United States. After that, we cease to observe migrants in the 2000 cohort, due to right truncation, while the return rate for the 1990 cohort starts increasing again, albeit erratically. The hazard ratios for the early years after entry, however, may be underestimated. This is because we produced the graph by setting *Current student status* equal to zero, while in reality it should be equal to one from entry in the United States until graduation (notice that the odd ratios for *Current student status* in table 1.4 are always greater than one). As a partial remedy, we have replicated regression (3) in table 1.4, but with duration t counted from the end of the migrant's first student spell in the United States. Results for the estimated return hazard ratios are reported in figures 1.7a and 1.7b, which we can compare with figures 1.6a and 1.6b. We notice how the estimation of return hazard ratios with respect to time now

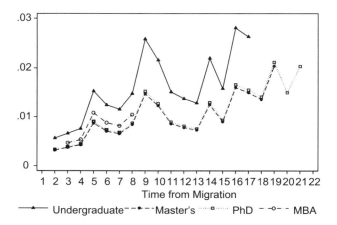

Fig. 1.6a   Estimated hazard ratios since entry into the United States by education level: education migrants, 1990 cohort

Note: Within-sample estimations from regression (3) in table 1.4 for age at migration = 23 and student status = 0 (all remaining regressors at mean values).

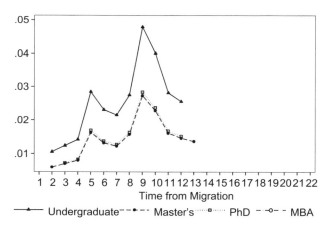

Fig. 1.6b   Estimated hazard ratios since entry into the United States, by education level: education migrants, 2000 cohort

Note: Within-sample estimations from regression (3) in table 1.4 for age at migration = 23 and student status = 0 (all remaining regressors at mean values).

changes: the inverted U-shape profile we initially observed is significantly smoothed, and the return hazard ratio appears first to increase and then to flatten down.

Overall, however, we find some signs of a positive time dependence of the return hazard on time for education migrants, which may imply positive self-selection with respect to unobservable skills. We further discuss these results in the conclusions.

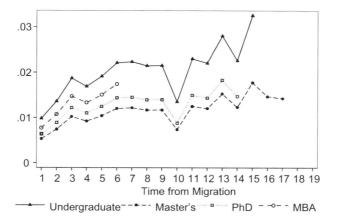

Fig. 1.7a   Estimated hazard ratios since completion of studies in the United States by education level: education migrants, 1990 cohort

Note: Within-sample estimations (unreported regression) for age at migration = 23 and student status = 0 (all remaining regressors at mean values).

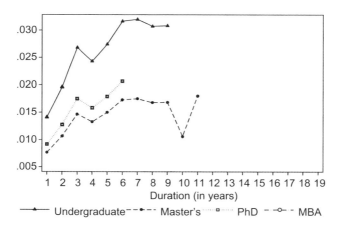

Fig. 1.7b   Estimated hazard ratios since completion of studies in the United States by education level: education migrants, 2000 cohort

Note: Within-sample estimations (unreported regression) for age at migration = 23 and student status = 0 (all remaining regressors at mean values).

1.5   Conclusions

Return migration is a much understudied topic, especially when it comes to its implications for innovation in both the host and home countries. Lack of data is a major cause of this situation due to the virtual absence of official statistics and the technical difficulties that stand in the way of large-scale data mining.

In this chapter, we have presented the outcome of an ambitious attempt to overcome such difficulties based on linking inventor information from patent data to biographical information from an important web-based social network. We focused on Indian inventors with professional experiences of various lengths at one or more US ICT companies and obtained rather reliable data for those among them who moved to the United States in the 1990s and 2000s. Based on biographical information, we could draw a clear distinction between work and education migrants and analyze separately the related return events. In particular, we applied event history analysis and explored the issue of returnees' self-selection with respect to observable and unobservable skills.

Both the distinction between work and education migrants and the study of self-selection may contribute to evaluating the effectiveness of US migration policies, with special reference to scientists, engineers, and other innovation-relevant professional categories.

As stressed by Koslowski (2018), US immigration policies are often compared unfavorably to those of countries such as Canada and Australia, whose selective, point-based visa systems are held responsible for their records of attracting high proportions of high-skilled migrants. But the comparison is biased by its exclusive focus on migrants first entering their host countries with permanent visas, which accounts for a very limited share of entries in the United States. When considering migrants entering with temporary visas, whether work- or education-based, the United States appears the most attractive country, also in view of the large share of temporary migrants turning into permanent ones over the years. In this respect, it becomes crucial to estimate the stay rates of highly skilled permanent immigrants, which our study on Indian migrants finds rather high and in accordance with the limited evidence available in the literature, especially for education migrants.

Besides assessing the highly skilled migrants' length of stay, it is crucial to assess whether the host countries manage to retain the best and brightest among them—namely, those who can contribute most to innovation. In this respect, Wadhwa et al. (2009) give voice to widespread concerns on the difficulties supposedly met by the United States in this respect. Our results, albeit exploratory, go against such concerns for work migrants and leave room for debate on education migrants.

Concerning work migrants, Indian returnees in our sample appear to be negatively selected with respect to education as well as, most likely, to the working experience they accumulate in the United States (as inferred by the negative time dependence of their hazard ratios). Admittedly, we also find a positive relationship between the return hazard and the number of patents they produce while in the United States, but we have suggested how this may have more to do with specialization in managerial functions or entrepreneurship than with positive self-selection.

As for education migrants, Indian returnees in our sample are also negatively selected with respect to education but also appear increasingly at risk of return the longer their permanence in the United States, especially over the first 10 years after migration. This can be interpreted as positive self-selection with respect to unobservable skills, at least over the first few years after graduation. But we should bear in mind that our return migration measure does not distinguish between individuals who settle permanently back in their home countries or become engaged in circular migration patterns and/or parallel professional activities in their home and host countries.

Further research is clearly needed to both assess the strength of these initial results and extend them. Further codification of the information contained in our data set will let us assess the quality and location of the educational institutions attended by migrants so as to test whether the return hazard is positively or negatively associated with the prestige of the institution and/or its links with a vibrant labor market for the highly skilled. We also plan to fully disambiguate the name of companies reported by work migrants in their LinkedIn profiles so as to distinguish between intracompany and intercompany mobility. We expect the former to generate short-term temporary migrants, not much exposed to the risk of turning permanent, while the latter should be at the origin of longer stays and more interesting phenomena of negative versus positive self-selection.

More generally, our methodology may be extended to other countries of origin of migrants besides India and to other professional categories besides those related to ICT.

While a large amount of the knowledge we may gather on highly skilled return migration will pass through the refinement and sharing of our data, we think that some ad hoc theorizing is also necessary to adapt the emerging theoretical literature on temporary and circular migration we discussed in section 1.2 to the specificities of STEM workers and students.

References

Allison, P. D. 2014. *Event History and Survival Analysis: Regression for Longitudinal Event Data*. Vol. 46. Los Angeles: SAGE.

Baruffaldi, S. H., and P. Landoni. 2012. "Return Mobility and Scientific Productivity of Researchers Working Abroad: The Role of Home Country Linkages." *Research Policy* 41 (9): 1655–65.

Bijwaard, G. E., C. Schluter, and J. Wahba. 2014. "The Impact of Labor Market Dynamics on the Return Migration of Immigrants." *Review of Economics and Statistics* 96 (3): 483–94.

Borjas, G. J. 1989. "Immigrant and Emigrant Earnings: A Longitudinal Study." *Economic Inquiry* 27 (1): 21–37.

Bönisch, P., P. Gaffert, and J. Wilde. 2013. "The Impact of Skills on Remigration Flows." *Applied Economics* 45 (4): 511–24.

Borjas, G. J., and B. Bratsberg. 1996. "Who Leaves? The Outmigration of the Foreign-Born." *Review of Economics and Statistics* 78 (1): 165–76.

Breschi, S., F. Lissoni, and E. Miguelez. 2017. "Foreign-Origin Inventors in the US: Testing for Diaspora and Brain Gain Effects." *Journal of Economic Geography* 17 (5): 1009–38.

Choudhury, P. 2016. "Return Migration and Geography of Innovation in MNEs: A Natural Experiment of Knowledge Production by Local Workers Reporting to Return Migrants." *Journal of Economic Geography* 16 (3): 585–610.

Constant, A., and D. S. Massey. 2002. "Return Migration by German Guestworkers: Neoclassical versus New Economic Theories." *International Migration* 40 (4): 5–38.

Constant, A. F., O. Nottmeyer, and K. F. Zimmermann. 2013. "The Economics of Circular Migration." In *International Handbook on the Economics of Migration*, edited by A. F. Constant and K. F. Zimmermann, 55–74. Cheltenham: Edward Elgar.

Constant, A. F., and K. F. Zimmermann. 2016. "Diaspora Economics: New Perspectives." *International Journal of Manpower* 37 (7): 1110–35.

De Rassenfosse, G., H. Dernis, D. Guellec, L. Picci, and B. v. P. de la Potterie. 2013. "The Worldwide Count of Priority Patents: A New Indicator of Inventive Activity." *Research Policy* 42 (3): 720–37.

Desai, M., D. Kapur, and J. McHale. 2005. "The Fiscal Impact of High Skilled Emigration: Flows of Indians to the US." Mimeo, Harvard University.

Dustmann, C., I. Fadlon, and Y. Weiss, Y. 2011. "Return Migration, Human Capital Accumulation and the Brain Drain." *Journal of Development Economics* 95 (1): 58–67.

Dustmann, C., and J.-S. Görlach. 2016. "The Economics of Temporary Migrations." *Journal of Economic Literature* 54 (1): 98–136.

Dustmann, C., and Y. Weiss. 2007. "Return Migration: Theory and Empirical Evidence from the UK." *British Journal of Industrial Relations* 45 (2): 236–56.

Filatotchev, I., X. Liu, J. Lu, and M. Wright, M. 2011. "Knowledge Spillovers through Human Mobility across National Borders: Evidence from Zhongguancun Science Park in China." *Research Policy* 40 (3): 453–462.

Finn, M. G. 2014. "Stay Rates of Foreign Doctorate Recipients from US Universities, 2011." Oak Ridge, TN: Oak Ridge Institute for Science and Education (ORISE).

Finn, M. G., and L. A. Pennington. 2018. "Stay Rates of Foreign Doctorate Recipients from US Universities, 2013." Oak Ridge, TN: Oak Ridge Institute for Science and Education (ORISE).

Gaulé, P. 2014. "Who Comes Back and When? Return Migration Decisions of Academic Scientists." *Economics Letters* 124 (3): 461–64.

Ge, C., K. W. Huang, and I. P. L. Png. 2016. "Engineer/Scientist Careers: Patents, Online Profiles, and Misclassification Bias." *Strategic Management Journal* 37 (1): 232–53.

Gibson, J., and D. McKenzie, D. 2014. "Scientific Mobility and Knowledge Networks in High Emigration Countries: Evidence from the Pacific." *Research Policy* 43 (9): 1486–95.

Hawthorne, L. 2018. "International Student Mobility: Sending Country Determinants and Policies." In *High-Skilled Migration: Drivers and Policies*, edited by M. Czaika, chap. 11. Oxford: Oxford University Press.

Hunt, J. 2011. "Which Immigrants Are Most Innovative and Entrepreneurial? Distinctions by Entry Visa." *Journal of Labor Economics* 29:417–57.

Hunt, J., 2013. "Are Immigrants the Best and Brightest U.S. Engineers?" NBER

Working Paper no. 18696. Cambridge, MA: National Bureau of Economic Research.

Jenkins, S. P. 2005. "Survival Analysis." Unpublished manuscript, Institute for Social and Economic Research, University of Essex, Colchester, UK.

Jones, B. F. 2009. "The Burden of Knowledge and the 'Death of the Renaissance Man': Is Innovation Getting Harder?" *Review of Economic Studies* 76 (1): 283–317.

Jonkers, K., and L. Cruz-Castro. 2013. "Research upon Return: The Effect of International Mobility on Scientific Ties, Production and Impact." *Research Policy* 42 (8): 1366–77.

Kahn, S., and M. MacGarvie. 2016. "Do Return Requirements Increase International Knowledge Diffusion? Evidence from the Fulbright Program." *Research Policy* 45 (6): 1304–22.

Kapur, D. 2010. "Indian Higher Education." In *American Universities in a Global Market*, edited by C. T. Clotfelter, 305–34. Chicago: University of Chicago Press.

Kapur, D., and J. McHale. 2005. *Give Us Your Best and Brightest: The Global Hunt for Talent and Its Impact on the Developing World*. Washington, DC: Center for Global Development.

Kerr, W. R. 2017. "US High-Skilled Immigration, Innovation, and Entrepreneurship: Empirical Approaches and Evidence." In *The International Mobility of Talent and Innovation: New Evidence and Policy Implications*, edited by C. Fink and E. Miguelez, 193–221. Cambridge: Cambridge University Press.

Kerr, S. P., W. R. Kerr, and W. F. Lincoln. 2015. "Skilled Immigration and the Employment Structures of US Firms." *Journal of Labor Economics* 33 (S1): S147–S186.

Kerr, W. R., and W. F. Lincoln. 2010. "The Supply Side of Innovation: H-1B Visa Reforms and U.S. Ethnic Invention." *Journal of Labor Economics* 28 (3): 473–508.

Kirdar, M. G. 2009. "Labor Market Outcomes, Savings Accumulation, and Return Migration." *Labour Economics* 16 (4): 418–28.

Koslowski, R. 2018. "Shifts in Selective Migration Policy Models." In *High-Skilled Migration: Drivers and Policies*, edited by M. Czaika, chap. 6. Oxford: Oxford University Press.

Lowell, B. L. 2000. "H-1B Temporary Workers: Estimating the Population." UC San Diego Working Papers. Working Paper no. 12.

Luo, S., M. E. Lovely, and D. Popp. 2013. "Intellectual Returnees as Drivers of Indigenous Innovation: Evidence from the Chinese Photovoltaic Industry." NBER Working Paper no. 19518. Cambridge, MA: National Bureau of Economic Research.

Nanda, R., and T. Khanna. 2010. "Diasporas and Domestic Entrepreneurs: Evidence from the Indian Software Industry." *Journal of Economics and Management Strategy* 19 (4): 991–1012.

OECD. 2008. *International Migration Outlook*. Paris: Organisation for Economic Co-operation and Development.

OECD. 2017. *International Migration Outlook*. Paris: Organisation for Economic Co-operation and Development.

Oettl, A., and A. Agrawal. 2008. "International Labor Mobility and Knowledge Flow Externalities." *Journal of International Business Studies* 39 (8): 1242–60.

Teitelbaum, M. S. 2014. *Falling Behind? Boom, Bust, and the Global Race for Scientific Talent*. Princeton, NJ: Princeton University Press.

Trippl, M. 2013. "Scientific Mobility and Knowledge Transfer at the Interregional and Intraregional Level." *Regional Studies* 47 (10), 1653–67.

UN. 1998. *Recommendations on Statistics of International Migration, Revision 1*. New York: United Nations Statistics Division.

Wadhwa, V. 2009. "A Reverse Brain Drain." *Issues in Science and Technology* 25 (3): 45–52.

Wadhwa, V., A. Saxenian, R. B. Freeman, and A. Salkever. 2009. "Losing the World's Best and Brightest: America's New Immigrant Entrepreneurs, Part 5." Mimeo. http://ssrn.com/abstract=1362012.

Zagheni, E., and I. Weber. 2015. "Demographic Research with Non-representative Internet Data." *International Journal of Manpower* 36 (1): 13–25.

Will the US Keep the Best and the Brightest (as Postdocs)?
Career and Location Preferences of Foreign STEM PhDs

Ina Ganguli and Patrick Gaulé

2.1 Introduction

A key factor behind the emergence and persistence of US leadership in science, technology, engineering, and mathematics (STEM) fields has been its ability to attract and retain top-tier talent from other countries. Foreign students represent half or more of PhD students, and they tend to be more productive during the PhD than natives (Gaulé and Piacentini 2013). More generally, the foreign-born make disproportionate contributions to US science and engineering (Stephan and Levin 2001).

Talented foreigners have typically come to the US as graduate students and have stayed in the US in academic or industry careers. An especially common career path among foreign PhD students is obtaining a postdoctoral position upon graduation. Postdocs, while an important part of the scientific labor force, are characterized by low pay and uncertain career trajectories. The NSF estimates that over 57 percent of postdocs in STEM fields were in the US on temporary visas in 2015; in chemistry, 64 percent of postdocs were temporary visa holders (NSF 2016). Yet relatively little is

Ina Ganguli is associate professor of economics at the University of Massachusetts, Amherst.

Patrick Gaulé is senior lecturer in economics at the University of Bath and a research affiliate of IZA.

We thank Jeff Furman, Delia Furtado, Jeff Grogger, Shulamit Kahn, Megan MacGarvie, seminar participants at the EPFL, and conference participants at the AEA Session on Foreign STEM Students and Immigration Policy, the Triple-I-Research Workshop on the Geographical and Organizational Mobility of Scientists, and the NBER conference on the Role of Immigrants and Foreign Students in Science, Innovation, and Entrepreneurship for comments and suggestions. We appreciate assistance from Danijela Vuletic in designing the survey. Gaulé and Ganguli acknowledge financial support by the Czech Science Foundation (GACR grant no 16–05082S). For acknowledgments, sources of research support, and disclosure of the authors' material financial relationships, if any, please see https://www.nber.org/chapters/c14108.ack.

known about both postdoc careers in general and the transition from the doctoral program to postdocs for foreign students in particular.

A few prior studies have used survey data collected at the end of the doctoral program to document the career and location choices of foreign STEM doctoral students. In another chapter in this volume, Roach, Sauermann, and Skrentny (chapter 8) compare foreign and native STEM doctoral students in terms of their entrepreneurial intentions, with foreign PhDs being more likely to express founder intentions or career preferences to join start-ups. They also report that 70 percent to 80 percent of foreign PhD students have intentions of working in the US, at least temporarily. Others have shown that individuals in US graduate programs with foreign bachelor's degrees and/or on temporary visas are more likely to take postdoc positions or other academic positions after graduation compared to US counterparts, likely because individuals in the US on temporary visas are constrained in their employment opportunities due to visa restrictions (Stephan and Ma 2005; Amuedo-Dorantes and Furtado 2019). One reason foreign students may prefer and ultimately end up in postdoc positions is that academic institutions are not subject to H-1B visa caps. For example, Amuedo-Dorantes and Furtado (2019) provide evidence suggesting that visa restrictions lead students to "settle" for academia. Grogger and Hanson (2015) also show using the Survey of Earned Doctorates that the foreign-born STEM doctoral students who report that they are intending to stay in the US in the year after they finish their degree are positively selected, measured indirectly through indicators such as having received fellowships during their studies. Finally, Finn (2010) measures stay rates of foreign-born doctorate recipients by country of origin and field of study using tabulated data from Social Security records.

An important aspect of using survey data collected only at the end of the PhD program—as well as aggregate estimates—is that these measures are the result of both supply- and demand-side factors.[1] For instance, students may plan to return to their home countries because they have failed to secure positions in the US. Similarly, a student may report planning to do a postdoc because no industry position was actually available to that student. Thus it is problematic to interpret these plans as necessarily reflecting preferences. By contrast, in this chapter we analyze a novel survey of currently enrolled doctoral students using a hypothetical choice methodology in order to elicit preferences among a set of options that are assumed to be available.[2]

---

1. A related literature has studied preferences for academic versus industry careers among currently enrolled doctoral students without focusing on differences between foreign and domestic students. See, e.g., Roach and Sauermann (2010).

2. Closest to the approach of our study is the work of Zeithammer and Kellogg (2013), who use conjoint analysis to study return migration preferences among US-educated Chinese STEM doctoral students. They ask approximately 300 Chinese STEM doctoral students studying at US universities questions about a series of hypothetical job choices with varying job attributes, such as salary, US location, public versus private firm, and job role (e.g., scientist manager). They find that Chinese doctoral graduates tend to remain in the United States because of a

Our study thus contributes to the existing literature by focusing on the supply side of the market by identifying and comparing the preferences of foreign and US graduate students for an academic versus industry career and for a US versus foreign location for a postdoc position. We leverage data from an original survey we conducted in the fall of 2017 of 1,605 current doctoral students in a major STEM field—chemistry—studying at 54 US institutions about their career and location preferences.

First, we estimate the career preferences of foreign and US STEM students for different types of postgraduation jobs—postdocs, industry, or teaching positions—using both hypothetical choice methods and more standard Likert-scale measures of preferences for different careers. Using a large sample of students across a range of departments, we are able to compare the preferences of foreign and US students within the same PhD program and area of specialization. We find that foreign students are much more likely to prefer a postdoc position upon graduation, reporting an 11-percentage-point higher likelihood of accepting a postdoc position at a top university compared to US students on average. US and foreign students both similarly place the highest preferences on industry jobs, but our results point to a notable difference in the types of academic jobs they prefer; foreign students value research-oriented academic careers more than US students (postdoc jobs), while US students value teaching more.

Since neither research nor teaching institutions would be subject to H-1B caps, it is unlikely that the differences in preferences for teaching versus research are due to potential visa restrictions. A potential explanation for the preference of foreigners toward academic careers may be that they are more able (e.g., due to a differential selection mechanism). However, controlling for proxies for ability, such as GRE scores or publications during the PhD, does not noticeably affect the results.

Second, we examine students' location preferences using a novel revealed preference approach based on a hypothetical choice method. Here we ask each respondent to report how likely (in terms of percent chances out of 100) they are to choose a postdoc position when given pairs of postdoc offers, where the offers include postdoc positions in top-50 chemistry departments in either US or non-US universities (based on the Shanghai Ranking). Our empirical strategy is based on comparing foreign and domestic students who are presented with the same hypothetical choice. While respondents across the board have a strong preference for US locations, foreign students are even more likely to prefer US locations. We estimate that foreign students are 13 percentage points more likely to choose a (hypothetical) postdoc offer in the US than in a non-US department even when controlling for the

large salary disparity between the two countries rather than because of an inherent preference for locating in the United States. In contrast to their work, we focus on choices among post-doctoral offers, varying only the employer (and implicitly location) on a larger sample covering both domestic and foreign students from different countries studying in the US. This enables us to directly compare the preferences of foreign students to those of US domestic students.

difference in the rank of the programs and baseline preferences for doing a postdoc and when comparing students within the same PhD program.

In sum, our findings show that foreign and US chemistry PhD students have significantly different preferences for careers, with foreign students being more likely to prefer academic careers and doing a postdoc. Foreign students also value a US location more than US students. Our results suggest that while the US is currently managing to retain talented foreign graduate students as postdocs, it is important for future research to understand why foreign students have greater preferences for postdoc positions in the US than native students and to what extent these preferences are driven by visa policies. We discuss possible explanations and directions for future research in the final section of the chapter.

2.2   Methodology

In this chapter, we are interested in measuring graduate students' preferences for different careers and different locations through an original survey. To measure preferences for academic careers, we use two types of questions. First, we use more standard Likert measures by asking respondents to rate the attractiveness of academic and other careers "leaving job availability aside." This approach follows closely that of Roach and Sauermann (2010) in their study of PhD career preferences.

Second, we use a hypothetical choices methodology. This methodology echoes conjoint analysis in marketing (see Zeithammer and Kellogg 2013 as discussed earlier) and has recently been used in labor economics to measure preferences over job attributes (e.g., Wiswall and Zafar 2017; Mas and Pallais 2017). This methodology essentially presents respondents with sets of jobs that vary in their attributes and asks them to state their probabilistic choices. To measure career preferences, we ask students to imagine that they have three job offers and then select how likely they are (percent chance out of 100) to accept one offer over the other. Importantly, the total chances the student allocates to the three offers should add up to 100. This ensures that they can't report a preference for each type of career. The choices are (1) Research Scientist/Engineer at Private Sector Firm (e.g., DuPont, Novartis); (2) Postdoctoral Research Fellow at Top US University (e.g., Berkeley, MIT); and (3) Assistant Professor at Top Liberal Arts College (e.g., Swarthmore College). Here we will interpret choosing the option to do a postdoc as a preference for an academic career.[3] The exact wording of both questions is

3. In many STEM fields, faculty placements out of graduate school are almost unheard of and postdocs are a necessary step in an academic career. While a sizeable number of students do postdocs and then go on to industry careers, we offer an industry career as an option in the counterfactual question. We thus interpret choosing a postdoc as a preference for an academic career, since those who have a preference for industry can choose the industry research scientist job offer.

available in appendix A. To estimate preferences for academia, we will run regressions of the type

$$PreferAcademia_i = \beta Foreign_i + \partial X_i + \varepsilon_i,$$

where i indexes students, $PreferAcademia_i$ is one of the three preferences measures as described previously, $Foreign_i$ is an indicator variable for foreign student, and X_i is a vector of controls including graduate school fixed effects, gender, marital status, enrollment year, and field of study.

To measure preferences for different locations, we also use a hypothetical choices methodology. Here we ask respondents to choose between two post-doctoral job offers that only differ in the employer (university) and hence location. We view STEM postdoctoral positions as being well suited for this type of analysis, since these positions are very similar across universities in terms of content (heavy research focus) and salary.

We are interested in the choices that involve a US university and a foreign university and whether foreign students report different preferences than native students when confronted with such choices. More specifically, we are interested in the propensity of foreign and native students to choose the US university when presented with the same two alternative choices. For instance, we might offer students a hypothetical choice between a post-doctoral position at Harvard and the University of Toronto and then see whether foreign students are more or less likely to choose Harvard, holding the counterfactual opportunity set fixed. We will be running regressions of the following type:

$$PreferUS_{i,jk} = \beta Foreign_i + \partial X_i + \gamma_{jk} + \varepsilon_{i,jk},$$

where i indexes students and j and k index the universities in the postdoc offers. $PreferUS_{i,jk}$ is an indicator variable for choosing the US option with a high probability (70 percent or more), $Foreign_i$ is an indicator variable for foreign student, X_i is a vector of student characteristics (graduate school fixed effects, gender, marital status, enrollment year, field of study), and γ_{jk} is a fixed effect for the university pair.

2.3   Data: Survey of Chemistry Doctoral Students

Our main data source is an original survey of US chemistry PhD students conducted in the fall of 2017. To construct our sampling frame, we first identified a set of 54 research-intensive US universities that grant PhDs and are internationally renowned in the field of chemistry (see list in appendix B).[4] We gathered the names and emails of all individuals (approximately 9,000)

---

4. This set corresponds to all US universities listed in the top 200 universities in the world according to the Academic Ranking of World Universities (Shanghai Ranking) in its chemistry subject ranking.

that were listed as graduate students in the chemistry departments of these universities either on graduate student directory websites or on individual laboratory websites.[5] We then sent email invitations to these students asking them to answer an online survey on the Qualtrics survey platform. To ensure a reasonable response rate, we sent two rounds of reminders and provided incentives to complete the survey in the form of a lottery to win Amazon gift certificates. We obtained approximately 1,600 complete responses corresponding roughly to an 18 percent response rate, which is quite consistent with survey response rates of this population (see, e.g., Sauermann and Roach 2013). However, collecting survey data prior to graduation comes with a tradeoff, as we have lower response rates than in the end-of-degree surveys.

The survey included a set of basic demographic questions as well as questions on undergraduate education, year of enrollment in the PhD program, progress in the PhD program, field of specialization, and career preferences questions discussed previously. Additionally, each respondent was presented with five consecutive hypothetical postdoc offer choices.

We coded each respondent as a foreign or a US student using a question in the survey about the country of the respondent's undergraduate institution. If the country was in the US, we coded the student as US, and if not, we coded the student as a foreign student. While we do not know each student's country of birth, the assignment of foreign status based on the country of undergraduate studies is commonly done in the literature (see, e.g., Gaulé 2014; Kahn and MacGarvie 2016).[6]

Table 2.1 provides summary statistics for the sample for US and foreign students. Approximately 30 percent of the sample are foreign, and most of the foreign respondents are from China (30 percent), followed by India (13 percent) and then Canada (5 percent).

We find a few differences between the US and foreign students in our raw data, with US students having slightly more women (8 percent higher) and being more likely to have enrolled in 2013. US and foreign respondents are similarly distributed across subfields within chemistry.

To assess the representativeness of our sample, we can compare our data with data collected by the National Science Foundation (NSF) and the

5. One issue we encountered is that some of the individuals we contacted reported having already graduated, reflecting, for example, the fact that some online directories and websites are not entirely up to date. We excluded such responses from our analysis sample.

6. While a growing number of foreign students have been pursuing undergraduate studies in the US, the vast majority of foreign students enrolled in US doctoral programs have a foreign undergraduate degree. For instance, Gaule and Piacentini (2013) report that in a large sample of chemistry PhD students graduating from a US department between 1999 and 2008, 88 percent of students with Chinese first and last names had received their undergraduate degrees in China (and a further 5 percent in Taiwan). We additionally checked in our sample whether we are missing a large number of respondents who are international students but did their undergraduate degree in the US using a name-matching algorithm. There are only a small number of respondents (18, or 1 percent of our sample) who have a Chinese/Indian/Korean last name, have a Chinese/Indian/Korean first name, and reported a US undergraduate institution.

Table 2.1   **Summary statistics at the student level (sample means)**

	US student	Foreign student	Difference
Female	0.465	0.379	0.086**
Married	0.161	0.193	−0.032
Enrolled 2015	0.209	0.205	0.004
Enrolled 2014	0.187	0.210	−0.023
Enrolled 2013	0.187	0.131	0.056**
Enrolled 2012	0.101	0.082	0.019
Enrolled 2011	0.022	0.017	0.004
Field of study			
Analytical	0.119	0.087	0.032
Biological/biochemistry	0.168	0.193	−0.025
Inorganic chemistry	0.172	0.146	0.025
Organic chemistry	0.180	0.173	0.007
Physical	0.154	0.146	0.008
Polymer	0.046	0.047	−0.001
Theoretical/computational	0.061	0.094	−0.033*
Other	0.101	0.114	−0.013
Country of undergraduate			
Canada		0.050	
China		0.302	
India		0.134	
Observations	1,201	404	

Note: Asterisks indicate the results of tests for equality of means. * $p < 0.10$, ** $p < 0.05$, *** $p < 0.01$.

National Institutes of Health (NIH) through the 2016 Survey of Graduate Students and Postdoctorates in Science and Engineering, which is an annual census of all US academic institutions granting research-based graduate degrees (NSF 2016) for chemistry.[7] We find that our survey data include somewhat fewer foreign students/temporary visa holders (33.6 percent vs. 37.6 percent) and slightly more female respondents (44.3 percent vs. 40.9 percent). Given that the NSF/NIH Survey includes students enrolled at all US graduate degree–granting academic institutions, whereas our survey was limited to the top 54 chemistry programs, the numbers are quite close.

For the location preferences, we offered each student five randomly selected counterfactual choices of postdoctoral positions. These choices were drawn from each possible pairwise combination of universities in the top 50 universities in the world in chemistry according to the Shanghai Rankings (see appendix C for a list). However, we focus here on the choices involving a foreign university and a US university—4,030 observations. We define "Strongly Prefer the US University" as selecting the chance of accepting the US postdoctoral position with a probability of 70 percent or more. Conversely, "Strongly Prefer the Foreign University" is defined as selecting

7. In this survey, the academic departments complete the questionnaire.

Table 2.2   Summary statistics at the choice level (sample means)

	US student	Foreign student	Difference
Strongly prefer US university	0.481	0.605	−0.124***
Strongly prefer foreign university	0.220	0.149	0.070***
Difference in university rank between US university and foreign university (lower rank corresponds to a better position in the Shanghai Rankings)	−6.93	−7.581	0.642
Location of foreign university			
Japan	0.277	0.277	−0.001
Germany	0.185	0.176	0.014
UK	0.130	0.128	0.012
Switzerland	0.099	0.121	0.011
China	0.085	0.083	0.010
Canada	0.047	0.040	0.007
France	0.049	0.045	0.008
Israel	0.047	0.035	0.008
Australia	0.042	0.045	0.007
Saudi Arabia	0.039	0.049	0.001
Observations	3,023	1,007	

Note: Asterisks indicate the results of tests for equality of means. * $p < 0.10$, ** $p < 0.05$, *** $p < 0.01$.

the chance of accepting the foreign US postdoctoral position with a probability of 70 percent or more. Table 2.2 presents descriptive statistics on the choice-level data.

We observe that both US and foreign students tend to prefer the US university (with a considerably higher mean for "Strongly Prefer the US University" compared to "Strongly Prefer the Foreign University"). This may reflect some intrinsic preference for being located in the US, but it may also reflect a preference for higher-ranked universities, as the US universities in the choices tend to have a lower (i.e., better) rank. Perhaps surprisingly, we observe that foreign students have a stronger preference for US postdoctoral positions than do US students.

2.4   Results

We first investigate whether foreign and domestic students have different career preferences using our three main measures of career preferences: (1) the attractiveness of the tenure-track faculty job on a one- to five-point Likert scale, (2) the overall percent chance they will do a postdoc after the PhD, and (3) the percentage chance of choosing a postdoc versus an industry research position or teaching-focused position in the hypothetical job offer question. In figure 2.1, we show the raw means for US and foreign students for the third measure based on the three hypothetical job offers. While both

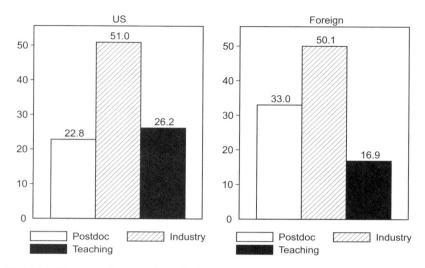

Fig. 2.1   Career preferences: hypothetical job offer question

Notes: See appendix A for text of survey question. Respondents were asked to rate how likely they were to accept one of three hypothetical job offers, reporting the percent chance (out of 100) of choosing each one. The choices were research scientist/engineer at private-sector firm (e.g., DuPont, Novartis), postdoctoral research fellow at top US university (e.g., Berkeley, MIT), and assistant professor at top liberal arts college (e.g., Swarthmore College).

Table 2.3   Estimates of career preferences

	Attractiveness of tenure-track faculty job (1–5 Likert) (1)	Chances of choosing postdoc option (among 3 choices) (2)	Likelihood of doing a postdoc (3)
Foreign student	0.829***	9.864***	12.410***
	(0.081)	(1.504)	(1.962)
Mean of DV	2.971	25.283	54.017
Observations	1,590	1,585	1,517

Note: Controls: Graduate school fixed effects, gender, marital status, enrollment year, field of study. Standard errors in parentheses. * $p < 0.1$, ** $p < 0.05$, *** $p < 0.01$.

US and foreign students overall prefer the industry choice, we can see that foreign students are more likely than US students to choose the postdoc and less likely to choose the teaching position.

Next we regress our measures of preferences for academia on an indicator variable for whether the respondent is a foreign student and control for a broad range of student characteristics, including gender, marital status, enrollment year, field of study, and graduate school. In table 2.3, we show that foreign students consistently report finding tenure-track faculty jobs more attractive than do US students and that they are 10 percentage points

Table 2.4   **Estimates of career preferences: Chinese versus other foreign students**

	Attractiveness of tenure-track faculty job (1–5 Likert) (1)	Chances of choosing postdoc option (among 3 choices) (2)	Likelihood of doing a postdoc (3)
Chinese student	0.882***	6.724***	8.749***
	(0.129)	(2.379)	(3.175)
Other foreign student	0.804***	11.310***	13.964***
	(0.093)	(1.726)	(2.229)
Mean of DV	2.971	25.283	54.017
Observations	1,590	1,585	1,517

Note: Controls: Graduate school fixed effects, gender, marital status, enrollment year, field of study. The number of observations may vary due to missing answers for some questions. Standard errors in parentheses. * $p < 0.1$, ** $p < 0.05$, *** $p < 0.01$.

Table 2.5   **Ability differences between foreign and US students**

	GRE score (self-reported) (1)	Publication in *Nature/Science/Cell* (2)	Pub in top chemistry journal (3)
Foreign student	82.838***	0.008***	0.006
	(5.424)	(0.003)	(0.012)
Mean of DV	770.461	0.004	0.095
Observations	1,780	4,030	4,030

Note: Controls: Graduate school fixed effects, gender, marital status, enrollment year, field of study. Standard errors in parentheses. * $p < 0.1$, ** $p < 0.05$, *** $p < 0.01$.

more likely to choose a postdoc option when being offered a choice between postdoc, an industry research position, or a teaching-focused position. Foreign students also rate their chance of doing a postdoc overall as 12 percentage points higher.[8] These patterns hold for both Chinese students and other foreign students, although the effect is somewhat weaker for Chinese students (see table 2.4).

One possible explanation for the fact that foreign students are more interested in academic careers is that they may be of higher ability or more science-oriented due to selection into emigration or selection into US PhD programs. To investigate this possibility, we first estimate whether foreign students in our sample appear to be higher ability or more science-oriented (table 2.5). We find that even when controlling for student characteristics, including gender, enrollment year, field of study, and graduate school, for-

8. One should bear in mind that the self-assessed chance of doing a postdoc may already incorporate expectations about what type of options will be available.

eign students have significantly higher (self-reported) GRE scores and are more likely to have already published during the PhD in one of the premier journals (*Nature*, *Science*, or *Cell*). This finding is consistent with other studies finding that foreign students—particularly Chinese students, who make up the largest share of our foreign student sample—are higher ability and more productive in terms of publications during the PhD (see, e.g., Gaulé and Piacentini 2013).

Next we repeat the regressions of academic career preferences in table 2.4 and now control for ability, where we proxy for ability with the publications of the student and the self-reported GRE scores (see table 2.6). While the inclusion of these controls somewhat weakens the point estimate for foreign students, the estimate remains large and significant. This suggests that other factors may play a role in the differing preferences for academic careers between foreign and native US students. For instance, it may be the case that foreign students envision an academic career in their home countries, or there may be important cross-cultural differences in the attractiveness of academic careers.

Next we turn to the analysis of location preferences, where we consider the hypothetical choices respondents made between pairs of postdoctoral offers described previously. Here we regress whether the respondent reported a strong preference for the US postdoctoral option on an indicator variable for whether the respondent is a foreign student while controlling for student characteristics (gender, marital status, enrollment year, field of study, graduate school) as well as a fixed effect for the pair of universities being presented to the student (choice fixed effects). We are thus effectively comparing foreign and domestic students who are asked to choose between the exact same two postdoctoral options. We also report the results of another specification where the dependent variable indicates having a strong preference for the non-US postdoctoral option.

As was already the case in the raw descriptive statistics, foreign students have a *stronger* preference for US universities (table 2.7). This is especially true for Chinese students but also holds for other foreign students (table 2.8).

Table 2.9 presents some heterogeneity analysis to try to shed light on why this difference in preferences may arise. Already having a publication is associated with a greater preference for the US university (column 1) but does not have a differential effect for foreign and domestic students. There is some limited evidence that foreign students with high GRE scores are less likely to have a preference for the US university (column 2), although the estimates are very noisy here. Interestingly, foreign students who have a stronger preference for an academic career are less likely to strongly prefer the US university (column 3).

Finally, we examine whether foreign and US students vary in their preferences depending on the difference in the Shanghai Rankings of the institutions offered. In figure 2.2, we show that foreign students strongly prefer the

Table 2.6   Estimates of career preferences: controlling for ability

	Attractiveness of tenure-track faculty job (1–5 Likert) (1)	Attractiveness of tenure-track faculty job (1–5 Likert) (2)	Likelihood of doing a postdoc (3)	Likelihood of doing a postdoc (4)	Chances of choosing postdoc option (among 3 choices) (5)	Chances of choosing postdoc option (among 3 choices) (6)
Foreign student	0.829***	0.721***	12.410***	11.246***	9.864***	8.405***
	(0.081)	(0.085)	(1.962)	(2.059)	(1.504)	(1.585)
Publication in *Nature/ Science/Cell*		0.636		22.426		24.470**
		(0.593)		(15.812)		(11.037)
Publication in top chemistry journal		0.295**		3.063		4.056*
		(0.118)		(2.927)		(2.206)
GRE dummies	No	Yes	No	Yes	No	Yes
Mean of DV	2.971	2.971	54.017	54.017	25.283	25.283
Observations	1,590	1,590	1,517	1,517	1,585	1,585

Note: Controls: Graduate school fixed effects, gender, marital status, enrollment year, field of study. Standard errors in parentheses. * $p < 0.1$, ** $p < 0.05$, *** $p < 0.01$.

Table 2.7   **Estimates of location preferences**

	Strongly prefer US university (1)	Strongly prefer foreign university (2)
Foreign student	0.131***	−0.072***
	(0.023)	(0.017)
Mean of DV	0.512	0.202
Obs	4,030	4,030
R^2	0.309	0.277

Note: Controls: Choice fixed effects, graduate school fixed effects, gender, marital status, enrollment year, field of study. Standard errors in parentheses. * $p < 0.1$, ** $p < 0.05$, *** $p < 0.01$.

Table 2.8   **Estimates of location preferences: Chinese versus other foreign students**

	Strongly prefer US university (1)	Strongly prefer foreign university (2)
Chinese student	0.177***	−0.102***
	(0.037)	(0.027)
Other foreign student	0.111***	−0.059***
	(0.026)	(0.019)
Mean of DV	0.512	0.202
Obs	4,030	4,030
R^2	0.310	0.277

Note: Controls: Choice fixed effects, graduate school fixed effects, gender, marital status, enrollment year, field of study. * $p < 0.1$, ** $p < 0.05$, *** $p < 0.01$.

US university across all ranks, and the difference in research rank between the domestic and foreign universities does not seem to have a differential effect for domestic and foreign students (table 2.9, column 4).

2.5   Discussion

In this chapter, we have reported the results of a novel survey of chemistry doctoral students enrolled at the top 54 US institutions aimed at understanding to what extent foreign and US students differ in their career and location preferences. Unlike previous studies focused on estimating career and location choices of foreign and US students, which have tended to rely on either survey data collected after students have completed their degrees or administrative data after students have obtained their first position, our data provide a measure of preferences before students are faced with demand-side factors.

We have documented that foreign and US students indeed appear to have significantly different career preferences, with foreign students being much more likely to prefer doing a postdoc and generally preferring academic

Table 2.9   Estimates of location preferences: controlling for ability and career preferences

	Strongly prefer US university (1)	Strongly prefer US university (2)	Strongly prefer US university (3)	Strongly prefer US university (4)	Strongly prefer US university (5)
Foreign student	0.132***	0.146***	0.137***	0.137***	0.131***
	(0.024)	(0.026)	(0.025)	(0.024)	(0.029)
Foreign student × has published	−0.022				0.001
	(0.073)				(0.073)
Has published	0.089**				0.080**
	(0.040)				(0.040)
Foreign × high GRE		−0.094*			−0.094*
		(0.056)			(0.055)
High GRE		0.067*			0.063
		(0.038)			(0.038)
Foreign × academic orientation			−0.111*		−0.151**
			(0.068)		(0.071)
Academic orientation			0.111**		0.087*
			(0.044)		(0.047)
Foreign × rank difference between the two schools				0.001	0.001
				(0.001)	(0.001)
Mean of DV	0.512	0.512	0.512	0.512	0.512
Obs	4,030	4,030	4,030	4,030	4,030
R^2	0.311	0.311	0.311	0.310	0.320

Note: Controls: Choice fixed effects, graduate school fixed effects, gender, marital status, enrollment year, field of study. Standard errors in parentheses. Academic orientation is proxied by an indicator variable taking value one for those respondents rating "faculty with research focus" as strictly more attractive than other career options. The main effect of rank difference between the two schools is not shown as it is absorbed into the fixed effect. * $p < 0.1$, ** $p < 0.05$, *** $p < 0.01$.

careers more than US students. We also show using a hypothetical choice method that foreign students also value a US location more than US students, even controlling for the ability and career preferences of the students. The high value placed on US location by foreign students is consistent with high rates of intentions to stay (Roach, Sauermann, and Skrentny, forthcoming) and high aggregate stay rates (Finn 2010).

One interpretation of our finding that foreign students have a stronger preference for US postdocs is linked to the availability of subsequent career options. Industry careers are the most likely eventual outcome, even for students who pursue postdocs, and it may be that access to industry careers in the US is differently impacted by a foreign postdoc across foreign and domestic students. Specifically, foreign students may be concerned that a foreign postdoc will limit their subsequent access to the US industry market if US postdocs are preferred in the US private sector. Conversely, US students may perceive foreign postdocs as enhancing their CVs without worsening their US industry career options.

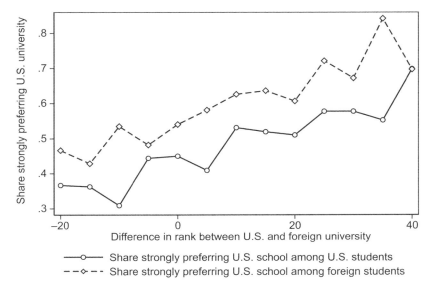

Fig. 2.2   Preferences for US location and university rank

Notes: Strongly preferring the US university means choosing the US option with a probability of 70 percent or more. The difference in rank of each pair of choices is calculated using the Shanghai Rankings of the institutions. A positive difference in rank corresponds to the US university having a better ranking than the foreign university.

Foreign students may also believe that leaving the US for a foreign postdoc will limit future private-sector options due to visa concerns. Foreign students are potentially "locked in" to a US location, as they have already incurred the costs of getting a visa or started the green card application process in the US. If they would like to eventually return to the US, then leaving the US for a two- or three-year postdoc, even if at a higher-ranked institution, may not be worth it if they eventually would like to pursue the US immigration path.

Another potential explanation is that the foreign students have ipso facto experienced migration to another country, while the US students would typically not already have had such an experience. Having a second migration to a different country might be relatively less appealing than a first migration experience.

While we cannot distinguish between these explanations for why foreign students prefer US locations for a postdoc more than US students with the data we have collected, we believe that our study points to important avenues for future research on these issues, particularly surrounding the role of visa policies in driving the preferences of foreign students. Moreover, the methodology we used in this chapter could be used in future research to tackle a wider range of questions regarding the preferences of foreign and domestic students. Some of the important questions we see as extensions of our study include the following: What are the preferences of foreign students who have not yet arrived in the US? How do location preferences evolve over time in the same set of students? Among students enrolled in doctoral programs in other countries, do they have preferences for being located in those countries? Or did they have a preference for US doctoral programs but did not have the opportunity to study there? The answers to such questions would shed further light on our understanding of the allocation of talented and skilled individuals across countries—the global "market for talent."

Appendix A
Selected Survey Questions

[Question 1]

Q. Putting job availability aside, how attractive do you personally find each of the following careers?

	Not at all attractive (1)	Mostly not attractive (2)	Neutral (3)	Mostly attractive (4)	Very attractive (5)
Academic faculty with an emphasis on research (1)	O	O	O	O	O
Academic faculty with an emphasis on teaching (2)	O	O	O	O	O
Government research and development position (3)	O	O	O	O	O
Government (other) (6)	O	O	O	O	O
Industry position with an emphasis on research and development (4)	O	O	O	O	O
Industry (other) (5)	O	O	O	O	O

[Question 2]

Q. Now we want to ask you to do some simple evaluations of potential job offers. Imagine that you have just completed your dissertation and are looking for a **full-time position**. First, suppose you have the following job offers and you need to choose between them. Please rate how likely you are to accept one of them rather than the other. For each job offer, choose the percent chance (out of 100) of choosing each one. **The total chances given to each offer should add up to 100.**

_____   **Job Offer #1:** Research Scientist/Engineer at Private Sector Firm (e.g. DuPont, Novartis) **Annual Salary:** $90,000 (1)

_____   **Job Offer #2:** Postdoctoral Research Fellow at Top U.S. university (e.g. Berkeley, MIT) **Annual Salary:** $50,000 (2)

_____   **Job Offer #3:** Assistant Professor at top liberal arts college (e.g. Swarthmore College) **Annual Salary:** $70,000 (3)

[Question 3]

Q. Now, we will ask you to evaluate a series of job offers. Suppose you had the following two job offers. Please rate how likely you are to accept one of them rather than the other.

Job Offer #1
Employer: University X
Location: Location of University X
Job Title: Postdoctoral Research Fellow

Job Offer #2
Employer: University Y
Location: Location of University Y
Job Title: Postdoctoral Research Fellow

	Strongly Prefer Left (1)	Somewhat Prefer Left (2)	Indifferent (3)	Somewhat Prefer Right (4)	Strongly Prefer Right (5)

	0	10	20	30	40	50	60	70	80	90	100

Which job offer do you prefer? (1)

Note: University X and Y are two of the top 50 universities worldwide according to a bibliometric ranking of universities in chemistry (Shanghai Academic Ranking of World Universities ranking in chemistry). Each respondent was presented with five such choices, with the choices randomly selected among all pairwise combinations of the top 50 universities in chemistry. The analysis focuses on the choices that involve one US and one foreign university.

Appendix B

Universities Included in the Sampling Frame

Table 2B.1   Universities included in the sampling frame

Arizona State University	University of California, Irvine
California Institute of Technology	University of California, Los Angeles
Carnegie Mellon University	University of California, Riverside
Colorado State University	University of California, San Diego
Columbia University	University of California, Santa Barbara
Cornell University	University of Chicago
Duke University	University of Colorado
Emory University	University of Delaware
Georgia Institute of Technology	University of Florida
Harvard University	University of Houston
Indiana University	University of Illinois at Urbana-Champaign
Iowa State University	University of Maryland, College Park
Johns Hopkins University	University of Massachusetts Amherst
Massachusetts Institute of Technology	University of Michigan
North Carolina State University	University of Minnesota
Northwestern University	University of North Carolina at Chapel Hill
Ohio State University	University of Pennsylvania
Pennsylvania State University	University of Pittsburgh
Princeton University	University of South Florida
Purdue University	University of Southern California
Rice University	University of Utah
Stanford University	University of Virginia
State University of New York at Buffalo	University of Washington
Texas A&M University	University of Wisconsin–Madison
University of Texas at Austin	Washington State University
University of California, Berkeley	Washington University in St. Louis
University of California, Davis	Yale University

Appendix C

Top 50 Universities in the World in Chemistry according to the Shanghai Rankings

Table 2C.1   Top 50 universities in the world in chemistry according to the Shanghai Rankings

1 University of California, Berkeley	26 University of Texas at Austin
2 Harvard University	27 University of California, Irvine
3 Stanford University	28 Georgia Institute of Technology
4 California Institute of Technology	29 University of Michigan-Ann Arbor
5 Northwestern University	30 University of Minnesota, Twin Cities
6 Massachusetts Institute of Technology (MIT)	31 Peking University
7 University of Cambridge	32 University of Wuerzburg
8 Swiss Federal Institute of Technology Zurich	33 University of Colorado at Boulder
9 Kyoto University	34 University of Illinois at Urbana-Champaign
10 University of Pennsylvania	35 Tohoku University
11 University of California, Los Angeles	36 King Abdulaziz University
12 Yale University	37 University of Florida
13 University of California, Santa Barbara	38 Zhejiang University
14 Technical University Munich	39 Osaka University
15 Cornell University	40 Texas A&M University
16 Columbia University	41 University of California, Riverside
17 University of Oxford	42 Weizmann Institute of Science
18 University of California, San Diego	43 University of Wisconsin–Madison
19 University of Strasbourg	44 Monash University
20 Purdue University–West Lafayette	45 University of Chicago
21 Heidelberg University	46 University of Muenster
22 Rice University	47 University of Southern California
23 Swiss Federal Institute of Technology Lausanne	48 Tokyo Institute of Technology
24 University of Toronto	49 Nagoya University
25 University of Tokyo	50 Imperial College London

References

Amuedo-Dorantes, C., and D. Furtado. 2019. "Settling for Academia? H-1B Visas and the Career Choices of International Students in the United States (No. 1705)." *Journal of Human Resources* 54 (2): 401–29.

Finn, M. 2010. "Stay Rates of Foreign Doctorate Recipients from the U.S. Universities 2010." Oak Ridge, TN: Oak Ridge Institute for Science and Education.

Gaulé, P. 2014. "Who Comes Back and When? Return Migration Decisions of Academic Scientists." *Economics Letters* 124 (3): 461–64.

Gaulé, P., and M. Piacentini. 2013. "Chinese Graduate Students and US Scientific Productivity." *Review of Economics and Statistics* 95 (2): 698–701.

Grogger, J., and G. H. Hanson. 2015. "Attracting Talent: Location Choices of Foreign-Born PhDs in the US." *Journal of Labor Economics* 33 (S1): S5–S38.

Kahn, S., and M. J. MacGarvie. 2016. "How Important Is US Location for Research in Science?" *Review of Economics and Statistics* 98 (2): 397–414.

Mas, A., and A. Pallais. 2017. "Valuing Alternative Work Arrangements." *American Economic Review* 107 (12): 3722–59.

National Science Foundation. 2016. Survey of Graduate Students and Postdoctorates in Science and Engineering. National Center for Science and Engineering Statistics. Fall. https://www.nsf.gov/statistics/srvygradpostdoc/.

Roach, M., and H. Sauermann. 2010. "A Taste for Science? PhD Scientists' Academic Orientation and Self-Selection into Research Careers in Industry." *Research Policy* 39 (3): 422–34.

Roach, M., H. Sauermann, and J. Skrentny. Forthcoming. "Entrepreneurial Characteristics, Preferences and Outcomes of Native and Foreign Science and Engineering PhD Students."

Sauermann, H., and M. Roach. 2013. "Increasing Web Survey Response Rates in Innovation Research: An Experimental Study of Static and Dynamic Contact Design Features." *Research Policy* 42 (1): 273–86.

Stephan, P., and J. Ma. 2005. "The Increased Frequency and Duration of the Postdoctorate Career Stage." *American Economic Review* 95 (2). Papers and Proceedings of the 117th Annual Meeting of the American Economic Association, Philadelphia, PA, January 7–9, 2005, 71–75.

Stephan, P. E., and S. G. Levin. 2001. "Exceptional Contributions to US Science by the Foreign-Born and Foreign-Educated." *Population Research and Policy Review* 20 (1–2): 59–79.

Stuen, E. T., A. M. Mobarak, and K. E. Maskus. 2012. "Skilled Immigration and Innovation: Evidence from Enrolment Fluctuations in US Doctoral Programmes." *Economic Journal* 122 (565): 1143–76.

Wiswall, M., and B. Zafar. 2017. "Preference for the Workplace, Investment in Human Capital, and Gender." *Quarterly Journal of Economics* 133 (1): 457–507.

Zeithammer, R., and R. P. Kellogg. 2013. "The Hesitant Hai Gui: Return-Migration Preferences of US-Educated Chinese Scientists and Engineers." *Journal of Marketing Research* 50 (5): 644–63.

II

Immigration Policy and Innovation

3

High-Skill Immigration, Innovation, and Creative Destruction

Gaurav Khanna and Munseob Lee

3.1 Introduction

Recent political and academic discussions have shone a spotlight on issues related to high-skill immigration. This discourse could have far-reaching implications for US policy, the profitability of firms, the welfare of workers, and the potential for innovation in the economy as a whole. Yet the effects of high-skill immigration on receiving countries are theoretically ambiguous. On the one hand, skilled migrants may increase the profitability and innovative capacity of the firm (Kerr and Lincoln 2010) and raise wages of native workers who are complements to production (Peri and Sparber 2009). On the other hand, migrants may crowd out domestic workers (Doran, Gelber, and Isen 2017) and lower the wages of close substitutes (Bound, Braga, Golden, and Khanna 2015).

What has been missing so far from this discourse is a discussion about how migrants may affect the product mix produced by a firm and the innovation involved in creative destruction. The entry and exit of products have long been seen as important determinants of firm-level innovation and

Gaurav Khanna is assistant professor of economics at the University of California, San Diego.

Munseob Lee is assistant professor of economics at the University of California, San Diego.

We are grateful to seminar participants at the NBER Immigration and Innovation Conferences and the University of California, San Diego, for valuable comments and to Patricia Cortes and Shulamit Kahn for insightful feedback. We thank Alireza Eshraghi and Olga Denislamova for excellent research assistance and the Center for Global Transformation for support. The conclusions drawn from the Nielsen data are those of the researchers and do not reflect the views of Nielsen. Nielsen is not responsible for, had no role in, and was not involved in analyzing and preparing the results reported herein. For acknowledgments, sources of research support, and disclosure of the authors' material financial relationships, if any, please see https://www.nber.org/chapters/c14105.ack.

Schumpeterian growth (Aghion, Akcigit, and Howitt 2014). Hiring high-skill workers from abroad may have a meaningful impact on such innovation, and this has implications not only for firm profits but also for consumer welfare. For instance, hiring more engineers and programmers from abroad, perhaps at a lower cost, allows firms to implement incremental innovations that may lead to newer products on the market. In this chapter, we fill this gap by studying the impact of H-1B worker applications on firm-level product reallocation, defined broadly as the entry of new products and the exit of outdated products.

We create a new data set by combining data on H-1B worker applications and firm production. Our H-1B data consists of publicly available labor condition applications (LCAs).[1] Our product-level data from the Nielsen Retail Scanner Data are combined with firm characteristics from the Compustat database. Together, a combination of these data sets at the firm-by-year level between 2006 and 2015 allows us to comprehensively examine the impact of wishing to hire foreign workers on firm production and innovation.

Our analysis consists of a few different methods. We first describe the entry and exit of products over the business cycle and across a firm's baseline propensity to hire H-1B workers.[2] We find that product reallocation falls precipitously in times of recession and rises in periods of economic recovery. Moreover, product reallocation is strongly associated with the baseline propensity to hire H-1B workers: firms that applied for H-1B workers in the first year of our LCA data are more likely to consistently have high product reallocation rates over the business cycle. Indeed, this association is invariant to a firm's research and development (R&D) expenditure, size, or revenue share. R&D expenditures and revenues are no longer strong determinants of product entry and exit after accounting for baseline propensities to hire H-1B workers.

We then use panel regressions, where we account for firm-level characteristics that are stable over time and for shocks that widely affect the economy with the help of fixed effects. Our preferred specifications look at outcomes in the following period, as they are less likely to be affected by contemporaneous shocks, and we would expect firm dynamics to change with a lag. We show that an increase in product reallocation is strongly associated with higher firm revenue growth.

We find that the number of LCAs, the number of certified workers, and the number of workers as a fraction of the total firm employment base are strongly associated with reallocation rates.[3] A 1 percentage point increase in the share of workers from certified LCAs is associated with a 5 percent-

---

1. LCAs are filed with the Department of Labor when a firm wishes to hire H-1B workers, and a single LCA may list many workers.
2. Our baseline propensity is whether or not a firm applied to hire H-1B workers in the first year of our LCA data (2000–2001).
3. A firm can file one LCA for many workers, and this LCA may be either denied, withdrawn, or certified. We define "certified workers" as the number of workers on certified LCAs.

age point increase in the reallocation rate. This association is stronger for software workers than for other occupation groups. In a distributed lead and lag setup, we also see that even as future H-1B certification does not affect current reallocation rates, current H-1B certification does affect future reallocation rates.

Our results speak to the innovative capacity of the firm by focusing on product reallocation, which is found to be highly correlated with firm growth and productivity (Argente, Lee, and Moreira 2018b). Previous work on high-skill immigrants and innovation focus on patenting activity (Kerr and Lincoln 2010; Hunt and Gauthier-Loiselle 2010; Moser, Voena, and Waldinger 2014). The propensity to patent may be affected by rulings of the Federal Court of Appeals, the firm's industry and products, and changes in state policies and taxes (Lerner and Seru 2018). Indeed, many important innovations are never patented (Fontana, Nuvolari, Shimizu, and Vezzulli 2013). While patents may be a good measure of newer production processes and inputs into production, our measure of innovation captures the final products produced by firms. The major advantage of a product reallocation measure is that it captures incremental innovations that are not usually patented. Previous work using patent data might have underestimated the benefits of having additional high-skilled immigrant workers by not being able to capture these incremental innovations.

Such changes affect not just firms but also consumers. Changes in a firm's production portfolio are strongly linked to a firm's revenue generation ability and profitability. In concurrent work, we examine how changes in consumer goods products affect the welfare of US consumers (Khanna and Lee 2018). Together these results have striking implications for the overall consequences of H-1B migration on the US economy.

Our chapter is organized into five sections. In section 3.2, we provide a background on the H-1B program and how that may relate to innovation and product reallocation. In section 3.3, we describe the data that we use and how we combine our data sets. Our primary analysis is in section 3.4, where we first describe trends over the business cycle, the association between reallocation rates and revenue growth, and then the association between H-1Bs and product reallocation. Section 3.5 concludes.

3.2 Background

3.2.1 The H-1B Program

The Immigration Act of 1990 established the H-1B visa program for temporary workers in "specialty occupations" with a college degree.[4] In order to

---

4. Specialty occupations are defined as requiring *theoretical and practical application of a body of highly specialized knowledge in a field of human endeavor including, but not limited to, architecture, engineering, mathematics, physical sciences, social sciences, medicine and health, education, law, accounting, business specialties, theology, and the arts.*

hire a foreigner on an H-1B visa, a firm must first file a LCA to the Department of Labor (DOL) and pay them the greater of the actual compensation paid to other employees in the same job or the prevailing compensation for that occupation.

After which, the H-1B prospective must demonstrate to the US Citizenship and Immigration Services Bureau (USCIS) in the Department of Homeland Security (DHS) that he or she has the requisite amount of education and work experience for the posted position.[5] USCIS then may approve the petitions up to the annual cap. H-1Bs are approved for a period of up to three years and can be extended up to six years. Once the H-1B expires, employers can sponsor a green card, and each country is eligible for only a specific number of those. The US General Accounting Office 2011 survey estimates the legal and administrative costs associated with each H-1B hire to range from 2.3 to 7.5 thousand dollars. It therefore seems reasonable to assume that employers must expect some cost or productivity advantage when hiring high-skill immigrants.

In the early years, the H-1B cap of 65,000 new visas was never reached, but by the time the IT boom began in the mid-1990s, the cap started binding, and the allocation was filled on a first-come, first-served basis. The cap was raised to 115,000 in 1999 and to 195,000 for 2000–2003 and was then reverted back to 65,000 thereafter. The 2000 legislation that raised the cap also excluded universities and nonprofit research facilities from it, and a 2004 change added an extra 20,000 visas for foreigners who received a master's degree in the US. Renewals of visas up to the six-year limit are not subject to the cap, and neither is employment at an institution of higher education or a nonprofit or governmental research organization.

When the cap is reached, USCIS conducts a lottery to determine who receives an H-1B visa. For instance, in the 2014 fiscal year, USCIS received approximately 124,000 petitions in the first five days of open applications for 85,000 visas. A computer-generated lottery first determines the visas for petitions of applicants who received a master's degree in the US (a quota of 20,000 visas), and then the remaining 65,000 visas are granted. Those not selected in the lottery may file again the next year. Those who are selected will eventually also receive an I-129 form from USCIS.

According to the United States Immigration and Naturalization Service (USINS 2000), the number of H-1B visas awarded to computer-related occupations in 1999 was about two-thirds of the visas, and the US Department of Commerce (2000) estimated that during the late 1990s, 28 percent of programmer jobs in the US went to H-1B visa holders. H-1B visas, therefore, became an important source of labor for the technology sector. Yet many

---

5. Workers may be educated in the US. The National Survey of College Graduates (NSCG) shows that 55 percent of foreigners working in computer science fields in 2003 arrived in the US on a temporary working (H-1B) or student-type visa (F-1, J-1).

non-IT firms also hire those with H-1B visas. Such workers may be in-house programmers but also scientists, mathematicians, and engineers.

3.2.2 The Impact of High-Skill Immigrants on the US

Work by economists on the impacts of the H-1B program is mostly focused on the wages and employment of native-born workers. Some argue that employers find hiring foreign high-skilled labor an attractive alternative and that such hiring either "crowds out" natives from jobs or puts downward pressure on their wages (Doran, Gelber, and Isen 2017). Given the excess supply of highly qualified foreigners willing to work and given the difficulty in the portability of the H-1B visa, immigrant workers may not be in a position to search for higher wages, allowing firms to undercut and replace US workers (Matloff 2003; Kirkegaard 2005). On the other hand, negative wage effects may be muted as native workers switch to complementary tasks (Peri and Sparber 2009).

Importantly, immigrants may affect the innovative capacity of the firm. Kerr and Lincoln (2010) and Hunt and Gauthier-Loiselle (2010) provide evidence on the link between variation in immigrant flows and innovation measured by patenting, suggesting that the net impact of immigration is positive rather than simply substituting for native employment. Kerr and Lincoln (2010) also show that variation in immigrant flows at the local level related to changes in H-1B flows does not appear to adversely impact native employment and has a small, statistically insignificant effect on their wages. Indeed, in other research, it is evident that changes in the size of the science, technology, engineering, and mathematics (STEM) workforce at the city level may raise wages for US-born workers (Peri, Shih, and Sparber 2015).

Even though much of the theoretical analysis underlying studies of immigration are about firms, a large fraction of the literature focuses on variation across states or metro areas.[6] Yet for high-skilled migrants sponsored by firms in specialty occupations, we may expect that effects on receiving firms will be rather different from the impacts on the larger labor market. Kerr and Lincoln (2010) and Kerr, Kerr, and Lincoln (2015) are among the first to focus on the firm, and more recently working papers using publicly traded firms (Mayda et al. 2018) or administrative tax data (Doran, Gelber, and Isen 2017) look at employment outcomes for native workers and the patenting propensity of the firm.

Yet focusing on either the labor market or innovative capacity may miss overall productivity changes in the US economy. Bound, Khanna, and Morales (2016) and Khanna and Morales (2018) take a different approach and set up a general equilibrium model of the US economy. Doing so allows them to conduct a comprehensive welfare analysis and study the distribu-

---

6. As Kerr, Kerr, and Lincoln (2015) point out, the word *firm* does not appear in the 51 pages of the seminal Borjas (1994) review of the immigration literature.

tional implications of the H-1B program. Importantly, by modeling the firms' decisions, including the spillovers from technological innovation, they find that even though US computer scientists are hurt by immigration, there are substantial benefits to consumers, entrepreneurs, and workers that are complements to computer scientists.

3.2.3   Innovation and Product Reallocation

Work on high-skill immigrants and innovation often focuses on patenting activity (Kerr and Lincoln 2010; Hunt and Gauthier-Loiselle 2010; Moser, Voena, and Waldinger 2014). Such pioneering work highlights the importance of immigrants in innovation. Although patents are a rich measure, they capture a specific type of innovation. While patents may capture larger significant innovations, product reallocation often captures incremental innovations that are rarely patented.

Certain features of patent data make it important to study alternative measures of innovation as well. First, immigration status is not directly observed in the patenting data, and often ethnicity needs to be inferred by name, and one needs to compare traditionally Indian or Chinese names to more Anglo-Saxon or European names. Second, changes to patenting over time may be a result of changes in intellectual property laws (such as the Computer Software Protection Act of 1980 and the Semiconductor Chip Protection Act of 1984) and rulings of the Court of Appeals for the Federal Circuit rather than actual innovation. Furthermore, there are gaps when a patent is filed and when it is granted, and any contemporary analysis like ours would need to limit itself to filing information and ignore granting status or citations to avoid issues with truncation.

The propensity to patent and cite innovations also varies widely across types of products and industries. Some patents are heavily cited due to their industry rather than "fundamental innovativeness" (Lerner and Seru 2018). Indeed, a relatively low number of important innovations may ever be patented.[7] Lastly, patenting propensities may differ across regions due to changes in state intellectual property policies and taxes or differences in industrial composition across regions, and analyses that use cross-state and -city variation need to account for such changes.

To complement the literature using patenting data, we investigate an alternative measure of innovation. For decades, economists have identified product entry and exit as one of the key mechanisms through which product innovation translates into economic growth (Aghion and Howitt 1992; Grossman and Helpman 1991). In the consumer goods sector, recent developments in point-of-sale systems allow us to investigate barcode-level trans-

---

7. Fontana, Nuvolari, Shimizu, and Vezzulli (2013) find that 91 percent of R&D award-winning inventions between 1977 and 2004 were never patented. Some inventions, like penicillin, may never be patented, as inventors may never wish to patent them.

actions and therefore product entry and exit. We calculate firm-level product creation and destruction by identifying manufacturers of each barcode-level product and aggregating transactions from about 35,000 stores in the United States. Following the idea of creative destruction, where new and better varieties replace obsolete ones, we define firm-level product reallocation as the sum of firm-level product creation and destruction. Most product reallocation is driven by surviving incumbent firms that add or drop products in their portfolios. The speed of product reallocation is strongly related to the innovation efforts of firms and several innovation outputs, such as revenue growth, improvements in product quality, and productivity growth (Argente, Lee, and Moreira 2018b). The major advantage of product reallocation as a measure of innovation outcomes is that it captures incremental innovations that are not usually patented. Under the presence of incremental innovations, previous work only with patent data might have underestimated the benefits of having additional high-skilled immigrant workers.

3.3   Data

We combine data at the firm-by-year level from multiple sources. We first obtain publicly available H-1B data on LCAs between 2000 and 2016. We merge this H-1B data with firm-level data from the Nielsen Retail Scanner Data (2006 to 2015), which provides us with information on products produced at the firm level, and also Compustat firm-level characteristics for a subset of large publicly listed firms.

3.3.1   Data on High-Skill Immigration

Data on H-1B visas come from the publicly available list of 2000–2001 LCAs, which firms file with the US DOL when they wish to hire a foreign high-skill worker. Attached to each LCA are an employer name, address (including city, zip code, and state), work start date and end date, occupation and job title, and number of workers requested. The LCA database also documents whether the application was denied, withdrawn, or certified. For our analysis, we only use certified applications and count the "certified workers" as the number of workers on certified LCAs. We aggregate the LCA-level data to the firm-by-year level, counting not just the number of LCAs and workers but also the types of workers for broad occupational categories. These categories, in descending order of prevalence, are (1) software workers (including computer programmers, software engineers, and software developers), (2) scientists / mathematicians / statisticians and engineers (including electrical and mechanical engineers), (3) managers (and administrators), and (4) those working in finance or marketing. Together, these categories account for more than 90 percent of all LCAs in each year of our data.

Due to the H-1B caps, not all certified LCAs lead to actual H-1B hires. However, since they are necessary for approved H-1Bs, these LCAs measure

Table 3.1   **Facts on Nielsen Retail Scanner Data**

		Nielsen Retail Scanner Data
	Time period	2006–2015
	Coverage	1,071 modules, 114 groups
	Observational units	Store
	# of stores	35,510
	# of states	49
	# of counties	2,550
	# of products in 2006	724,211
	Frequency	Weekly, average
	Tag on temporary sales	None

the firms' desire to hire H-1Bs and therefore are likely to be highly correlated with actual H-1Bs. Since our analysis is only for for-profit firms that produce consumer goods, none of the H-1B LCAs we eventually match to our products data set are cap exempt. Importantly, our data set should not be thought of as being representative of H-1B firms. Instead, it is only representative of consumer goods–producing firms. Since about 2011, there has been an increase in outsourcing firms grabbing the majority of H-1B visas and filing a lot of LCAs—yet such firms are not a part of our sample and are not the focus of our analysis.

With the help of these data, we compute a few important variables: we count (1) the number of LCAs filed by a firm each year, (2) the number of workers under certified LCAs, (3) the number of workers in each of the four broad occupational categories mentioned above, and (4) the number of workers normalized by the total employment in the firm (from Compustat).

3.3.2 Data on Products

For data on products, we use the Nielsen Retail Scanner Data provided by the Kilts Center for Marketing at the University of Chicago. Each individual store reports weekly prices and quantities of every UPC (Universal Product Code) that had any sales during that week. The data are generated by point-of-sale systems from approximately 35,000 distinct stores from 90 retail chains across 371 Metropolitan Statistical Areas (MSAs) and 2,500 counties between January 2006 and December 2015. The data are organized into 1,070 detailed product modules aggregated into 114 product groups that are then grouped into 10 major departments.[8] Table 3.1 summarizes basic facts on the data.

---

8. The ten major departments are Health and Beauty Aids, Dry Grocery (e.g., baby food, canned vegetables), Frozen Foods, Dairy, Deli, Packaged Meat, Fresh Produce, Non-Food Grocery, Alcohol, and General Merchandise.

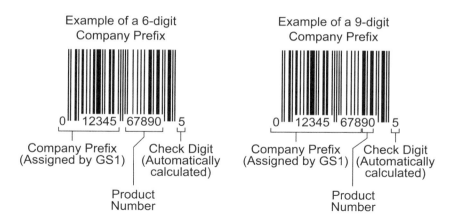

Fig. 3.1   Example of a company prefix

Note: This figure shows examples of a six- and a nine-digit firm prefix. The source is the GS1-US website (http://www.gs1-us.info/company-prefix).

Our data set combines all sales of products at the national and annual levels. As in Broda and Weinstein (2010) and Argente and Lee (2016), we use the UPC as the level of analysis. A critical part of our analysis is the identification of entries and exits, for which we mostly follow Argente, Lee, and Moreira (2018a, 2018b). For each product, we identify the entry and exit periods. We define entry as the first year of sales of a product and exit as the year after we last observe a product being sold.

We link firms and products with information obtained from GS1 US, the single official source of UPCs. In order to obtain a UPC, firms must first obtain a GS1 company prefix. The prefix is a 5- to 10-digit number that identifies firms and their products in more than 100 countries where the GS1 is present. In figure 3.1, we show a few examples of different company prefixes. Although the majority of firms own a single prefix, it is not rare to find that some own several. Small firms, for instance, often obtain a larger prefix first, which is usually cheaper, before expanding and requesting a shorter prefix. Larger firms, on the other hand, usually own several company prefixes due to past mergers and acquisitions. For instance, Procter & Gamble owns the prefixes of firms it acquired, such as Old Spice, Folgers, and Gillette. For consistency, in what follows, we perform the analysis at the parent-company level.

Given that the GS1 US data contains all the company prefixes generated in the US, we combine these prefixes with the UPC codes in the Nielsen Retail Scanner Data. Less than 5 percent of the UPCs belong to prefixes not generated in the US. We were not able to find a firm identifier for those products.

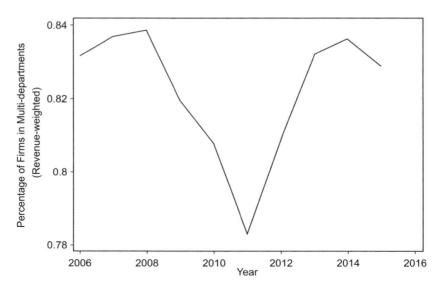

Fig. 3.2   Share of firms in multiple departments

Note: This figure shows the share of firms operating in more than one product department. The share is calculated with real revenue weights. The 10 major departments are Health and Beauty Aids, Dry Grocery (e.g., baby food, canned vegetables), Frozen Foods, Dairy, Deli, Packaged Meat, Fresh Produce, Non-Food Grocery, Alcohol, and General Merchandise.

With this data set on products and firms, we can compute how firm-level product creation and destruction evolve over time.

Note that typical firms in the data produce multiple products in several different categories. Over the sample period, about 82.2 percent of revenue has been generated by firms operating in more than one product department. Figure 3.2 shows that the share of firms in multiple departments has been between 78 and 84 percent from 2006 to 2015, declining a bit during the Great Recession.

3.3.3   Data on Other Firm Characteristics

We obtain other firm-level characteristics from Compustat. The Compustat is a database of financial and market information on global companies throughout the world. For the purpose of this research, we bring in information on employment and R&D expenditures over the sample period from the fundamental annual North American database. This limits the number of firms in analysis but provides much more detailed information on firms. For instance, with information on the number of employees, we can calculate the share of high-skill immigrant worker applications instead of just the number of high-skilled migrant applications. Additionally, data on R&D expenditures allow us to test the importance of H-1B workers to product reallocation relative to R&D investments.

Table 3.2   **Descriptive statistics for two merged samples**

Merged samples	LCA-Nielsen (1)	LCA-Nielsen-Compustat (2)
Number of firms	36,218	482
Years	2006–15	2006–15
Variables from LCA		
Average # of certified workers	0.79	20.72
Variables from Nielsen		
# of observations	235,522	4,022
Average firm revenue (USD)	6.25 million	154 million
Average reallocation rates (0–2)	0.1944	0.2585
Variables from Compustat		
# of observations	—	4,565
Average # of employees	—	43,841
Average R&D to sales	—	0.251

3.3.4   Combining Data Sets

We merge our data sets at the firm-by-year level using a string matching algorithm for firm names. When there is uncertainty in name matching, we consult city and/or zip codes. We do not expect a matching error to be correlated with our main variables of interest. For our analysis, we create two different merged samples: (a) the LCA-Nielsen sample and (b) the LCA-Nielsen-Compustat sample. Table 3.2 reports descriptive statistics for all three merged samples.

The first sample combines LCAs and Nielsen Retail Scanner Data. As table 3.2 shows, the LCA-Nielsen sample contains 36,218 distinct firms for 2006 to 2015. This covers both small and large firms, where the average annual number of certified workers from LCAs is 0.79 (many firms file no LCAs in some years), and the average annual revenue in the Nielsen data is $6.25 million.

The second sample adds Compustat to the LCA-Nielsen sample in order to obtain other firm characteristics. As table 3.2 shows, the LCA-Nielsen-Compustat sample has 482 distinct firms for 2006 to 2015. Due to the limited coverage of the Compustat database, this sample mostly covers large companies, where the average annual number of certified workers from LCAs is 20.7 and the average annual revenue in the Nielsen data is $154 million. From the Compustat database, we additionally know that the average number of employees is 43 and the average R&D expenditure-to-sales ratio is 0.25.

3.3.5   Measurement of Creative Destruction

We start with a description of the measures that we use to identify the degree of creative destruction by firms in the product space.

To capture the importance of product entry and exit, we use information on the number of new products and exiting products and the total number of products for each firm i over year t. We define firm-level entry and exit rates as follows:

$$(1) \qquad\qquad n_{it} = \frac{N_{it}}{T_{it}}$$

$$(2) \qquad\qquad x_{it} = \frac{X_{it}}{T_{it-1}},$$

where N_{it}, X_{it}, and T_{it} are the numbers of entering products, exiting products, and total products, respectively. The entry rate is defined as the number of new products for each firm i in year t as a share of the total number of products in period t. The exit rate is defined as the number of products for each firm i that exited in year t as a share of the total number of products in year $t - 1$.

From the idea of creative destruction at the firm level, the overall change in the portfolio of products available to consumers can be captured by the sum of firm-level entry and exit rates. We refer to this concept as the product reallocation rate:

$$(3) \qquad\qquad r_{it} = n_{it} + x_{it}.$$

With this measure, we can investigate the extent of changes in the status of a product in our data from either the entry or the exit margin.

3.4   Empirical Analysis

3.4.1   Product Reallocation and Firm Outcomes

To understand the importance of product reallocation, we first study the association between reallocation and firm revenue growth. This is simply a replication of the results found in Argente, Lee, and Moreira (2018b) and is theoretically similar to results in Aghion, Akcigit, and Howitt (2014). We test for this association in our sample with the following regression specification:

$$(4) \qquad \Delta\mathrm{Log}(Revenue)_{i,t+1} = \alpha + \beta r_{i,t} + \mu_i + \tau_t + \varepsilon_{i,t},$$

where $\Delta\mathrm{Log}(Revenue)_{i,t}$ is growth in the sum of revenue over all products in firm i's portfolio between years t and $t - 1$. μ_i are firm fixed effects, and τ_t are year fixed effects. With the help of fixed effects, our associations account for firm characteristics that are stable over time and for annual shocks that affect the entire US economy. Our resulting variation is driven by changes over time within firms. Here and elsewhere, we cluster our standard errors at the firm level.

In table 3.3, we study this association. Product reallocation has a strong

Table 3.3   **Reallocation activities and revenue growth**

DV: $\Delta\ Log(Revenue)_{i,t+1}$	(1)	(2)	(3)
Product reallocation rate	0.432		
	(0.0235)***		
Product entry rate		1.240	
		(0.0210)***	
Product exit rate			0.355
			(0.0377)***
Observations	147,723	179,502	147,723
R^2	0.013	0.063	0.009
Number of firms	27,574	31,626	27,574
Fixed effects	Year and firm	Year and firm	Year and firm
Cluster	Firm	Firm	Firm

Note: The table reports the coefficients of OLS regressions with the LCA-Nielsen merged sample. The dependent variable is the revenue growth rate in the next year: the change in revenues between year t and $t + 1$. The product reallocation rate is defined as the product entry rate plus the product exit rate at the firm level, as defined in the main text. Reallocation rates range from 0 to 2, whereas entry and exit rates range between 0 and 1. Revenue growth rates are winsorized at the 1% level. Standard errors are clustered at the firm level and presented in parentheses. ***, **, and * represent statistical significance at 1%, 5%, and 10% levels, respectively.

positive association with firm revenue growth. When we look at product entry and exit separately, once again it is clear that both entry and exit of new products are strongly associated with firm revenue growth; however, firm entry has a much stronger association than firm exit. While these associations are not causal, they are suggestive as to how product reallocation is important for firm revenue growth.

3.4.2   Reallocation and Immigration over the Business Cycle

Our period of study, 2006 to 2016, encapsulates the Great Recession of 2008–10. This is an ideal setting to understand how the business cycle affects product reallocation and how high-skill migration interacts with this relationship. In much of this subsection, we divide firms by whether they have a propensity to apply for H-1B workers. Any firm that filed an LCA that was certified in the first year of our LCA data (2000–2001) is categorized as a firm that has a propensity to hire H-1B workers. We use the earliest possible year (2000–2001) rather than our sample period (2006–15) for our classification so as to ensure that contemporaneous changes in firm characteristics are not driving much of our analysis.[9] The aim is to capture baseline propensities of the firm that may not be related to differential trends over time in

9. The propensity to hire H-1B workers in 2000–2001 is also strongly predictive of the propensity to hire H-1B workers between 2006 and 2015. However, it is important to note that the propensity to hire may not be actual hiring given the caps.

A   Reallocation Rates

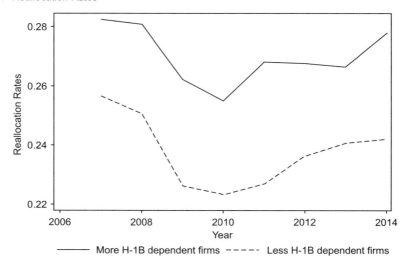

Fig. 3.3   Product entry, exit, and reallocation over the business cycle

Note: This figure shows product reallocation rates, entry rates, and exit rates by type of firm using the LCA-Nielsen sample. Reallocation rates range from 0 to 2, whereas entry and exit rates range between 0 and 1. More H-1B-dependent firms have at least one H-1B worker application in 2000–2001 (the first year of our LCA data), whereas less H-1B-dependent firms have no H-1B worker applications in 2000–2001.

reallocation rates, such as the ability of human resources (HR) departments within a firm to file H-1B paperwork or connections to employers in countries such as India.

In figure 3.3, we use the LCA-Nielsen sample to look at reallocation rates, product entry, and product exit over this period. We split the sample by H-1B dependent firms (defined as any firm that wished to hire H-1B workers in 2000–2001) and nondependent firms (no new H-1B LCAs certified in 2000–2001). Panel (a) of figure 3.3 highlights two important takeaways: (1) H-1B-prone firms have higher product reallocation rates, and (2) the business cycle is strongly correlated with product reallocation. Over the recession, product reallocation fell drastically only to rise again over the recovery. Firms that wished to hire H-1B workers started out with a higher reallocation rate, were not as adversely affected as non-H-1B-prone firms, and unlike non-H-1B-prone firms, recovered to their previous reallocation rates by 2015.

In panels (b) and (c) of figure 3.3, we look at product entry and exit rates. As expected, over the recession, product entry falls and exit rises. H-1B firms have higher entry and exit rates at baseline; however, by the end of the period, non-H-1B-prone firms have marginally higher exit rates. The fall in entries over the recession is not as strong for H-1B-dependent firms, and the

B Entry Rates

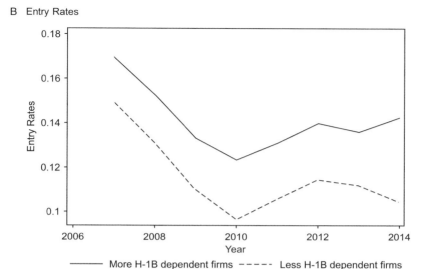

C Exit Rates

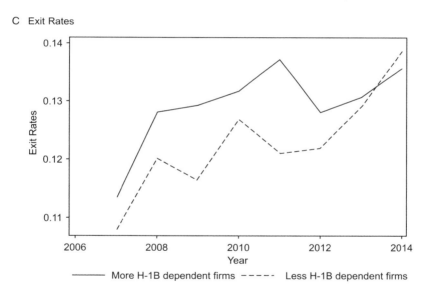

Fig. 3.3   (cont.)

recovery is mildly stronger—by the end of the business cycle, H-1B-prone firms have much higher entry rates than non-H-1B-prone firms.

The stark differences between H-1B and non-H-1B firms in product real-location may be driven by other factors correlated with H-1B visas. For instance, firms that spend more on R&D, or larger firms in general, may have more H-1B workers and also higher reallocation rates. Additionally, it

Table 3.4   Reallocation rates by firm H-1B status and R&D or revenue

	Low R&D	High R&D	Difference
Panel A: Reallocation rates by H-1B and R&D propensity			
High H-1B	0.289	0.286	–0.002
SE	(0.019)	(0.013)	(0.022)
N	48	62	
Low H-1B	0.247	0.242	–0.006
SE	(0.011)	(0.012)	(0.017)
N	78	63	
Difference	0.041	0.044	
SE	(0.021)	(0.018)	

	Low revenue	High revenue	Difference
Panel B: Reallocation rates by H-1B and revenue			
High H-1B	0.266	0.260	–0.005
SE	(0.008)	(0.003)	(0.007)
N	305	555	
Low H-1B	0.197	0.189	–0.008
SE	(0.001)	(0.001)	(0.001)
N	10,442	12,170	
Difference	0.069	0.072	
SE	(0.007)	(0.003)	

Note: Panel A compares reallocation rates across H-1B propensity and R&D expenditures (as a fraction of sales) using the LCA-Nielsen-Compustat sample. R&D expenditures as a fraction of sales are divided at the median. Panel B compares reallocation rates across H-1B propensity and firm revenue across all products in their portfolio using the LCA-Nielsen sample. Reallocation rates range from 0 to 2. Revenue is divided at the median. Low H-1B is defined as having no H-1B worker applications in 2000–2001. High H-1B is defined as having at least one H-1B worker application in 2000–2001.

is important to understand the interaction between H-1B dependency and R&D expenditures. Our analysis in table 3.4 and figure 3.4 investigates this interaction.

Table 3.4 is divided into two panels. In Panel A, we use the LCA-Nielsen-Compustat sample and divide firms into four groups by H-1B propensity and R&D expenditures. Low H-1B firms are those that did not apply for a new H-1B worker in the first year of our H-1B data (2000–2001), whereas high H-1B firms did. This division roughly splits the sample in half. We also split the firms by whether or not they are above the median level of R&D expenditures as a proportion of total sales (in 2000–2001). By construction, this division splits the sample in half.

In Panel A, it is clear that high H-1B firms have higher reallocation rates than low H-1B firms. This is true whether or not the firms have a high R&D expenditure share. Regardless of R&D share, high H-1B firms have a reallocation rate that is about 17 percent higher than that of low H-1B firms. Interestingly enough, within H-1B categories, R&D share is not as strong

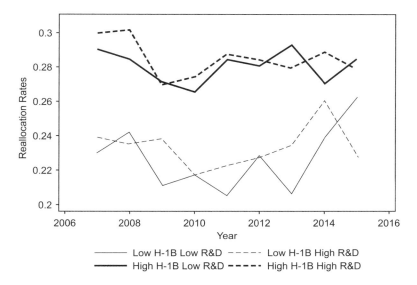

Fig. 3.4   Product reallocation by H-1B dependency and R&D propensity

Note: This figure shows the reallocation rates by type of firm using the LCA-Nielsen-Compustat sample. Reallocation rates range between 0 and 2. More H-1B-dependent firms have at least one H-1B worker application in 2000–2001 (the first year of our H-1B data), whereas less H-1B-dependent firms have no H-1B worker applications in 2000–2001. Low-R&D firms have below-median R&D expenditures as a proportion of sales in 2000–2001. High-R&D firms have above-median R&D expenditures as a proportion of sales.

a determinant of reallocation rates, since firms with low and high baseline R&D rates have similar reallocation rates.

In Panel B, we perform a somewhat similar exercise, but instead of R&D shares, we use baseline revenues from Nielsen. We use the larger LCA-Nielsen sample. Firms that did not apply for an H-1B worker in 2000–2001 far outnumber the firms that did apply for an H-1B worker. Once again comparing the means in reallocation rates suggests a meaningful difference between H-1B and non-H-1B firms: high H-1B firms have, on average, between 35 percent and 38 percent higher reallocation rates than low H-1B firms. On the other hand, baseline firm revenues are not predictive of reallocation rates over the period, as both large and small firms have similar reallocation rates.

Such differences are succinctly captured in figure 3.4, which splits up the sample by H-1B propensity and R&D expenditure share. Consistent with the tables, it shows that there is a substantial difference in reallocation rates between high and low H-1B firms. This difference is unaffected by R&D expenditure share, which in and of itself is less predictive of differences in reallocation rates.

Table 3.4 and figure 3.4 suggest that whether or not a firm has a higher propensity to hire H-1B workers is strongly associated with product real-

A   Reallocation Rates

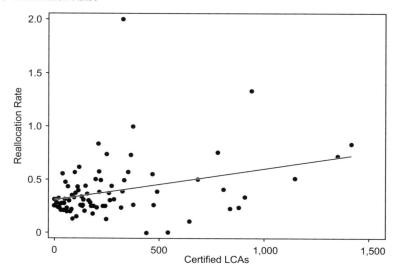

Fig. 3.5   Product entry, exit, and reallocation versus number of certified H-1B workers

Note: This figure shows product reallocation rates, entry rates, and exit rates by the number of certified workers in the LCA data. Reallocation rates range from 0 to 2, whereas entry and exit rates range between 0 and 1. LCAs that are certified (not withdrawn or denied) list the number of workers that a firm wishes to hire. This measure is the number of certified workers. The LCA-Nielsen sample pooled across firms and over 2006–15 is used. Values are binned at each unique point of the *x*-axis (number of certified LCA workers).

location rates. This association is somewhat independent of whether or not the firm has high R&D expenditures or is a large firm with high revenues. Indeed, in comparison to the association between H-1B workers and reallocation rates, it seems like R&D expenditures and firm revenues are less strongly associated with high product reallocation.

3.4.3   The Association between Immigration and Product Reallocation

We first study the association between high-skill immigration and product reallocation graphically in figure 3.5. Here we plot reallocation rates, entry rates, and exit rates across the number of workers on certified LCA applications. Each point is a firm-year observation. There seems to be a mildly positive association between reallocation rates and the number of certified workers. Yet such analyses may be confounded by firm-specific characteristics or annual shocks to the economy. To account for these, we perform a fixed effects regression:

$$(5) \qquad r_{i,t+1} = \alpha + \beta \mathrm{H1B}_{i,t} + \mu_i + \tau_t + \varepsilon_{i,t+1},$$

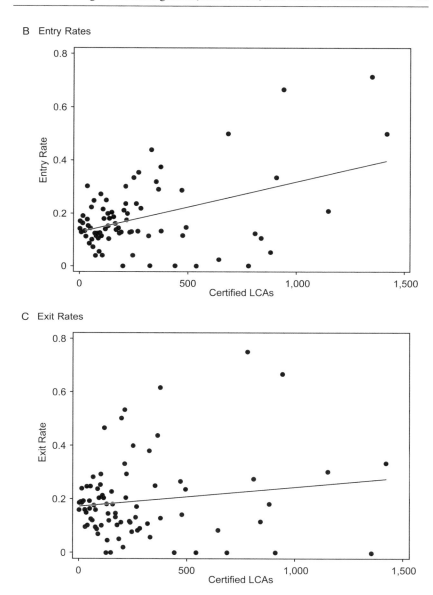

Fig. 3.5   (cont.)

where $r_{i,t}$ is the product reallocation rate for firm i in year t and H1B$_{i,t}$ is a measure of new H-1B worker certifications at firm i in year t. Even as we show results with both contemporaneous and next period's outcomes, our preferred specification looks at future reallocation. As proposed in other similar work (Argente, Lee, and Moreira 2018b), future product reallocation is less likely to be affected by contemporaneous shocks, and we expect that changes in firm dynamics occur with a lag. We include both firm μ_i and year τ_t fixed effects and cluster errors at the firm level.

Our measures of $H1B_{i,t}$ worker certifications take on a few different forms. We look at (1) the number of LCAs filed by a firm each year, (2) the number of workers on certified LCAs each year (called "certified workers"), and (3) the number of workers from certified LCAs in each broad occupational group. We use the LCA-Nielsen sample for such regressions. Additionally, using the LCA-Nielsen-Compustat sample, we can (4) normalize the number of certified workers by total employment in the firm using Compustat measures of employment.

Table 3.5 reports the coefficients of OLS regressions with the LCA-Nielsen merged sample. We find a strong positive association between the number of applications/certifications and reallocation rates in both the current and the following years. When we divide certifications into four occupational categories, science/math and engineering have the largest effect in magnitude, but this is imprecisely estimated. Software more precisely estimates and has a positive effect, which may be consistent with the type of innovations we capture with reallocation rates. Unlike patent data, we mostly capture incremental innovation, where it is possible that lower costs and a better quality of occupations that perform auxiliary functions may matter more.

Next we normalize our measures by the size of firms. The same number of high-skilled immigrants may affect firms differentially by firm size. We now calculate the share of applications/certifications by normalizing them with the number of employees from Compustat. Table 3.6 reports the coefficients of OLS regressions with the LCA-Nielsen-Compustat merged sample. Once again we find a positive association between shares of applications/certifications and reallocation rates. A 1 percentage point increase in the share of certifications is associated with a 5 percentage point increase in the reallocation rate.[10]

In interpreting these results with caution, we acknowledge that even as the number of H-1B visas granted over time is largely driven by changes to policy, the policy itself may respond to the aggregate demand for H-1Bs. Indeed, IT firms often lobby Congress to increase the cap as it often binds. As such, we find it important to compare changes across firms conditional on year fixed effects, which absorb aggregate changes in the cap. Additionally, our final results below test for pretrends in our main outcomes.

10. The mean share of certifications is 0.047 percent, so a 1 percentage point increase in the share of certified workers corresponds to more than double the mean. The reallocation rate in table 3.6 ranges from 0 to 200 with a mean of 25.85. A five percentage point increase in reallocation rates corresponds to a 20 percent increase at the mean. In other words, a 1 percent increase at the mean share of certified workers is associated with about a 0.2 percent increase at the mean of reallocation rates.

Table 3.5 LCA application/certification and reallocation activities

	Reallocation rate in year t			Reallocation rate in year $t + 1$		
DV:	(1)	(2)	(3)	(4)	(5)	(6)
Number of applications	0.00217 (0.000413)***			0.00118 (0.000615)*		
Number of certifications		0.00291 (0.000466)***			0.00140 (0.000767)*	
By occupations:						
Software			0.00217 (0.000471)***			0.00166 (0.000294)***
Science, math, and engineering			0.0300 (0.0446)			0.0206 (0.0274)
Manager			-0.00273 (0.00976)			0.000558 (0.0260)
Finance, analysis, and marketing			0.0359 (0.0196)*			-0.000832 (0.0228)
Observations	183,554	183,554	183,554	181,451	181,451	181,451
R^2	0.003	0.003	0.003	0.003	0.003	0.003
Number of firms	31,876	31,876	31,876	31,685	31,685	31,685
Fixed effects	Year and firm	Year and firm	Year and firm	Year and firm	Year and firm	Year and firm
Cluster	Firm	Firm	Firm	Firm	Firm	Firm
Type	OLS	OLS	OLS	OLS	OLS	OLS

Note: The table reports the coefficients of OLS regressions with LCA-Nielsen merged sample. The dependent variable is the product reallocation rates this and next year. Reallocation rates range from 0 to 200. The product reallocation rate is defined as the product entry rate plus the product exit rate at the firm level as defined in the main text. The number of applications is the number of LCAs filed by a firm. The number of certifications is the number of workers on LCAs that were certified. The occupation composition is the number of workers in each occupation from LCAs that were certified. Standard errors are clustered at the firm level and presented in parentheses. ***, **, and * represent statistical significance at 1%, 5%, and 10% levels, respectively.

Table 3.6   Applying/certified immigrant worker shares and reallocation activities

DV:	Reallocation rate in year t			Reallocation rate in year $t + 1$		
	(1)	(2)	(3)	(4)	(5)	(6)
Share of applications	3.910			5.077		
	(2.693)			(2.040)**		
Share of certifications		4.242			5.593	
		(2.789)			(2.034)***	
By occupations:						
Software			4.839			9.344
			(1.238)***			(0.732)***
Science, math, and engineering			−0.915			0.203
			(2.140)			(1.402)
Management			8.953			5.854
			(5.095)*			(4.384)
Finance, analysis, and marketing			0.771			1.098
			(2.016)			(2.221)
Observations	2,742	2,742	2,742	2,800	2,800	2,800
R^2	0.015	0.016	0.022	0.022	0.022	0.029
Number of firms	416	416	416	429	429	429
Fixed effects	Year and firm	Year and firm	Year and firm	Year and firm	Year and firm	Year and firm
Cluster	Firm	Firm	Firm	Firm	Firm	Firm
Type	OLS	OLS	OLS	OLS	OLS	OLS

Note: The table reports the coefficients of OLS regressions with LCA-Nielsen-Compustat merged sample. The dependent variable is the product reallocation rates this and next year. Reallocation rates range from 0 to 2. The product reallocation rate is defined as the product entry rate plus the product exit rate at the firm level as defined in the main text. The share of applications is the number of LCAs filed by a firm divided by the total employment base in Compustat. The share of certifications is the number of workers on LCAs that were certified divided by the total employment base in Compustat. The occupation composition is the number of workers in each occupation from LCAs that were certified divided by the total employment base in Compustat. Standard errors are clustered at the firm level and presented in parentheses. ***, **, and * represent statistical significance at 1%, 5%, and 10% levels, respectively.

3.4.4   The Timing of Effects

To further investigate the timing of effects, we use a distributed lead and lag model. Such a model allows us to check that future H-1B applications do not affect past reallocation rates and to also study whether our outcomes of interest react contemporaneously or with a lag. While informative, however, these results should be interpreted carefully, as we are not necessarily identifying a "shock" in the number of H-1B applications, which is instead a choice variable for the firm. In the following equation, we describe the model:

$$(6) \qquad r_{i,t} = \alpha + \beta_1 H1B_{i,t-1} + \beta_2 H1B_{i,t} + \beta_3 H1B_{i,t+1} + \mu_i + \tau_t + \varepsilon_{i,t}.$$

While we would expect that past H-1B certifications $H1B_{i,t-1}$ would affect reallocation rates, we can also test to ensure that the number of future H-1B certifications $H1B_{i,t+1}$ is not correlated with current reallocation rates. In figure 3.6, we can see that future H-1B applications do not affect lagged reallocation rates. Furthermore, the main impact on reallocation rates seems to show up with a one-period lag.

3.5   Conclusion

In this chapter, we highlight an important fact: H-1B applications are associated with higher rates of reallocation (entry and exit) of products at firms. Product reallocation is an integral part of Schumpeterian growth, driven by the discarding of older products and the generation of newer products. We complement the literature on patenting (capturing larger innovations) and highlight that smaller, incremental innovations are captured by measures of product reallocation.

At the firm level, we merge data on H-1B LCAs with Nielsen scanner data on products and Compustat data on firm characteristics. We find that H-1B LCAs are strongly associated with product reallocation, which in turn is associated with firm revenue growth.

Our work is consistent with other work showing that high-skill migrants are strongly associated with higher patenting activity (Kerr and Lincoln 2010; Hunt and Gauthier-Loiselle 2010). Measures of firm patenting and new product entry should be thought of as complementary yet capturing different aspects of a firm's innovation ladder. While patenting may be more associated with newer methods of production and newer inputs into final goods, we study the entry and exit of final goods as and when they show up in the consumer market. Yet other work that uses variation generated by the H-1B lottery finds little effect on patenting activity (Doran, Gelber, and Isen 2017). Therefore we find it important to study alternative measures of firm innovativeness to get a comprehensive picture of firm dynamics.

Importantly, as we look at consumer goods, we may expect that such

A   Reallocation Rates

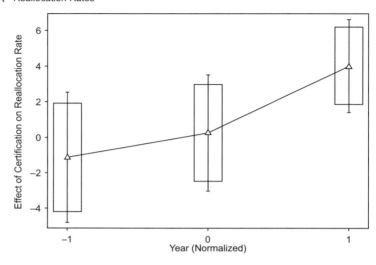

B   Entry Rates

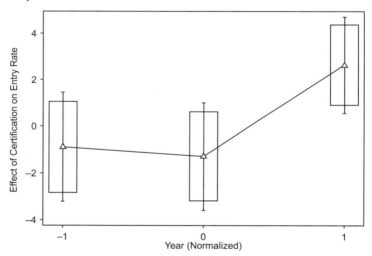

Fig. 3.6   Distributed lead and lag model

Note: This figure shows the impact of the number of certified workers from H-1B LCAs on product reallocation rates and entry rates. Reallocation rates range between 0 and 200, whereas entry rates range between 0 and 100. LCAs that are certified (not withdrawn or denied) list the number of workers that a firm wishes to hire. This measure is the number of certified workers. We use a distributed lead and lag model to estimate the coefficients. The LCA-Nielsen-Compustat sample over 2006–15 is used. Standard errors are clustered at the firm level.

activity affects consumer welfare as well. In Khanna and Lee (2018), we study how prices and the variety of products in the consumer goods market changes as firms introduce newer products and produce older products more efficiently when they wish to hire H-1B workers.[11] Such changes affect the welfare of consumers and alter quantitative estimates of the overall impacts of high-skill immigration on the US economy.

References

Aghion, Philippe, and Peter Howitt. 1992. "A Model of Growth through Creative Destruction." *Econometrica* 60 (2): 323–51.

Aghion, Philippe, Ufuk Akcigit, and Peter Howitt. 2014. "What Do We Learn from Schumpeterian Growth Theory?" In *Handbook of Economic Growth*, vol. 2, edited by Philippe Aghion and Steven N. Durlauf, 515–63. Oxford: North Holland.

Argente, David, and Munseob Lee. 2016. "Cost of Living Inequality during the Great Recession." Kilts Center for Marketing at Chicago Booth—Nielsen Dataset Paper Series 1-032.

Argente, David, Munseob Lee, and Sara Moreira. 2018a. "How Do Firms Grow? The Life Cycle of Products Matters." No. 1174, 2018 Meeting Papers, Society for Economic Dynamics.

Argente, David, Munseob Lee, and Sara Moreira. 2018b. "Innovation and Product Reallocation in the Great Recession." *Journal of Monetary Economics* 93:1–20.

Borjas, George. 1994. "Economics of Immigration." *Journal of Economic Literature* 33:1667–1717.

Bound, John, Breno Braga, Joseph Golden, and Gaurav Khanna. 2015. "Recruitment of Foreigners in the Market for Computer Scientists in the US." *Journal of Labor Economics* 33 (S1): 187–223.

Bound, John, Gaurav Khanna, and Nicolas Morales. 2016. "Understanding the Economic Impact of the H-1B Program on the US." In *High-Skilled Migration to the United States and Its Economic Consequences*, edited by Gordon H. Hanson, William R. Kerr, and Sarah Turner, 177–204. Chicago: University of Chicago Press.

Broda, Christian, and David E. Weinstein. 2010. "Product Creation and Destruction: Evidence and Price Implications." *American Economic Review* 100 (3): 691–723.

Cortes, Patricia. 2008. "The Effect of Low-Skilled Immigration on US Prices: Evidence from CPI Data." *Journal of Political Economy* 116 (3): 381–42.

Doran, Kirk B., Alexander Gelber, and Adam Isen. 2017. "The Effects of High-Skilled Immigration Policy on Firms: Evidence from H-1B Visa Lotteries." NBER Working Paper no. 20668. Cambridge, MA: National Bureau of Economic Research.

Fontana, Roberto, Alessandro Nuvolari, Hiroshi Shimizu, and Andrea Vezzulli. 2013. "Reassessing Patent Propensity: Evidence from a Dataset of R&D Awards 1977–2004." *Research Policy* 42 (10): 1780–92.

---

11. This work is closely related to the work of Cortes (2008), who finds that low-skill immigration lowers the prices of nontradable goods and services such as housekeeping and gardening. In contrast, we estimate the effects of high-skill migration at the firm level on prices and varieties of tradable products.

Grossman, Gene M., and Elhanan Helpman. 1991. "Quality Ladders in the Theory of Growth." *Review of Economic Studies* 58 (1): 43–61.

Hunt, Jennifer, and Marjolaine Gauthier-Loiselle. 2010. "How Much Does Immigration Boost Innovation?" *American Economic Journal: Macroeconomics* 2 (2): 31–56.

Kerr, Sari Pekkala, William R. Kerr, and William F. Lincoln. 2015. "Skilled Immigration and the Employment Structures of U.S. Firms." *Journal of Labor Economics* 33 (S1): S147–S186.

Kerr, William, and William Lincoln. 2010. "The Supply Side of Innovation: H-1B Visa Reforms and U.S. Ethnic Invention." *Journal of Labor Economics* 28 (3): 473–508.

Khanna, Gaurav, and Munseob Lee. 2018. "High-Skill Immigration and Consumer Welfare." Working Paper.

Khanna, Gaurav, and Nicolas Morales. 2018. "The IT Boom and Other Unintended Consequences of Chasing the American Dream." Working Paper.

Kirkegaard, J. 2005. "Outsourcing and Skill Imports: Foreign High-Skilled Workers on H-1B and L-1 Visas in the United States." Working Paper no. 05-15. Washington, DC: Peterson Institute for International Economics.

Lerner, Josh, and Amit Seru. 2018. "The Use and Misuse of Patent Data: Issues for Corporate Finance and Beyond." Harvard Business School Working Paper no. 18-042.

Matloff, Norman. 2003. "On the Need for Reform of the H-1B Non-immigrant Work Visa in Computer-Related Occupations." *University of Michigan Journal of Law Reform* 36 (4).

Mayda, Anna Maria, Francesc Ortega, Giovanni Peri, Kevin Shih, and Chad Sparber. 2018. "The Effect of H-1B Visas on Publicly Traded Firms." Working Paper.

Moser, Petra, Alessandra Voena, and Fabian Waldinger. 2014. "German Jewish Émigrés and US Invention." *American Economic Review* 104 (10): 3222–55.

Peri, Giovanni, Kevin Shih, and Chad Sparber. 2015. "STEM Workers, H-1B Visas, and Productivity in US Cities." *Journal of Labor Economics* 33 (S1): S225–S255.

Peri, Giovanni, and Chad Sparber. 2009. "Task Specialization, Immigration, and Wages." *American Economic Journal: Applied Economics* 1 (3): 135–69.

US Department of Commerce. 2000. "Digital Economy 2000." Technical Report.

USINS. 2000. "Characteristics of Specialty Occupation Workers (H-1B)." Washington, DC: US Immigration and Naturalization Service.

4

New Data and Facts on H-1B Workers across Firms

Anna Maria Mayda, Francesc Ortega, Giovanni Peri, Kevin Shih, and Chad Sparber

4.1 Introduction

Several researchers are using administrative data on petitions for H-1B workers (also known as I-129 forms) in their analyses of high-skilled immigrants in the United States. While potentially very useful, to date there has been no systematic analysis of the validity of these data. Such an exercise is important because these data are released without a detailed codebook and were not originally designed for use in academic research.

We obtained microdata from United States Citizenship and Immigration Services (USCIS) through a Freedom of Information Act (FOIA) request. These data contain the universe of approved petitions for H-1B workers, along with a substantial (though incomplete) number of denied petitions received during the period 1997–2012. The data set contains 3.72 million cases corresponding to roughly 300,000 companies.

Previous studies (e.g., Kerr and Lincoln 2010; Ghosh, Mayda, and Ortega

Anna Maria Mayda is currently senior advisor to the chief economist at the US State Department. She is on leave from Georgetown University, where she is an associate professor of economics. Francesc Ortega is the Dina Axelrad Perry Professor in Economics at Queens College CUNY. Giovanni Peri is professor and chair of the Department of Economics at the University of California, Davis, and a research associate of the National Bureau of Economic Research. Kevin Shih is assistant professor of economics at Queens College CUNY. Chad Sparber is professor of economics at Colgate University.

We thank Ina Ganguli, Jennifer Hunt, Shulamit Kahn, and Megan MacGarvie and all participants at the NBER conference on the Role of Immigrants and Foreign Students in Science, Innovation, and Entrepreneurship for helpful comments. All views contained herein are the authors' own. We are grateful to the National Science Foundation (award 1535561) for generously funding this project. For acknowledgments, sources of research support, and disclosure of the authors' material financial relationships, if any, please see https://www.nber.org/chapters/c14106.ack.

2014, among others) have relied on data on labor condition applications (LCAs), which need to be filed by any company intending to hire H-1B workers. In contrast to our I-129 data set, LCA data are publicly available from the Department of Labor. While LCAs are a useful proxy for a firm's general interest in hiring H-1B workers, they are much less useful as a measure of how many H-1B petitions that firm files or how many approvals it eventually obtains. The reason is that firms can file LCAs at virtually no cost, and there is an advantage in keeping LCA applications even if hiring foreign workers is simply one of many options. There is no LCA filing fee, for example, and LCA approval does not commit firms to subsequently conduct a job search. As a result, many companies submit LCA paperwork requesting approval to hire far more H-1B workers than they actually intend to hire.[1] In contrast, the H-1B data are worker-specific and necessarily imply that a firm has performed a job search and identified suitable candidates. Hence it is much closer to the concept of "vacancy" or "labor demand" for a firm. Moreover, each petition is accompanied by a positive (and substantial) marginal cost in the form of an I-129 filing fee.[2]

This chapter has three goals. First, we examine the validity of the administrative USCIS microdata on petitions for H-1B workers by comparing these data to the aggregate totals published in the USCIS annual reports on *Petitions and Characteristics of the H-1B Population*. After showing that the microdata are highly consistent with the aggregate statistics, we use string-matching techniques to build a longitudinal, company-level data set for approved H-1B petitions. This turned out to be a very arduous process, and our results in this chapter represent a preliminary summary of work in progress. Nonetheless, we describe a number of important facts in these data, distinguishing between applications for initial employment and those for continuing employment at the firm level. Last, we match our data set on approved petitions to Compustat data on all publicly traded companies. The resulting panel data set contains a wealth of information on firm-level outcomes along with the number of yearly approved H-1B petitions. We use this data set to compare the characteristics of Compustat companies that received H-1B workers to those that did not and describe trends at the industry level in H-1B usage.

Our main findings are as follows. First, we show that the annual counts of petitions in the microdata closely match the totals in the USCIS reports for most, though not all, years. We also show that the microdata account fairly well for the total numbers of approved petitions, with a higher degree

---

1. The LCA data show multiple instances of companies that request the exact same number of applications every year for several years.

2. Originally, we intended to use the number of LCAs filed by a company in a particular year together with the number of approved H-1B petitions to build firm-specific annual success rates in order to exploit the randomization introduced by the lottery assignment. However, for the reasons outlined earlier, we abandoned such an approach.

of accuracy when focusing on issuances for initial employment (as opposed to continuing-employment applications).

Next we establish the following facts on the three million approved H-1B petitions in the period 2000–2012. First, 46 percent of all initial-employment H-1Bs were issued to workers in computer-related occupations. The bulk of the remaining approved petitions were issued to firms hiring managers, officials, and occupations in administrative specializations (13 percent); architects and engineers (11.3 percent); education-related occupations (9.9 percent); and workers in occupations in medicine and health (6.3 percent). Second, about 1 in 5 approved petitions for initial-employment originated in the metropolitan area of *New York/Northeastern New Jersey*. Other important metropolitan areas were *San Jose, CA*; *Washington, DC/MD/ VA*; *Boston, MA/NH*; *Chicago, IL*; and *Dallas–Fort Worth, TX*. Together, these six metropolitan areas account for 60 percent of all initial-employment petitions. Third, our firm-level data set contains approximately 398,000 companies with an annual average for approved petitions of 1.6 for initial-employment and 1.9 for continuing employment. Fourth, we document a very large increase in the concentration of approved petitions. The data show a fourfold increase in the top-20 share for new-employment H-1B petitions over the period 2000–2012, with a sharp acceleration between 2008 and 2012. During this period, we also observe a clear trend toward a ranking dominated by global IT consulting companies. Fifth, public school districts and research universities enter the top-20 ranking in some years. Among not-for-profit institutions, in most years the top petitioner for initial-employment H-1B workers was the New York City Public School District.

Regarding publicly traded (Compustat) companies, our data reveal the following facts. Compustat companies account for about 13 percent of all approved petitions in our data set. Roughly 42 percent of Compustat companies had at least one approved petition over the period 2000–2012, and in any given year, only 20 percent of Compustat companies had at least one approved petition for an initial-employment H-1B. We also find that firms using the H-1B program are larger on average and have higher growth rates than nonusers. In our data, the main H-1B-receiving industries are business services, electronic equipment, and machinery and computers. The data also show the explosion in the number of new-employment H-1Bs received by the business services sector between 2009 and 2012. Moreover, this growth has been largely driven by an increase in the intensity of H-1B use (relative to overall employment in the industry) as opposed to an increase in the size of the industry. Between 2000 and 2008, the business services industry received about 1.5 initial-employment issuances per 1,000 employees. However, this intensity grew by 133 percent between 2008 and 2012.

This chapter is most directly related to the growing research on the economic effects of the H-1B program. Some studies have focused on the impact on innovation and patenting (Hunt and Gauthier-Loiselle 2010; Kerr and

Lincoln 2010; Kerr, Kerr, and Lincoln 2015). In our use of string-matching techniques, our chapter is closely related to the studies aimed at linking patenting data to other firm-level data sets (such as Compustat), as in Hall, Jaffe, and Trajtenberg (2001) and Bessen and Hunt (2007). Others have focused on labor market effects (Peri, Shih, and Sparber 2015; Mayda et al. 2018), company performance (Doran, Gelber, and Isen 2014; Ghosh, Mayda, and Ortega 2014), or educational and career choices (Kato and Sparber 2013; Amuedo-Dorantes and Furtado 2016; Shih 2016).

To our knowledge, this chapter, together with Mayda et al. (2018), is the first to utilize data on the universe of H-1B visas at the firm level (over several years). The other papers in the literature on H-1B visas either use aggregate data (e.g., state-level or city-level data) or use data on labor condition applications (LCAs) or focus on a small sample of firms. Hunt and Gauthier-Loiselle (2010) exploit cross-state variation for the United States and find that a 1 percentage point increase in the share of immigrant college graduates in the population leads to an increase in patents per capita of 9 percent to 18 percent—the main reason being that they disproportionately hold science, technology, engineering, and mathematics (STEM) degrees. Peri et al. (2015) use variation in the H-1B cap to identify the effect of increases in the population of STEM workers in a city on the wages of skilled and unskilled workers in the same city. This chapter finds that H-1B-driven increases in STEM workers are associated with increases in the wages paid to skilled workers (in both STEM and non-STEM occupations) and finds no evidence of effects on the wages of unskilled workers.

Kerr and Lincoln (2010) focus on the effects of H-1B visas on patenting activity and carry out the analysis, for the most part, at the city level—the firm-level analysis in Kerr and Lincoln (2010) is based on LCA data for a very small sample of companies (77 firms). On the other hand, Ghosh et al. (2014) use data on LCAs for the universe of publicly traded firms in the US (almost 4,000 firms) and investigate a different set of firm-level outcomes, including firm productivity, sales, profits, and total-factor productivity. Kerr, Kerr, and Lincoln (2015) exploit the same empirical strategy as Kerr and Lincoln (2010) to analyze the impact of hiring young skilled immigrants on the hiring and employment of several groups of skilled native workers. This chapter uses administrative microdata from the US Census Bureau, which is extremely accurate. However, as in Kerr and Lincoln (2010), the focus is on a subset of firms—specifically an unbalanced panel of 319 firms selected on the basis of employment and patenting activity.

An important recent contribution to the literature is the work by Doran et al. (2014), which exploits the visa lottery in fiscal years 2006 and 2007 to analyze the effects of H-1B visas on patenting and overall firm employment. This paper finds no evidence of an effect on patenting and at most a moderate effect on overall employment in the firm. Clemens (2013) analyzes internal personnel data from an anonymous Indian-based IT firm to study the effects on earnings for workers who migrate to the US on H-1B status relative to those who remain in India. He finds a large effect stemming primarily from the change in location. It has been argued that H-1B status holders are tied to their employers and subject to some degree of exploitation. Depew et al. (2013) revisit this question by focusing on worker separations in a data set containing six large Indian IT firms. They show that quit rates are significant and procyclical, suggesting a substantial degree of mobility toward other employers.

The structure of this chapter is as follows. Section 4.2 describes our microdata on H-1B petitions. Section 4.3 describes the procedure to create the company-level data set on approved petitions. Section 4.4 summarizes the procedure to match the H-1B data to Compustat and presents the main facts arising from these data. Section 4.5 concludes.

4.2   H-1B Petitions for 1997–2012

4.2.1   Data Source

The starting point of our analysis is a microdata set provided by USCIS (through an FOIA request) on the universe of processed I-129 petitions for H-1B workers from 1997 to 2012. H-1B status provides foreign citizens a legal right to temporarily work in highly skilled specialty occupations in the United States. Although it is awarded to individuals, a person must have a qualifying job offer to receive H-1B status, and the I-129 petition for H-1B employment is filed by the employer. Thus the program creates a strong employer/employee link. This motivates us to create a firm-level data set on H-1B employment.

Our data set contains 3.72 million individual petitions for H-1B employment. Petitions for fiscal years 1997 and 1998 are severely incomplete for unknown reasons, and we do not use them in our analysis.[3] Each petition provides the date on which it was received as well as the status date and decision (i.e., if the H-1B application was approved, denied, rejected, pending, or administratively closed). In principle, all approved H-1Bs are included in our data set. We have limited information on nonapproved petitions, however. This is because new H-1B issuances have been subject to an annual cap since the program's inception. Cap exemptions exist for H-1B renewals and employees of universities and nonprofit research institutions. But USCIS stops processing and recording petitions for cap-bound new H-1B employment after the annual cap has been reached, so these unprocessed petitions

3. The 1,501 petitions for fiscal year (FY) 1997 and 21,324 for FY 1998 account for only 0.61 percent of all petitions in our data.

are not in our data set. Among the 3.64 million petitions processed in fiscal years 1999–2012, 82.4 percent (3 million) were approved.[4]

Our data set includes individual- and firm-level information for each petition. Firm-level information includes company name, state, and zip code. In theory, it also identifies whether the employer is a cap-exempt educational or nonprofit research organization. Individual-level information includes country of birth, age, education level, salary, occupation, and principal field of study. It also identifies whether the individual is requesting new H-1B status (24.4 percent), a change in status (24.1 percent), an extension of an existing H-1B status (49.6 percent), or an amendment (1.7 percent). Petitions can be for new employment (55.7 percent), continuation of employment (27 percent), change in previous approved employment (7.1 percent), change of employer (8.2 percent), or an amendment (1.5 percent).

We use this information to distinguish between petitions for new employment (which can be cap-bound) and for cap-exempt continuing employment. Specifically, we define a petition to be for *initial employment* when (a) the applicant's job status is new employment and (b) the petition is not requesting an extension or an amendment of an existing H-1B. Among the 3 million *approved* petitions, 1.60 million were for new employment. Among these, 251,000 petitions requested either an extension or an amendment of established H-1B employment. Thus according to our definition, 1.35 million approved petitions were for *initial employment*. We refer to all other approved H-1Bs (1.65 million) as pertaining to *continuing employment*.

4.2.2   Comparison with USCIS Reports

Validation. The data on petitions (I-129 forms) we obtained from USCIS lacked detailed documentation and had some awkward features. It is therefore important to check validity. To do so, we compare our microdata to the reports published annually by USCIS (*Petitions and Characteristics of the H-1B Population*). We restrict our comparison to fiscal years 2000–2012.

The figures in the annual reports correspond to the figures of USCIS in terms of H-1B petitions, filings, and approvals. The timing of their data is not directly linked to the lotteries or application deadlines in any given year. In our microdata, for each petition we know the receipt date and a status date. The latter probably corresponds to the time the last recorded decision on that petition was made. It is not obvious which of these two dating conventions best matches the data in the annual reports. It seems natural that *receipt date* should be the best criterion for classifying petitions filed. However, we believe *status date* is probably best to classify approvals because we understand that when a petition being processed is turned into an approval, that will be the status date reported. We think this dating convention matches

---

4. Among the remaining petitions, 16.2 percent were denied, 0.35 percent rejected, 0.64 percent pending, and 0.44 percent administratively closed.

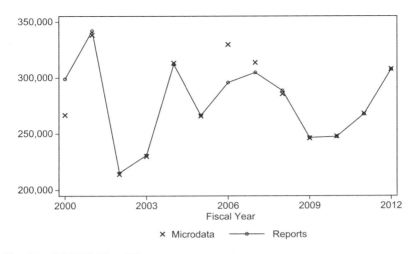

Fig. 4.1   I-129 H-1B petitions

Note: Microdata sorted by receipt year. "Reports" refers to the annual USCIS reports on Petitions and Characteristics of H-1B Workers. The R^2 of this simple linear regression is 0.88.

the spirit of the output of USCIS in terms of H-1B workers in a particular quarter, and we use it in our analysis in this section.

Counting Petitions. First, we aggregate all petitions in our microdata by fiscal (receipt) year and compare them to the annual aggregates reported in the USCIS reports. As seen in figure 4.1, in many cases the microdata exactly fits the total in the reports. However, there are significant discrepancies in years 2000, 2006, and 2007. The overall goodness of fit is 0.88, and the average ratio of petition counts in the microdata relative to the report is 1, although it varies from 0.89 to 1.11 in the years in our sample.

Approved Petitions. The data set includes petitions that were approved as well as petitions in another status (e.g., denied, rejected, or pending). So now we turn to approved petitions sorted by status date. Figure 4.2 reports the result. As before, the fit is fairly good (with an R^2 of 0.89). However, the counts for approved petitions based on our microdata are uniformly lower than the total in the reports. The ratio of approved petitions in the microdata relative to the report ranges from 0.76 to 0.94 and takes a value of 0.88 in an average year. We suspect that the larger figure in the USCIS reports may be due to the fact that when an application is amended, it might be counted as an additional processed item, even though in our microdata it might simply be recorded as a status update to an existing petition.

Approved Petitions for Initial Employment. We now turn to initial-employment petitions as defined in the previous section. As shown in figure 4.3, the match is somewhat improved relative to all approvals, but we still observe a uniformly lower count in our microdata relative to the published totals in the USCIS reports. The ratios between counts in the micro-

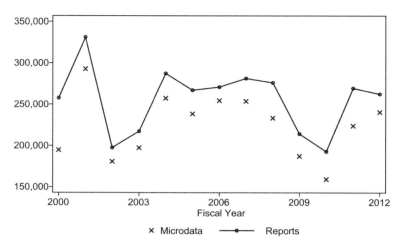

Fig. 4.2   Approved petitions for H-1B workers (I-129s)

Note: Microdata sorted by status year. Reports refer to the annual USCIS reports on Petitions and Characteristics of H-1B Workers. The R^2 of this simple linear regression is 0.89.

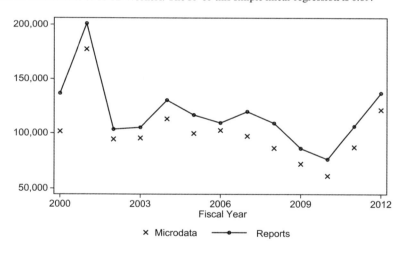

Fig. 4.3   Approved H-1B petitions for initial employment

Note: Microdata sorted by status year. Initial employment petitions (*jobstatus* = 1) excluding those referring to extensions or amendments (*request* = 3,4). "Reports" refers to the annual USCIS reports on Petitions and Characteristics of H-1B Workers. The R^2 of this simple linear regression is 0.94.

data and reported totals range between 0.74 and 0.94 and take the value 0.85 on average (the R^2 is 0.94). Obviously, the undercount of initial-employment approved petitions can be reduced by using a broader definition—that is, by defining initial-employment as any petition listing the applicant's job status as new employment regardless of whether it is simply requesting an exten-

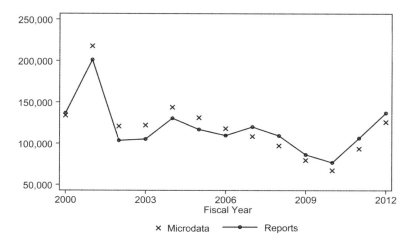

Fig. 4.4   Approved H-1B petitions for initial employment (2)

Note: Microdata sorted by status year. All initial employment petitions (*jobstatus* = 1). "Reports" refers to the annual USCIS reports on Petitions and Characteristics of H-1B Workers. The R^2 of this simple linear regression is 0.89.

sion or amendment. Clearly, in this case (figure 4.4) the number of approved initial-employment petitions increases, and we obtain a better fit of the totals in the annual reports. Nonetheless, we think that the narrower definition is more relevant for our analysis.[5]

Verdict. In summary, our comparison between our I-129 microdata and the aggregate figures in the USCIS annual reports turns out to be quite successful. Our data contain all filed petitions for most years. However, there is a small degree of discrepancy in the status of the petitions. The total approved petitions according to the annual reports is somewhat higher than what is implied by the microdata, but the two variables co-move very strongly. Agreement between the two sources of data improves when we restrict the sample to approved petitions for initial employment. Altogether, our microdata are strongly validated by the totals in the annual USCIS reports, although some discrepancies exist between the two sources.

4.3   Firm-Level Panel for Petitions

4.3.1   Aggregation

The largest data challenge we face is the aggregation of individual H-1B petitions to the company level. For each individual case, we know the

---

5. The average gap is now nonexistent, ranging between undercounts in some years (0.87) and overcounts (1.16) in others, with an R^2 of 0.89.

name and zip code of the company submitting the application, but we lack the exact address or, more importantly, a numerical identifier such as the employer identification number (EIN). Thus we need to rely on the company name to link individual cases within and across years. This is a challenging endeavor because a single firm will often file separate I-129 petitions under several name variants with a high prevalence of typos and misspellings. For example, there are 52 separate variants of the name "MICROSOFT" in Redmond, Washington, including "MICROSOFT CORP," "MICROSOFT COPORATION" [sic], "MICROSOFT CO," and just "MICROSOFT." We need to inspect the data and employ a harmonization routine to assign a common firm name to these separate entries.

We proceed in two steps. First, we conduct an extensive process of manual name harmonization in which we review the entries with company names that clearly pertain to the top H-1B-receiving firms. Specifically, we harmonize common words (e.g., "INCORPORATED," "GLOBAL," "RESEARCH") for all petitions. In addition, we manually assign a common company name to the petitions that appear to correspond to the same company in the top 3,000 firms in terms of filed petitions.[6] For instance, we aggregate records with company names "INFOSYS T," "ILNFOSYS T," and "INFORSYS TECH LIMITED" under the common name "INFOSYS TECH LIMITED." When collapsing the petitions by the harmonized name, the 3.72 million petitions in the raw data go down to 1.35 million company-year observations.

The second step conducts automatic name harmonization applied to all companies. Specifically, we parse company names to separate the company's official name from other names included in the same field (such as doing-business-as and formerly-known-as names), standardize the entity type (e.g., INC, CORP, etc.), and create numerical identifiers for groups of observations with similar names.[7] We then collapse observations using the numerical identifier, which results in 1.23 million company-year observations. When restricting to (status) fiscal years 2000–2012, the number of observations falls to 1.17 million.

An important caveat is how to deal with affiliates. We aggregate petitions under a common name in cases where company names indicate clear affiliation. For instance, we combined "IBM" with its foreign affiliate "IBM India" under the common name "INTL BUSINESS MACHINES CORP." Likewise, we also aggregated clearly recognizable affiliates within the country,

6. This ranking was built on the basis of the petitions filed in fiscal years 2008 and 2009. In these years, all new H-1B issuances were assigned through a lottery. These 3,000 firms account for more than 60 percent of all petitions filed in those years.

7. The parsing of company names is done using *Stata's* command *STND_COMPNAME*. String-grouping is conducted using *Stata's* STRGROUP command (Reif 2010) on the standardized name field. The command computes the Levenshtein distance between all bilateral pairs of standardized names. Pairs with a distance normalized by the number of characters corresponding to the shorter name string in the pair that is lower than 10 percent are grouped together under a common numerical identifier.

such as "AMAZON CORPORATE," "AMAZON DIGITAL," "AMAZON FULFILLMENT," "AMAZON TECH," and "AMAZON WEB," which were aggregated under the common name "AMAZON." However, we do not have systematic information on affiliates that do not share similar names.

The resulting longitudinal, firm-level data set for approved petitions contains almost 400,000 companies and 1.17 million company-year observations for the fiscal years 2000–2012. For short, we will refer to these data as the *H-1B Data Set*. For each of these companies, we have constructed the number of H-1B workers (approved I-129s) received annually in period 2000–2012, distinguishing between approvals referring to initial employment and those referring to continuing employment.[8]

4.3.2   Facts on H-1B Petitioners

Let us now examine the main facts pertaining to the *H-1B Data Set* for the period 2000–2012.

Occupation. Across all years and companies, 46 percent of all initial-employment H-1Bs were awarded to workers in *computer-related occupations.* The other most important occupations are *managers, officials, and occupations in administrative specializations* (13 percent); architects and engineers (11.3 percent); education-related occupations (9.9 percent); and occupations in *medicine and health* (6.3 percent). Together, these groups account for 87 percent of all initial-employment H-1Bs.

Metropolitan Area. It is also interesting to examine the geographical distribution of H-1B workers. This is based on the zip code listed in the I-129 form, which we matched with the corresponding metropolitan area. In many cases, this will identify the area of employment of the worker, but in others, this might simply be the headquarters of the company. Among initial-employment issuances, we observe a large concentration (21 percent) in *New York / Northeastern New Jersey*. The remaining H-1Bs are distributed much more uniformly, with 6.3 percent in *San Jose, CA*; 6.3 percent in *Washington, DC/MD/VA*; 4.7 percent in *Boston, MA/NH*; 4.5 percent in *Chicago, IL*; and 4.5 percent in *Dallas–Fort Worth, TX*. Together these six metropolitan areas account for 60 percent of all initial-employment issuances.

Rankings. Collapsing our data by company and year renders 0.82 million observations (corresponding to approximately 398,000 companies), with an annual average of 1.6 new-employment petition approvals and 1.9 continuing-employment approvals. However, there is a large degree of dispersion. Across years and companies, approved new-employment H-1Bs range between 0 and 9,483. It is also interesting to examine the rankings for a few selected years. Table 4.1 reports the top 20 receivers of new (initial-

---

8. These data could be used to estimate the stocks of H-1B workers at the firm level and their evolution over time. However, doing so requires making some assumptions regarding the depreciation of these stocks. For relevant information in this respect, see Depew et al. (2013) and Clemens (2013).

Table 4.1   Ranking by approved initial employment: years 2000, 2004, 2008, and 2012

Rank	2000 Firm	2000 Initial	2004 Firm	2004 Initial	2008 Firm	2008 Initial	2012 Firm	2012 Initial
1	TATA CONSULT	983	INFOSYS TECH	4,406	INFOSYS TECH	2,706	COGNIZANT TECH SOL	9,483
2	MICROSOFT	819	SATYAM COMPUTER	2,190	WIPRO LIMITED	2,683	TATA CONSULT	7,727
3	MOTOROLA	672	TATA CONSULT	1,879	TATA CONSULT	1,274	INFOSYS TECH	6,808
4	TEKEDGE	555	WIPRO	1,430	SATYAM COMPUTER	1,209	WIPRO LIMITED	4,002
5	INFOSYS TECH	652	COGNIZANT TECH SOL	1,196	MICROSOFT CORP	1,063	ACCENTURE LLP	3,548
6	INTEL	519	PATNI COMPUTER INC	941	ACCENTURE LLP	712	HCL AMERICA	2,133
7	ACE TECH	505	IBM GLOBAL INDIA	766	CISCO SYSTEMS INC	471	LARSEN & TOUBRO INFOTECH	1,703
8	MASTECH	493	MICROSOFT CORP	646	COGNIZANT TECH SOL	417	IBM INDIA PRIVATE	1,427
9	CISCO SYS	477	TATA INFOTECH	607	IBM GLOBAL INDIA	401	SATYAM COMPUTER	1,293
10	ALPHASOFT SVC	425	NYC PUBLIC SCHOOLS	540	LARSEN & TOUBRO INFOTECH	398	MICROSOFT	1,231
11	WIPRO	403	MPHASIS CORPORATION	516	INTEL CORP	377	PATNI AMERICAS	1,227
12	HTC GLOBAL SVC	394	LARSEN & TOUBRO INFOTECH	461	QUALCOMM	238	SYNTEL CONSULT	1,104
13	TECHSPACE SOL	368	SYNTEL	418	MPHASIS CORP	229	DELOITTE CONSULT	909
14	DATA CONVERSION	354	DELOITTE & TOUCHE LLP	346	BALTIMORE PUBLIC SCHOOLS	229	TECH MAHINDRA AMERICAS	826
15	BIRLASOFT	346	HEXAWARE TECH INC	298	PRINCE GEORGE PUBLIC SCHOOLS	213	MPHASIS	704
16	PEOPLE COM CON	342	DELOITTE CONSULTING	270	UST GLOBAL INC	199	AMAZON CORP	611
17	COGNIZANT TECH	327	POLARIS SOFT LAB INDIA	267	ERNST & YOUNG LLP	198	INTEL	552
18	SYNTEL	298	PWC	253	VERINON TECH SOL	176	GOOGLE	512
19	LUCENT TECH	291	UNIVERSITY OF PENN	238	GOOGLE	174	PRICEWATERHOUSECOOPERS	487
20	SATYAM COMPUTER	271	CAMBRIDGE RESOURCE GROUP	229	TERRA INFOTECH	166	UST GLOBAL INC	445
TOTAL		112,071		109,662		86,470		116,099
Share top 10		5.4%		13.3%		13.1%		33.9%
Share top 20		8.5%		16.3%		15.7%		40.3%
Share IT top 20		4.5%		15.0%		12.3%		37.7%

Note: The names of some of the companies have been shortened slightly to accommodate the formatting of the table. The row TOTAL refers to the total number of initial-employment visas approved in the corresponding year taking into account all petitions (not just those submitted by the firms in the ranking presented here. The bottom row reports the number of initial-employment visas that went to business and technology consulting firms that are part of the ranking presented in the table, as a share of the TOTAL initial-employment visas.

employment) H-1B issuances in the years 2000, 2004, 2008, and 2012. The top 3 companies by approved (initial-employment) visas in year 2000 were TATA CONSULTANCY SERVICES, MICROSOFT, and MOTOR- OLA. From 2004 onward, the top 3 companies have been business and information-technology consulting companies based in India, alternating between INFOSYS TECH, SATYAM COMPUTER SERVICES, WIPRO LIMITED, and TATA CONSULTANCY SERVICES. In addition, the number of H-1B visas obtained by these firms has grown enormously as a result of growing demand for their services. More generally, with the exception of MICROSOFT, AMAZON, INTEL, and GOOGLE, all other companies in the 2012 top-20 ranking by approved petitions for initial-employment issuances were business and technology consulting firms.

Increased Concentration. Between 2000 and 2012, the data show a sharp increase in the concentration of new visas in the hands of a small number of companies. In 2000, the top 20 receivers obtained 8 percent of the 112,071 issuances for initial employment granted in that year. In 2004, the degree of concentration increased further, with the top 20 firms receiving 16 percent of the 109,662 H-1Bs for new employment granted in that year. The share of these workers being granted to the top 20 companies remained at 16 percent in 2008 despite the lower total of 86,470 H-1Bs. However, there was another sharp increase in concentration in 2012, with the top-20 share increasing to 40 percent for a total of 116,099 H-1Bs granted in that year. In sum, the data reveal a fourfold increase in the top-20 share for new-employment H-1Bs over the period 2000–2012.

The rise in concentration has been fundamentally driven by business and IT consulting companies. As can be seen at the bottom of table 4.1, the IT consulting companies among the top 20 receivers accounted for 4.5 percent of new-employment visas in year 2000, slightly over half of the share among all the top 20 receivers. However, in year 2012, IT companies among the top 20 receiving companies accounted for 37.7 percent of all new-employment H-1B visas, or 94 percent of the visas awarded to the top 20 receivers.

Educational and Research Institutions. We also note that public school districts (e.g., New York City Public Schools) and universities (e.g., University of Pennsylvania) enter the top-20 ranking in some years. In table 4.2, we present the top-10 ranking of petitioners for initial-employment H-1Bs in years 2004, 2008, and 2012, distinguishing between for-profit and nonprofit organizations. This distinction is important because the latter are generally exempt from the annual cap. In the three selected years, the top petitioner of initial-employment H-1B issuances was the New York City Public School District. In addition, leading research universities are also part of the top 10, such as Yale, Stanford, University of Michigan, and University of Pennsylvania.

In recent work, we show that the above facts are consistent with evidence based on a triple difference estimation strategy. In particular, Mayda et al.

Table 4.2   Ranking by approved new-employment H-1B petitions by exemption status

Year 2004	Year 2008	Year 2012
Cap-bound		
INFOSYS TECH LIMITED	INFOSYS TECH LIMITED	COGNIZANT TECH SOLUTIONS US CORP
SATYAM COMPUTER SERVICES LIMITED	WIPRO LIMITED	INFOSYS TECH LIMITED
MICROSOFT CORP	MICROSOFT CORP	WIPRO LIMITED
TATA CONSULTANCY SERVICES LIMITED	SATYAM COMPUTER SERVICES LIMITED	TATA CONSULTANCY SERVICES LIMITED
WIPRO LIMITED	COGNIZANT TECH SOLUTIONS US CORP	MICROSOFT CORP
COGNIZANT TECH SOLUTIONS US CORP	TATA CONSULTANCY SERVICES LIMITED	ACCENTURE LLP
PATNI COMPUTER SYSTEMS INC	CISCO SYSTEMS INC	LARSEN & TOUBRO INFOTECH LIMITED
CISCO SYSTEMS INC	IBM CORP	HCL AMERICA INC (HCL TECH)
IBM GLOBAL SVCS IGS INDIA PVT	INTEL CORP	IBM INDIA PRIVATE LIMITED
INTEL CORP	ORACLE USA INC	INTEL CORP

Year 2004	Year 2008	Year 2012
Cap-exempt		
NEW YORK CITY PUBLIC SCHOOLS	NEW YORK CITY PUBLIC SCHOOLS	NEW YORK CITY PUBLIC SCHOOLS
YALE UNIVERSITY	PRINCE GEORGE'S COUNTY PUBLIC SCHOOLS	STANFORD UNIVERSITY
UNIVERSITY OF MICHIGAN	YALE UNIVERSITY	UNIVERSITY OF MICHIGAN
COLUMBIA UNIVERSITY	UNIVERSITY OF MICHIGAN	YALE UNIVERSITY
UNIVERSITY OF FLORIDA	UNIVERSITY OF PENNSYLVANIA	CLEVELAND CLINIC FOUNDATION
STANFORD UNIVERSITY	COLUMBIA UNIVERSITY	JOHNS HOPKINS UNIVERSITY
BAYLOR COLLEGE OF MEDICINE	HOUSTON INDEPENDENT SCHOOL DISTRICT	UNIVERSITY OF PITTSBURGH
DUKE UNIVERSITY MED CENTER & HOSPITAL	UNIVERSITY OF PITTSBURGH	COLUMBIA UNIVERSITY
UNIVERSITY OF PA	STANFORD UNIVERSITY	DUKE UNIVERSITY UNIVERSITY MED CENTER & AFFIL
HOUSTON INDEPENDENT SCHOOL DISTRICT	DUKE UNIVERSITY UNIVERSITY MED CENTER & AFFIL	EMORY UNIVERSITY

Note: Ranking on the basis of new-employment approved I-129 petitions in our *H-1B Data Set.*

(2018) empirically analyze the intended and unintended effects of the 2004 reduction in the H-1B quota. The policy change created a sudden discontinuity in the maximum supply of H-1B visas for the "treated" group of new H-1B workers of for-profit firms relative to the "control" group of experienced H-1B workers of for-profit firms and of (new and experienced) H-1B workers of nonprofit firms. We find that the cap restrictions significantly reduced the aggregate employment of new H-1B workers in for-profit firms relative to what would have occurred in an unconstrained environment. In addition, our results show that the quota reduction implied no change in employment of H-1B workers, respectively, in computer-related occupations, from India, and in firms that employ more than ten H-1B workers. As a consequence, the quota reduction redistributed H-1Bs toward computer-related occupations, Indian-born workers, and firms using the H-1B program extensively. This, in turn, produced a much higher concentration of the H-1B visas in the hands of a few employers, as shown in Lorenz curves of the inequality of H-1B issuances across firms (see figure 4.5: H-1B Concentration in Firms in Mayda et al. 2018).

4.4   H-1Bs among Publicly Traded Firms

Unfortunately, our *H-1B Data Set* does not contain any firm-level information beyond its name and geographic location. In order to learn more about the trends regarding the demand for H-1B workers as a function of firm-level characteristics, we merge our data set with Compustat. Once again, this needs to be done on the basis of company name.

4.4.1   Merging with Compustat

After some basic cleaning, our Compustat data contains 7,067 companies.[9] As noted earlier, the *H-1B Data Set* contains nearly 400,000 companies. To match the companies in this data set to the companies in Compustat, we make use of probabilistic record-linking techniques.[10] In essence, we examine all pairs (n,m), where n refers to the name in Compustat and m to the name in the *H-1B Data Set*. As before, for each pair of names, we compute a measure of similarity between the two character strings.

The code produces more than 11,000 potential matches, with associated scores ranging between 0.60 and 1. There are 3,070 perfect matches with a (perfect) score of 1. Clerical review of the potential fuzzy matches is time

---

9. We restricted the Compustat sample to companies with nonmissing, nonzero employment in 2012, which results in 7,067 companies. Interestingly, only 5,294 of these companies have an employer identification number (EIN), and in fact, several of the top recipients of H-1B workers, such as INFOSYS, SATYAM, WIPRO, or ERICSSON, lack an EIN. Hence some degree of record-linking error based on company names is unavoidable.

10. The specific record-linking protocol we use is Stata's *reclink2* command. This code is an extension of Blasnik's (2010) procedure carried out by Wasi and Flaaen (2014).

Table 4.3   **Record-linking** *H-1B Data Set* **and** *Compustat*

	1	2	3	4	5	6
Threshold RLSC	1	0.99	0.98	0.97	0.96	0.95
perfect matches	3,070	3,070	3,070	3,070	3,070	3,070
potential fuzzy matches	.	900	991	1,101	1,237	808
accepted fuzzy matches	.	454	327	207	223	68
success rate	.	0.50	0.33	0.19	0.18	0.08
total matches	3,070	3,524	3,851	4,058	4,281	4,349
collapsed by firm	2,169	2,489	2,687	2,823	2,957	3,002
share of Compustat comp. with approved I-129s	0.31	0.35	0.38	0.40	0.42	0.42

Note: The RLSC (record-linking score) is the key output of the *reclink2* probabilistic record-linking routine. It is a measure of similarity between the two company name strings. The similarity score is based on the number of characters that need to be changed in one of the strings in order to perfectly match the other string. The shares of the last row are computed on the basis of the 7,067 Compustat companies (with nonmissing, nonzero employment in 2012). Column 1 considers only perfect matches. Columns 2–6 also include fuzzy matches, with a gradually decreasing threshold for the record-linking score in order to be considered.

consuming—it takes about one hour to review 500 candidate pairs. As a result, we conduct clerical review in stages, gradually lowering the similarity score threshold.[11] As reported in table 4.3, there are 3,070 pairs with a perfect match by company name (column 1). The next column also includes the (roughly 900) potential matches with a similarity score above 0.99. After manually reviewing each of them, we conclude that 454 of those are correct, amounting to a 50 percent success rate. We then proceed to review the candidate pairs with scores above 0.98, which results in a 33 percent success rate. Columns 4 to 6 gradually lower the similarity score threshold to 0.97, 0.96, and 0.95. As expected, the success rates decline to 19 percent, 18 percent, and 8 percent, respectively. At this point we deem the success rate to be too low to merit further clerical review. We have matched 4,349 pairs of company names. However, some of these pairs refer to the same firm. When collapsing by firm, we end up with 3,002 Compustat firms having approved I-129s, which amounts to 42 percent of all Compustat firms (with nonzero, nonmissing employment).

It is also worth noting that Compustat companies are only a small fraction

11. Some pairs have very similar names, which is why they are over the similarity threshold, but it is unclear whether they refer to the same company. For example, (ANDERSON,ANDERSONS) could very well refer to two different companies, so we verify that they exist. Typically, in ambiguous cases where both companies exist, we do not accept the match. We only assume there was a typo when the name for the I-129 data entry corresponds to a company that does not seem to exist according to Google searches. We are fairly confident of the quality of our matches. Keep in mind that some pairs will have been rejected despite being true matches. This type of measurement error is, by construction, random and should not bias our estimates.

Table 4.4   **Examples of the evolution of approved initial-employment petitions**

Year	gvkey	Approved petitions: initial employment	Approved petitions: continuing employment
GOOGLE			
2000	160329	6	2
2001	160329	16	9
2002	160329	11	9
2003	160329	36	31
2004	160329	71	52
2005	160329	184	120
2006	160329	148	149
2007	160329	178	217
2008	160329	174	180
2009	160329	252	215
2010	160329	298	388
2011	160329	573	495
2012	160329	512	579
COGNIZANT			
2000	111864	327	131
2001	111864	451	222
2002	111864	185	197
2003	111864	599	273
2004	111864	1,197	685
2005	111864	817	482
2006	111864	586	1,457
2007	111864	663	1,347
2008	111864	417	1,329
2009	111864	1,308	1,319
2010	111864	4,050	2,510
2011	111864	4,963	3,501
2012	111864	9,484	6,152

Note: Based on approved I-129 forms for initial-employment H-1B issuances on the basis of our USCIS microdata merged with Compustat. To save on space, we have shortened the company names.

of all companies based in the United States. Summing over all years in our data, Compustat firms account for roughly 412,000 approved H-1B petitions for H-1B, with 40 percent of these referring to initial-employment issuances. This figure accounts for only 13 percent of the three million approved H-1B petitions over the period 2000–2012.

Next we report two specific examples of companies that have substantially increased their use of H-1B workers over our period of analysis. The top panel in table 4.4 reports the data for GOOGLE. In year 2000, GOOGLE obtained merely six and two initial and continuing employment workers, respectively. Over the next 12 years, GOOGLE has received an increasing number of initial-employment issuances, peaking at 573 in 2011. The bottom panel reports the data for COGNIZANT. This company obtained a few

Table 4.5   **Approved H-1B petitions: sum of initial and continuing employment**

Approved H-1B	2000 percentage	2012 percentage
None	77	80
1 to 10	18	15
11+	5	5
Total firms	3,419	7,067

Note: Distribution of Compustat companies in year 2000 (or 2012) with nonmissing employment over the number of approved H-1B petitions (pooling initial and continuing employment). The lower number of firms in 2000 is due to the fact that our Compustat sample conditions on nonmissing, nonzero employment in year 2012.

hundred initial-employment issuances every year between 2000 and 2008. From 2009 onward, the growth in the number of this type of H-1B has been exponential. In 2012, COGNIZANT received 9,484 initial-employment H-1Bs compared to only 327 in year 2000.

4.4.2   Facts on Compustat H-1B Petitioners

As noted earlier, our matched H-1B-Compustat data set is a longitudinal data set containing 7,067 companies and 12 years.[12] We were able to match about 42 percent of the firms in Compustat through our string-matching algorithm, and we imputed zero issuances to the unmatched firms.

4.4.2.1   *Characteristics of H-1B-Using Companies*

The first exercise we carry out is a comparison between the matched (i.e., H-1B users) and unmatched Compustat companies. We focus on employment, revenue, and market value, both in levels and in growth rates.

Our starting point is to build the distribution of Compustat companies by usage of the H-1B program. Specifically, we consider the companies with nonmissing, nonzero employment in 2000 (as well as in 2012) and classify them in three groups: companies with no approved petitions in 2000, companies with 1 to 10 approved petitions (for initial or continuing employment), and companies with 11 or more approved petitions in 2000. The resulting distribution is summarized in table 4.5: 77 percent, 18 percent, and 5 percent, respectively, among the 3,419 companies satisfy the restrictions. The table also presents the H-1B usage distribution for the 7,067 firms with nonzero, nonmissing employment in 2012, with 80 percent of firms with no approved H-1B petitions in year 2012, 15 percent with 1 to 10 approved petitions, and 5 percent with 11 or more approved petitions in that year.[13]

---

12. The time dimension is restricted by the availability of data on H-1B petitions, which ranges from year 2000 to 2012. Among Compustat companies we have restricted to those that have nonmissing, nonzero employment in year 2012.

13. As noted earlier, there may be some unmatched firms that did receive H-1B workers. However, the size of this group is likely to be very small based on the statistics reported in table 4.3.

Table 4.6   **Characteristics of H-1B usage**

Year	2000	2000	2000	2012	2012	2012
H-1B	None	1 to 10	11+	None	1 to 10	11+
Employment (M)	10	16	44	8	13	35
Revenue ($MM)	2,462	3,744	12,593	3,103	4,296	17,330
Market value ($MM)	1,765	4,830	29,783	1,803	3,528	21,851
Growth employment	11.2%	12.4%	15.2%	6.0%	6.4%	8.8%
Growth revenue	32.4%	61.1%	85.3%	20.5%	19.3%	20.7%
Growth market value	.	.	.	30.1%	62.3%	40.1%
Mode SIC2d	60, 28	73, 36	73, 36	60, 73	73, 36	73, 36

Note: Employment counts are in thousands of employees. Revenue and market value are in millions of dollars (at current prices). The last row reports the top two mode industries (to-digit Standard Industrial Classification [SIC] code) in each column. The relevant SIC codes are as follows: chemicals and allied products (28); electronic and other electrical equipment and components, except computer equipment (36); depository institution (finance; 60); business services (73); engineering, accounting, research, management, and related services (87); and industrial and commercial machinery and computer equipment (35). In the bottom three rows, for year 2000, the growth rate is computed as the annualized 1997–2000 growth rate. For year 2012, the growth rate is computed as the annualized 2009–12 growth rate. To compute these growth rates, we restrict to companies with initial year (1997 or 2000) values of at least 1,000 employees and $1MM revenue and market values.

Size and Market Value. Next we compare the three groups of companies on the basis of H-1B usage. As reported in table 4.6 (columns 4–6), in year 2012, the average employment for Compustat companies that did not receive any (initial or continuing employment) H-1Bs in year 2012 was 8,000 workers. In comparison, companies that had 1 to 10 or 11 or more approved petitions had average employment of 13,000 and 35,000, respectively. Thus firms employing H-1B workers are much larger than nonusers. The same size gradient is also present in terms of revenue and market value. In year 2012, the average revenue among non-H-1B users in Compustat was $3.1 billion compared to $4.3 billion and $17.3 billion among moderate and heavy users of the program. These relationships are also confirmed when we focus on year 2000 (columns 1–3).

Firm Growth. The bottom part of the table examines firm-level growth rates by H-1B usage, which suggests there exists a positive relationship as well between the number of approved H-1B petitions and firm growth (over the previous three years). More specifically, the 2009–12 annualized growth rate in terms of employment was 6.0 percent among firms that did not receive any H-1B workers in year 2012 (measured by approved petitions for either initial or continuing employment). In comparison, moderate and heavy users of the program exhibited average employment growth rates of 6.4 percent and 8.8 percent, respectively. Revenue growth in this period was practically the same for the three groups of firms at around 20 percent per year. In terms of growth in market value, once again we see substantially

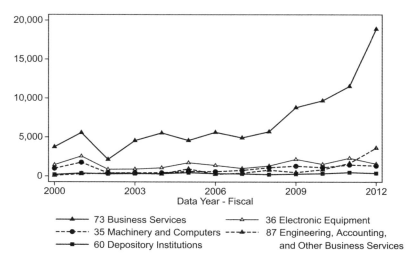

Fig. 4.5 Approved initial-employment H-1B petitions by industry

Note: Approved initial-employment H-1B petitions by two-digit SIC industry code. We plot only the data for the top five receiving industries in 2012.

higher growth rates among users of the H-1B program (40–60 percent) relative to nonusers (30 percent). The 1997–2000 growth rates also confirm these patterns, with clearer evidence of a monotonic relationship between H-1B usage and firm growth.

Clearly, these are purely descriptive facts. To a large extent, the differences in level and growth as a function of H-1B usage reflect differences in terms of industry composition. The last row in table 4.6 reports the mode two-digit Standard Industrial Classification (SIC) code by H-1B usage. The mode industries in the sample that did not receive approved petitions in 2012 were depository institutions (finance; 60) and business services (73). Among H-1B users, the mode industries were business services (73) and electronic and other electrical equipment and components, except computer equipment (36).

4.4.2.2   Industry Trends

Counts of Approved Petitions. In order to better understand industry trends in H-1B usage, we collapse our H-1B-Compustat data set by two-digit SIC industries. Figure 4.5 plots the counts of approved initial-employment H-1B petitions for the top five receiving industries. The top receiving industry is business services (73), followed by electronic equipment (36), machinery and computers (35), engineering, accounting and other business services (87), and depository institutions (60). Business services is by far the industry receiving the largest number of workers. Between years 2000 and 2008, Compustat companies in this industry received about 5,000 initial-employment H-1Bs annually. However, there has been an explosion in this figure since

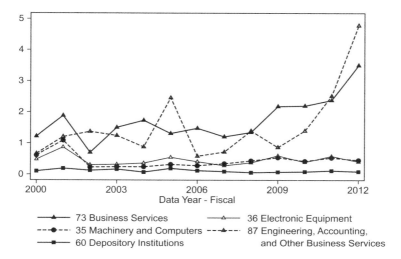

Fig. 4.6   H-1B Intensity at the industry level: approved initial-employment H-1B petitions per 1,000 employees by industry

Note: Approved initial-employment H-1B petitions by two-digit SIC industry code per 1,000 employees. We plot only the data for the top five receiving industries in 2012.

2009. In 2012, these companies hired close to 20,000 initial-employment H-1B workers.

Intensity of Use of H-1B Visas. Naturally, this increase may simply reflect a rise in the size of the business services industry, keeping the intensity of H-1B use constant. To examine this hypothesis, we compute the industry-level intensity, defined as approved initial-employment issuances per 1,000 employees, and plot it in figure 4.6. The figure suggests that the bulk of the increase in H-1B usage in the business services industry is due to an increase in intensity. The intensity of initial-employment H-1Bs in the business services industry has remained practically unchanged throughout the 2000–2008 period (at around 1.5 initial-employment issuances per 1,000 employees). However, it grew by 133 percent between 2008 and 2012. Interestingly, the engineering, accounting, and other business services (87) industry exhibits very similar behavior. In fact, in 2012, the H-1B intensity in this industry is 5 initial-employment H-1Bs per 1,000 employees, compared to a 3.5 intensity for business services (73).

4.5   Conclusions

As is often the case in merging large data sets based on names of firms with automated or semiautomated matching techniques, the quality of the matches improves at each iteration, and a perfect match is often infeasible. This is also the case here. While we believe that the general facts presented here will persist, we also note that our data set will continue to evolve as we continue improving the quality of our matching algorithm. False positives (matched firms that should not have been matched) and false negatives (unmatched firms that should have been matched) will continue to occur. Naturally, a nearly perfect match could be attained if USCIS agreed to release the employer identification number (EIN) associated with each petitioning firm, which so far has not been the case.

Possibly, the single most important fact regarding the aggregate economic effects of the current H-1B program is the large increase in the concentration of H-1Bs in the hands of a small number of global technology consulting companies. With little doubt, the large expansion of these firms derives from a pronounced trend toward outsourcing of information technology services. This trend may be fundamentally driven by technological developments in information and communication systems that have triggered this change in the boundaries of the firm. However, it is also possible that the increasing difficulty in obtaining and managing H-1Bs due to the increasing excess demand over the last few years has accelerated the tendency to outsource these tasks. At any rate, it is important to keep in mind that from its inception, the H-1B visa program has been intended as a vehicle for *trade in services*.[14]

Some recent papers (Peri et al. 2015) have argued that the H-1B program may have increased the productivity and wages of highly skilled *native* workers due to spillovers and increasing returns to innovation. However, the recent trend toward an increasing concentration of H-1B workers in the hands of companies engaged in outsourcing of information-technology services may reduce the scope for these spillovers even though it is likely to increase the profitability (and perhaps the productivity) of the firms contracting out IT services. Characterizing precisely the firm-level dynamics of H-1B users, which will be made possible by this data set and further iterations of it, is crucial to predict the potential impact of the H-1B visa program into the future.

References

Amuedo-Dorantes, Catalina, and Delia Furtado. 2016. "Settling for Academia? H-1B Visas and the Career Choices of International Students in the United States." IZA Discussion Papers 10166, August. Institute for the Study of Labor (IZA).

14. As part of the Uruguay Round (1986–1994) multilateral trade agreements, the US agreed to set up the H-1B visa program and committed to offering at least 65,000 visas. Similarly, the US also set aside specific numbers of visas during the negotiation of the North American Free Trade Agreement (NAFTA) and the US Free Trade Agreements with Chile (2,400 visas) and Singapore (1,600 visas). These agreements were also incorporated into the H-1B visa program. We thank Jennifer Hunt for pointing out the connection between the H-1B visa program and multilateral trade agreements.

Bessen, James, and Robert M. Hunt. 2007. "An Empirical Look at Software Patents." *Journal of Economics and Management Strategy* 16 (1): 157–89.

Blasnik, Michael. 2010. "RECLINK: Stata Module to Probabilistically Match Records." Working Paper.

Clemens, Michael A. 2013. "Why Do Programmers Earn More in Houston Than Hyderabad? Evidence from Randomized Processing of US Visas." *American Economic Review* 103 (3): 198–202.

Depew, Briggs, Peter Norlander, and Todd A. Sorensen. 2013. "Flight of the H-1B: Inter-firm Mobility and Return Migration Patterns for Skilled Guest Workers." IZA Discussion Papers 7456, June. Institute for the Study of Labor (IZA).

Doran, Kirk, Alexander Gelber, and Adam Isen. 2014. "The Effects of High-Skilled Immigration Policy on Firms: Evidence from H-1B Visa Lotteries." NBER Working Paper no. 20668. Cambridge, MA: National Bureau of Economic Research.

Ghosh, Anirban, Anna Maria Mayda, and Francesc Ortega. 2014. "The Impact of Skilled Foreign Workers on Firms: An Investigation of Publicly Traded U.S. Firms." IZA Discussion Papers 8684, November. Institute for the Study of Labor (IZA).

Hall, Bronwyn H., Adam B. Jaffe, and Manuel Trajtenberg. 2001. "The NBER Patent Citation Data File: Lessons, Insights and Methodological Tools." NBER Working Paper no. 8498. Cambridge, MA: National Bureau of Economic Research

Hunt, Jennifer, and Marjolaine Gauthier-Loiselle. 2010. "How Much Does Immigration Boost Innovation?" *American Economic Journal: Macroeconomics* 2 (2): 31–56.

Kato, Takao, and Chad Sparber. 2013. "Quotas and Quality: The Effect of H-1B Visa Restrictions on the Pool of Prospective Undergraduate Students from Abroad." *Review of Economics and Statistics* 95 (1): 109–26.

Kerr, Sari Pekkala, William R. Kerr, and William F. Lincoln. 2015. "Firms and the Economics of Skilled Immigration." In *Innovation Policy and the Economy*, vol. 15, edited by William R. Kerr, Josh Lerner, and Scott Stern, 115–52. Chicago: University of Chicago Press.

Kerr, William R., and William F. Lincoln. 2010. "The Supply Side of Innovation: H-1B Visa Reforms and U.S. Ethnic Invention." *Journal of Labor Economics* 28 (3): 473–508.

Mayda, Anna Maria, Francesc Ortega, Giovanni Peri, Kevin Shih, and Chad Sparber. 2018. "The Effect of the H-1B Quota on the Employment and Selection of Foreign-Born Labor." *European Economic Review* 108:105–12.

Peri, Giovanni, Kevin Shih, and Chad Sparber. 2015. "STEM Workers, H-1B Visas, and Productivity in US Cities." *Journal of Labor Economics* 33 (S1): 225–55.

Reif, Julian. 2010. "STRGROUP: Stata Module to Match Strings Based on Their Levenshtein Edit Distance." Statistical Software Components S457151, Boston College Department of Economics, Revised August 14, 2010.

Shih, Kevin. 2016. "Labor Market Openness, H-1B Visa Policy, and the Scale of International Student Enrollment in the United States." *Economic Inquiry* 54 (1): 121–38.

Wasi, N., and A. Flaaen. 2015. "Record Linkage Using Stata: Preprocessing, Linking, and Reviewing Utilities." *Stata Journal* 15 (3): 672–97.

Immigration and Invention
Does Language Matter?

Kirk Doran and Chungeun Yoon

5.1 Introduction

Economists have long noted several ways that immigration could affect innovation. Highly skilled immigrants may innovate directly, while low-skilled immigrants could affect the scale of production, thereby encouraging labor-complementary inventions and discouraging strongly labor-saving inventions (Acemoglu 2010). But the literature on immigration and innovation has failed to address the potential importance of one of the most obvious differences between immigrants and natives: language. On the one hand, immigrants may have a larger impact on innovation when there is a language similarity between the immigrants and natives. Strongly labor-complementary inventions may be incentivized more by a large homogeneous workforce that can easily work together rather than by heterogeneous labor inputs that have trouble communicating with each other. On the other hand, immigration may have a larger impact on innovation when there is a language dissimilarity between the immigrants and natives. After all, a large literature explores the possibility that a diverse ethnolinguistic mix "brings about variety in abilities, experiences, and cultures that may be productive and may lead to innovation and creativity" (Alesina and La Ferrara 2005).

Both of the above effects of language on innovation are plausible, so it

Kirk Doran is the Henkels Family Collegiate Chair and associate professor of economics at the University of Notre Dame.

Chungeun Yoon is a PhD student in the Department of Economics at the University of Notre Dame.

We thank Ina Ganguli, Megan MacGarvie, and especially Shu Kahn for very helpful comments on our preliminary draft. All errors are our own. For acknowledgments, sources of research support, and disclosure of the authors' material financial relationships, if any, please see https://www.nber.org/chapters/c14102.ack.

is helpful to consider them in light of theoretical models of what innovation actually is. According to many theories, innovation involves making new combinations from existing ideas and experiences (Weitzman 1998). An innovative society will thus *necessarily* involve people with diverse ideas communicating with each other to facilitate new combinations (innovations). Thus as the number of individuals increases, innovation may increase if (a) individuals communicate more and more and (b) they have a larger and larger number of unique things to communicate about.

Linguistic diversity of immigrants relative to the preexisting population can affect both of these channels but in opposite directions. Linguistic homogeneity increases the likelihood of (a) and decreases the likelihood of (b). Linguistic diversity decreases the likelihood of (a) and increases the likelihood of (b). It is therefore plausible that the optimal amount of immigrant linguistic diversity for building an innovative society will be somewhere in between complete linguistic homogeneity and complete linguistic diversity. The results in this chapter are consistent with this hypothesis.[1]

We bring empirical evidence to bear on this question through analyzing a setting in which the language of immigrants varies independently of the language mix of the people already living in the locations that the immigrants are immigrating to. This is difficult because shift-share style immigration instruments build on exactly that variation in immigration that is correlated with ethnolinguistic variation in the preexisting population across locations. In this chapter, we make use of immediate-onset 1920s US immigration quotas that suddenly ended ongoing immigrant flows to some cities but not others. Crucially, the quotas caused cities with a circa-1920 immigrant inflow from quota-affected countries to suddenly stop receiving as many immigrants; not every such city had a native-born population descended from long-past immigrant inflows that had kept speaking their family's language. As a result, among the quota-affected cities, some lost immigrants who spoke a common language among the preexisting population (because previous generations of immigrants had preserved their language across generations), while others lost immigrants who spoke an uncommon language among the population. These "off-diagonal" terms allow us to estimate the effects of immigrants on innovation in a city both when the immigrants speak a common language in the city and when they do not.

The results are striking. We find that native-born inventors whose cities lost immigrants who spoke uncommon languages apply for no fewer, and possibly more, patents after the quotas. Native-born inventors whose cities lost immigrants who spoke very common languages applied for somewhat fewer patents after the quotas. But native-born inventors whose cities lost

---

1. For a thorough overview of the theoretical tradeoffs between immigrant diversity and immigrant homogeneity in general, as well as important empirical results in this area, see Kemeny (2017).

immigrants with moderate linguistic diversity applied for many fewer patents after the quotas.

These results are thus consistent with a U-shaped curve for the effect of linguistic diversity on the innovativeness of a society. Too much linguistic diversity creates a "Tower of Babel" effect (Ballatore, Fort, and Ichino 2018) in which people have unique things to talk about but no common language to say them in. Too little linguistic diversity creates a homogeneous population (Alesina and La Ferrara 2005) in which people have a common language but nothing unique to share. The optimal amount of linguistic diversity for a creative society appears to be somewhere in between.

It is important to note that, as Doran and Yoon (2019) explain, the effect of these low-skilled immigrants on native inventors is to act through a change in the scale of production that incentivizes strongly labor-complementary inventions (Acemoglu 2010). The role of communication, therefore, is happening in the context of a low-skilled workforce, not in the context of highly skilled innovators themselves. The effects of linguistic diversity among highly skilled immigrants may therefore differ from those reported here. We also note that here, as with many recent papers, we rely on policy variation for our identification. We refer the reader to Doran and Yoon (2019) for historical evidence supporting the quota identification strategy. In particular, we there argue that "far from local efforts to reduce all immigration to some locations but not others, these laws were national efforts to reduce all immigration from some sources but not others" (Doran and Yoon 2019).

The chapter is organized as follows. In section 5.2, we review the literature on the 1920s quotas and explain where our results fit in the context of that literature. In section 5.3, we introduce the data set, referring especially to Doran and Yoon (2019). In section 5.4, we introduce our empirical strategy and estimating equations. In section 5.5, we describe our results. In section 5.6, we conclude.

5.2   Existing Economics Literature on the Quotas

Before 1921, United States law placed virtually no limitations on immigration from Europe to the United States. Starting in the 1890s, Protestant Americans of Northern and Western European descent became concerned about the increased flows of non-Protestant immigrants from Southern and Eastern Europe. These concerns eventually reached an expression in law with the 1921 and 1924 immigration quotas. The Emergency Quota Act of 1921 established annual quotas for Southern and Eastern European immigration that were considerably lower than the then-current flows while establishing quotas for Northern and Western European immigration that were barely binding. The Immigration Act of 1924 tightened the quotas on Southern and Eastern European immigration even further.

In the last several years, a total of seven papers have emerged studying the economic impacts of the 1920s US immigration quotas. After the initial work of Ager and Hansen (2018), these papers have been written almost simultaneously by separate teams of authors, with subtle differences in the implementation of the identification strategies and without planned consistency. Nevertheless, here we argue that in fact these seven papers tell a largely consistent history in which the reported economic impacts of the quotas correspond with those predicted by models such as those presented by Borjas (1987), Acemoglu (2010), and Tabellini (2018). In particular, it appears that these quotas (1) reduced immigration from some sources but not others, (2) reduced immigration to some locations but not others, (3) induced differential wage changes among natives in affected locations, (4) induced a native migration response to affected locations that was less than one for one with the immigration reductions, (5) decreased the scale and mechanization of production in affected locations, and (6) decreased natives' inventions in affected locations, especially those inventions relevant for industries that lost a large number of immigrant workers. This set of results is not only consistent with itself but also consistent with the new results reported here.

In this section, we review the results of this existing literature, summarizing the results and comparing them to models such as those in Borjas (1987) and Acemoglu (2010) and the model in appendix B by Tabellini (2018).

One of the most important papers in this literature is "Immigration in American Economic History" (Abramitzky and Boustan 2017). In this paper, Abramitzky and Boustan (2017) review the literature on historical and contemporary immigration. They focus on three major questions in the economics of immigration. First, they question whether immigrants are positively or negatively selected from their home countries over time. Second, they explore how immigrants assimilate into the US. Third, they examine the effects of immigration on the economy, especially native employment and wages. In particular, they cover the two main eras of mass immigration—the age of mass migration from Europe (1850–1920), an era of unrestricted migration, and a recent period of constrained mass migration from Asia and Latin America (1965–present).

First, they find that migrant selection was mixed in the past (with some migrants being positively selected and others being negatively selected from their home countries), while migrants are positively selected in the present. Specifically, migrant selection during the age of mass migration is consistent with a Roy model (Roy 1951) as developed by Borjas (1987). The Roy model would predict positive selection from Northern and Western Europe and negative selection from southern and eastern Europe, with differences in productive skills of migrants and income equality across sending countries. Historical evidence on income distribution supports their argument. Income distribution in Western European countries was similar to that of the US at that time, while income distribution in the European periphery was less equal than that of the US. Consistent with the model, historical evidence suggests that low-skilled workers from southern and eastern Europe immigrated to the US and that they were thus negatively selected. The positive selection of immigrants today can be explained by both the increase in income inequality in the US (as the model would predict) and the increasing selectivity of US immigration policy, which would favor high-skilled immigration.

Second, they find that assimilation of immigrants into the US economy is not consistent with the stereotypical "American Dream," whereby poor immigrants work hard and eventually become rich. During periods of mass migration, immigrants did not catch up with US natives in the past, and they do not do so today, because immigrants start behind natives, and their occupational upgrading and earnings grow at a similar pace to that of US natives over time. Although immigrants experience some earnings convergence, the immigrants themselves do not catch up with US natives in the labor market during their own lifetimes. However, these gaps diminish across generations because many children of immigrants are educated and grow up in the US.

Third, the authors argue that immigrants during the age of mass migration were more substitutable with natives in agriculture and manufacturing and that therefore there was some effect of immigration on native wages. They also find that immigration in the past contributed to the spread of large factories used for mass production. In addition, unskilled immigrants and assembly-line machinery were complementary at that time.[2]

The first paper to make use of the quotas as part of an identification strategy to determine the economic effects of low-skilled immigration appears to be "Closing Heaven's Door: Evidence from the 1920s U.S. Immigration Quota Acts" (Ager and Hansen 2018). Their first main finding is that the areas with a large decline in incoming immigrants due to the quotas experienced a decrease in the foreign-born share and lower population growth. Specifically, one additional missing immigrant per 100 inhabitants per year led to a decline in the foreign-born share by 1.6 percentage points and a decrease in the 10-year population growth rate by 6.7 percentage points at the county level. This suggests that any compensatory migration from non-quota-restricted immigrants or from natives was not enough to counteract the effects of the quotas on quota-affected immigration. Reinforcing the effects of this main finding is an associated decline in marriage rates in quota-affected regions. Second, they show that the quotas have a significant effect on the earnings of native workers. Natives in counties exposed to the quotas were more likely to change to lower-wage occupations, though the effect varies by gender and race. In particular, white workers experienced earning losses, while black workers benefited from the quotas. Earnings of white female workers were not affected, while black female workers gained significantly. These findings suggest that immigrant workers during the 1920s had a higher elasticity of substitution to black native workers. Third,

---

2. See also related papers, such as Ward (2017) and Greenwood and Ward (2015).

they find that labor productivity in manufacturing at the city level declined under the quotas.

A third important paper in this literature is Tabellini's (2018). This paper makes two main additional contributions above and beyond the points already made in the literature described above. First, Tabellini (2018) introduces a notion of linguistic distance adapted from Chiswick and Miller (2005). The results show that the impact of immigration is tied closely to the linguistic distance of the source country language compared to English. The second main contribution is to introduce a model (in online appendix B of Tabellini 2018) that makes the following predictions: (1) (unskilled) immigration favors capital accumulation in the unskilled sector, (2) "immigration has a positive and unambiguous effect on high-skilled wages," and (3) immigration has an ambiguous effect on low-skilled wages. This theoretical framework is consistent with Tabellini (2018) by construction, but it is clearly consistent with the results of Ager and Hansen (2018) as well.

A fourth study in this literature is by Doran and Yoon (2019). This study addresses the question of how mass migration affects innovation. In particular, it questions whether low-skilled immigrants could influence innovations through labor-complementary inventions or labor-saving inventions. The results show that incumbent inventors in cities exposed to fewer low-skilled immigration inflows due to the 1920s quotas applied for fewer patents. To be specific, inventors living in quota-exposed cities that experienced a 10 percent reduction in new immigrants reduced their patent applications by 0.5 percent per year. Further, the effect of quotas on patents is driven by fewer patent applications relevant to the quota-exposed industries that lost immigrant workers.

The papers above tell a consistent history of the quotas—a history that lays the groundwork for this chapter. The quotas reduced low-skilled immigration, this decrease affected the large scale manufacturing that had flourished in areas with many low-skilled immigrants, and inventors who supplied patented inventions relevant for the affected industries produced fewer such inventions after the quotas.

5.3   Data

Our analysis relies on a panel of individual inventors, a measure of how locations are exposed to quotas, and information on the primary languages spoken by new immigrants and the preexisting population of US cities circa 1920 (just before the quotas were enacted).

To obtain the inventor sample, we follow the method used in Doran and Yoon (2019). In particular, we use the European Patent Office's PATSTAT database, which provides characteristics such as the inventor's full name, year of patent application, and the number of citations of each patent application granted by the US Patent Office from 1899 to the present. We exploit a fuzzy matching procedure that merges patents at the individual-name level into the complete-count 1920 US Census with names. In the 1920 Census, 43 percent of the US population is made up of people with a unique combination of first name, middle name, and last name. If a person from this unique-name subsample is matched to a patent application made between the years 1919 and 1929, then, barring transcription errors, that person must be the author of the patent application unless someone with the exact same name immigrated after 1919 and patented soon after arrival. Furthermore, to increase the quality of the matches, we also restrict the matches to those with an implied age at the time of application of between 18 and 80 years old.

On this matched individual inventor sample, the variables from the complete-count 1920 US Census give us each individual's birth year, birthplace, citizenship, nationality, and geographic location at the city/county level, as well as other characteristics.

Our second data set measures how locations were differentially exposed to the quotas over time as well as other characteristics of these locations. In Doran and Yoon (2019), we digitize immigration inflows by source country and year, as well as the exact size of the quotas by country and year, from administrative data obtained from Willcox (1929) and the US Department of Commerce (1924, 1929, and 1931). Using data from the 1910 and 1920 US Censuses, we collect the following aggregated characteristics of each city: total population, foreign-born population, Southern and Eastern European immigrant population, Northern and Western European immigrant population, and immigrant populations by nationality and year of immigration to the US.

In the next section, we explain how unique features of the implementation of the quotas allow us to identify how the impact of low-skilled immigration on American innovation varies by how closely the immigrant languages mirror that of the preexisting population.

5.4   Empirical Strategy

Typically, a shift-share instrument for immigration relies on variation in the national origin of the preexisting population across locations and assumes that the new immigrants will have a tendency to choose locations where people of their ethnicity or nationality already live. In most cases, this would also imply linguistic sorting, in which immigrants who speak a given language (say, for example, Italian) end up sorting to locations full of people who already speak that language. Given such linguistic sorting, it would be difficult to use such an instrument to determine the differential impact of immigrants who speak a relatively common language among the preexisting population from that of immigrants who speak a relatively rare language among the preexisting population in a given city. We would need a natural experiment in which immigrants who speak Italian, for example, are often attracted to locations with relatively few Italian speakers and immigrants who do not speak Italian are often attracted to locations with relatively many Italian speakers. These "off-diagonal" sortings would enable us to determine whether immigrants have a differential impact when they are located in areas with relatively many or relatively few people speaking their language.

In this chapter, we exploit 1920s US immigration quotas that attracted speakers of a given language to locations with both relatively many and relatively few speakers of that language. In particular, the quotas suddenly cut off immigration to many cities that were "exposed" to the quotas because they had experienced recent flows of immigrants from quota-affected countries. But these cities were not all alike: some quota-affected cities were populated by the descendants of immigrants from previous generations whose families had preserved their native tongue (to the point of that language being their primary spoken method of communication). But other quota-affected cities were populated by the descendants of immigrants who preserved an ethnic kinship with the newcomers but had not preserved their language. While both types of cities attracted new immigrants of a similar background to the preexisting foreign-born population before the quotas were enacted and both types of cities subsequently lost these new flows of immigrants after the quotas were enacted, only the first type of city lost immigrants who spoke a language *commonly* spoken in their destination city. The second type of city lost immigrants who spoke a language *uncommonly* spoken in their destination city.

To identify the impact of low-skilled immigration on innovation in any given subsample, we follow the method in Doran and Yoon (2019), which built on Ager and Hansen (2018). To identify how these effects of low-skilled immigration on innovation vary depending on the linguistic distance between the new immigrants and the preexisting population in each city, we split the sample into four subsamples: (1) one in which the languages of the new immigrants had been preserved and were spoken widely among the preexisting population, (2) another in which the languages of the new immigrants were uncommon, (3) another in which the languages were moderately common, and (4) another in which the languages were moderately uncommon. We then replicate the main analysis in Doran and Yoon (2019) once for each subsample.

Our main estimation equations are

(1) $Y_{ict} = \alpha + \beta(Quota_c \times Post_t) + \theta X_{it} + \tau_t + \gamma_i + \varepsilon_{ict}$,

where Y_{ict} is the number of patents by incumbent inventor i in city c and year t. We include the quartic of age of person i in year t, individual fixed effects, and year fixed effects. The quota-exposure variable is defined as follows:

(2) $Quota_c = \dfrac{100}{P_{c,1920}} \sum_{j=1}^{J} \left(\widehat{Immig}_{j,22-30} - Quota_{j,22-30} \right) \dfrac{FB_{jc,1920}}{FB_{j,1920}}$,

where $P_{c,1920}$ is the 1920 population in city c, $\widehat{Immig}_{j,22-30}$ is the estimated average immigration inflows that would have occurred per year from country j to the United States during the postquota period from 1922 to 1930 if the quotas had not been enacted,[3] $Quota_{j,22-30}$ is the average quota for country j during the period from 1922 to 1930, $FB_{jc,1920}$ is the foreign-born population of country j in city c in 1920, and $FB_{j,1920}$ is the total foreign-born population of country j in the 1920 Census.

When a city's predicted immigration from 1922 to 1930 (predicted from the pre–World War I annual immigration flows from 1900 to 1914) is much higher than quotas for the years 1922 through 1930, then the quota exposure variable is high. Otherwise, it is low. This quota begins to affect quota-exposed cities sometime after the quota acts of 1921 and 1924 are implemented. We compare different options for the post-t variable, including 1922 and 1924. In this regression, β represents a difference-in-differences estimate of the effect of the quotas.

We can observe which languages the preexisting population spoke in each location by observing the individual responses in the 1920 US Census to the question in column 20: "person's mother tongue." Table 5.1 shows that in the US during 1920, there were considerable differences between the number of people born in a given country and the number of people whose mother tongue was the language of that country. Many US-born individuals continued to speak the language of their immigrant parents even though they were born in the United States. This tendency for foreign-language persistence across generations varied from city to city, and this variation allows us to divide locations into those in which the languages of the new immigrants were common and those in which the languages of the new immigrants were not.

Each city c has a vector of languages in which each element, $PreLang_{lc}$, is the share of the preexisting population in city c whose mother tongue is l:

$$(3) \qquad PreLang_{lc} = \frac{Lang_{lc,1920}}{TotalPopulation_{c,1920}}.$$

Each city c also has a vector of languages in which each element, $NewLang_{lc}$, is the share of the missing immigrants between 1922 and 1930 in city c whose mother tongue is l:

$$(4) \qquad NewLang_{lc} = \frac{ImmigLang_{lc}}{TotalMissingImmig_{c}}$$

To calculate how close the languages of the new immigrants were to the languages spoken by the preexisting population, we need to determine how "close" the vector $PreLang$ is to the vector $NewLang$. There is no mathematically unique way to determine how "close" two vectors are to each other. We

---

3. The estimates are predicted from the pre–World War I annual immigration flows from 1900 to 1914 based on the regression model $Immig_{jt} = \beta_1 lnt + \beta_2 (lnt)^2 + \varepsilon_{jt}$ (Ager and Hansen 2018; Doran and Yoon 2019).

Table 5.1   **Birthplace and mother tongue in the 1920 US Census**

Mother tongue	Birthplace							
	US (1)	UK (2)	Ireland (3)	Germany (4)	Italy (5)	Russia (6)	Poland (7)	Others (8)
English	53.12	83.38	73.37	0.93	0.33	0.52	0.25	15.99
German	17.34	0.52	0.34	95.96	0.17	8.62	7.53	8.54
Italian	4.35	0.13	0.02	0.10	99.03	0.12	0.13	0.54
Celtic	3.70	14.20	25.59	0.03	0.05	0.10	0.10	0.59
Polish	2.10	0.09	0.05	1.43	0.01	5.10	78.54	1.58
Spanish	2.51	0.04	0.02	0.05	0.05	0.05	0.02	9.67
French	2.63	0.08	0.08	0.10	0.08	0.06	0.03	7.85
Swedish	2.40	0.15	0.10	0.06	0.01	0.09	0.02	10.69
Jewish	1.52	0.83	0.07	0.23	0.04	49.98	8.56	2.68
Norwegian	1.37	0.01	0.01	0.04	0.00	0.01	0.00	5.99
Czech	1.03	0.01	0.00	0.08	0.00	0.08	0.07	3.63
Russian	0.79	0.11	0.00	0.04	0.00	23.91	1.15	0.14
Dutch	0.84	0.10	0.03	0.13	0.01	0.05	0.03	2.90
Danish	0.79	0.02	0.05	0.30	0.01	0.02	0.01	2.98
Hungarian	0.69	0.01	0.01	0.09	0.01	0.06	0.07	4.57
Others	4.80	0.32	0.26	0.43	0.20	11.23	3.49	21.64
Total	91,683,696	1,153,841	1,049,330	1,631,480	1,608,841	1,450,734	1,133,710	6,033,502

Note: This table shows the relationship between birthplace and mother tongue in the 1920 US Census. Each number indicates the percentage of people reporting a given mother tongue out of those born in a given birthplace. The UK numbers in column 2 exclude people born in Ireland. The last row shows the total number of individuals born in a given birthplace.

make use of two methods used in Borjas and Doran (2012): the correlation coefficient and the index of similarity.

The correlation coefficient is well known. The index of similarity of Borjas and Doran (2012) is based on the "Index of Dissimilarity" used by Cutler and Glaeser (1997) and introduced by Duncan and Duncan (1955). We calculate the index of similarity with the following formula:

(5) $$LangIndex_c = 1 - \frac{1}{2}\sum_{l=1}^{L} |PreLang_{lc} - NewLang_{lc}|$$

Clearly, the Index of Similarity will be one when the languages of the missing immigrants are distributed identically to the languages of the preexisting population. If the preexisting languages and the languages of the missing immigrants never match in the same city, then the index will be zero.[4] For each of these measures of linguistic "closeness" between the missing immigrants and the preexisting population, we divide the cities into four equal groups by quartiles. We report simple statistics in table 5.2. It is clear

4. If two vectors never match, then

$$LangIndex_c = 1 - \frac{1}{2}\sum_{l=1}^{L} |PreLang_{lc} - NewLang_{lc}|$$

$$= 1 - \frac{1}{2}\sum_{l=1}^{L} |PreLang_{lc}| - \frac{1}{2}\sum_{l=1}^{L} |NewLang_{lc}| = 0.$$

Table 5.2   **Summary statistics**

Variables	Quota exposed cities	Non-quota-exposed cities
Number of cities	1,668	1,669
Quota exposure	0.5805	0.0237
	(0.6110)	(0.0217)
Index of similarity	0.3021	0.2617
	(0.1356)	(0.2061)
Correlation coefficient	0.2015	0.2446
	(0.2259)	(0.3050)
Population in 1920 Census	46,128	19,902
	(130,596)	(12,276)
Southern and Eastern foreign-born in 1920	3,826	34
	(24,679)	(54)
New immigrants per year and city as a fraction of 1920	0.0039	0.0007
population, 1900–1921	(0.0052)	(0.0027)
Patents per year and inventor, 1900–1921	0.1200	0.1295
	(0.1270)	(0.1794)
Cities with linguistically close missing immigrants		
Quota exposure	0.9248	0.0204
	(0.8258)	(0.0212)
New immigrants	0.0054	0.0006
	(0.0060)	(0.0031)
Patents	0.1230	0.1273
	(0.1103)	(0.1819)
Cities with linguistically moderately close missing immigrants		
Quota exposure	0.5351	0.0304
	(0.4926)	(0.0240)
New immigrants	0.0039	0.0010
	(0.0051)	(0.0032)
Patents	0.1218	0.1183
	(0.1188)	(0.1359)
Cities with linguistically moderately far missing immigrants		
Quota exposure	0.3486	0.0268
	(0.3132)	(0.0224)
New immigrants	0.0031	0.0007
	(0.0044)	(0.0026)
Patents	0.1212	0.1207
	(0.1453)	(0.1548)
Cities with linguistically far missing immigrants		
Quota exposure	0.4764	0.0203
	(0.5201)	(0.0188)
New immigrants	0.0029	0.0004
	(0.0046)	(0.0022)
Patents	0.1073	0.1426
	(0.1359)	(0.2096)

Note: This table presents means and standard deviations (in parenthesis) of variables used in our analysis, in subsamples defined by quota exposure of cities (above and below the median) and by linguistic closeness (as measured through the correlation coefficient).

that there are similar inflows of new immigrants and similar rates of patent applications by incumbent native inventors across all quota-exposed cities regardless of the degree of linguistic closeness of the missing immigrants to that city.

In the next section, we determine whether the quota-induced change in immigration had differential impacts on innovation depending on whether the immigrants spoke a relatively common local language or not.

5.5   Results

We begin our analysis by showing that the quotas decreased immigration inflows in quota-exposed locations regardless of linguistic distance. In tables 5.3 and 5.4, we report the results when the outcome variable is newly arrived immigrants rescaled by the 1920 city population in a given location in a given year, after we split the sample into the four subsamples using the correlation coefficient and the index of similarity, respectively. It is apparent that regardless of which of the four subsamples partitioned by linguistic distance we consider, which of the two proxies (the correlation coefficient and the index of similarity) for linguistic distance we use to split the sample, which years we include in the sample, and which year we use as the posttreatment year, the quota-exposed cities experienced substantial reductions to their immigrant inflows. Next we determine how the quotas, which decreased immigration inflows to all four groups of cities, differentially affected innovation (as measured by patents) depending on the linguistic closeness of the missing immigrants to the preexisting population.

The quota-exposure variable represents the average annual number of immigrants per 100 inhabitants in a city who were "missing" due to the quotas (Ager and Hansen 2018; Doran and Yoon 2019). Doran and Yoon (2019) find that a one-unit increase in quota exposure decreases immigration inflows by approximately 100 percent and decreases patent applications by incumbent native-born inventors by about 5 percent. Thus for every 10 percent decrease in immigration inflows, patent applications per year decrease by 0.5 percent.

Here we explore how these results vary with respect to the linguistic closeness of the missing immigrants to the preexisting population. In table 5.5, we report the results of estimating equation (1) on the four subsamples of cities partitioned by linguistic closeness measured through the correlation coefficient. It is clear that the effect of the quotas on native patenting is most significant when the missing immigrants and the preexisting population are moderately close linguistically. Moderately far linguistic-distance cities experience the second-largest and second-most-significant effect on patenting. The linguistically close and linguistically far cities experience smaller and less significant effects.

In table 5.6, we report the results of the same estimation when we parti-

Table 5.3   **How the effect of the quotas on immigrant inflows varies with linguistic closeness, as measured by the correlation coefficient**

	Year of immigration			
	1900–1929		1919–29	
	Posttreatment year			
	1922 (1)	1924 (2)	1922 (3)	1924 (4)
A. Linguistically close missing immigrants				
Quota exposure × posttreatment	−0.0028***	−0.0029***	−0.0008***	−0.0010***
	(0.0002)	(0.0002)	(0.0001)	(0.0001)
Dependent variable mean	0.0025	0.0024	0.0018	0.0016
Number of observations	23,190	23,190	8,503	8,503
Number of cities	773	773	773	773
R²	0.5447	0.5409	0.6364	0.6422
B. Linguistically moderately close missing immigrants				
Quota exposure × posttreatment	−0.0024***	−0.0025***	−0.0006***	−0.0009***
	(0.0002)	(0.0002)	(0.0001)	(0.0001)
Dependent variable mean	0.0028	0.0027	0.0021	0.0020
Number of observations	23,850	23,850	8,745	8,745
Number of cities	795	795	795	795
R²	0.5576	0.5558	0.6972	0.7010
C. Linguistically moderately far missing immigrants				
Quota exposure × posttreatment	−0.0030***	−0.0032***	−0.0008***	−0.0011***
	(0.0004)	(0.0004)	(0.0002)	(0.0001)
Dependent variable mean	0.0024	0.0023	0.0016	0.0016
Number of observations	22,890	22,890	8,393	8,393
Number of cities	763	763	763	763
R²	0.5633	0.5604	0.6757	0.6821
D. Linguistically far missing immigrants				
Quota exposure × posttreatment	−0.0034***	−0.0035***	−0.0005***	−0.0009***
	(0.0003)	(0.0002)	(0.0002)	(0.0002)
Dependent variable mean	0.0016	0.0015	0.0009	0.0008
Number of observations	22,170	22,170	8,129	8,129
Number of cities	739	739	739	739
R²	0.5279	0.5227	0.6340	0.6439

Note: The dependent variable is new immigrants as a fraction of 1920 population. The outcome variable of new immigrants is constructed by combining information from the 1910, 1920, and 1930 US Census. Specifically, new immigrants per year between the years 1900 and 1909 are obtained from the 1910 Census data, those between 1910 and 1919 from the 1920 US Census, etc. We restrict data to cities that exist in all three censuses to obtain a balanced panel. The sample of cities is partitioned into four equally sized subsamples according to the quartile of linguistic closeness, as measured through the correlation coefficient.

Table 5.4

How the effect of the quotas on immigrant inflows varies with linguistic closeness, as measured by the index of similarity

	Year of immigration			
	1900–1929		1919–29	
	Posttreatment year			
	1922	1924	1922	1924
	(1)	(2)	(3)	(4)
A. Linguistically close missing immigrants				
Quota exposure × posttreatment	−0.0026***	−0.0027***	−0.0008***	−0.0010***
	(0.0002)	(0.0002)	(0.0001)	(0.0001)
Dependent variable mean	0.0033	0.0032	0.0022	0.0020
Number of observations	22,650	22,650	8,305	8,305
Number of cities	755	755	755	755
R^2	0.5905	0.5864	0.7680	0.7761
B. Linguistically moderately close missing immigrants				
Quota exposure × posttreatment	−0.0027***	−0.0029***	−0.0007***	−0.0012***
	(0.0003)	(0.0003)	(0.0002)	(0.0001)
Dependent variable mean	0.0028	0.0028	0.0021	0.0020
Number of observations	23,730	23,730	8,701	8,701
Number of cities	791	791	791	791
R^2	0.5351	0.5346	0.6228	0.6299
C. Linguistically moderately far missing immigrants				
Quota exposure × posttreatment	−0.0036***	−0.0039***	−0.0004*	−0.0012***
	(0.0003)	(0.0003)	(0.0002)	(0.0003)
Dependent variable mean	0.0020	0.0020	0.0014	0.0013
Number of observations	23,400	23,400	8,580	8,580
Number of cities	780	780	780	780
R^2	0.5127	0.5115	0.6444	0.6470
D. Linguistically far missing immigrants				
Quota exposure × posttreatment	−0.0034***	−0.0033***	−0.0001	−0.0003***
	(0.0003)	(0.0002)	(0.0001)	(0.0001)
Dependent variable mean	0.0011	0.0011	0.0007	0.0006
Number of observations	22,320	22,320	8,184	8,184
Number of cities	744	744	744	744
R^2	0.4990	0.4905	0.6076	0.6084

Note: The dependent variable is new immigrants as a fraction of 1920 population. The outcome variable of new immigrants is constructed by combining information from the 1910, 1920, and 1930 US Census. Specifically, new immigrants per year between the years 1900 and 1909 are obtained from the 1910 Census data, those between 1910 and 1919 from the 1920 US Census, etc. We restrict data to cities that exist in all three censuses to obtain a balanced panel. The sample of cities is partitioned into four equally-sized subsamples according to the quartile of linguistic closeness, as measured through the index of similarity.

Table 5.5	How the effect of the quotas on patents varies with linguistic closeness, as measured by the correlation coefficient

	Year of patent application			
	1900–1950		1919–29	
	Posttreatment year			
	1922	1924	1922	1924
	(1)	(2)	(3)	(4)
A. Linguistically close missing immigrants				
Quota exposure × posttreatment	−0.0011	−0.0031*	0.0004	−0.0027
	(0.0020)	(0.0019)	(0.0035)	(0.0025)
Dependent variable mean	0.1215	0.1173	0.1010	0.0906
Number of observations	1,217,491	1,217,491	292,122	292,122
Number of inventors	27,170	27,170	27,170	27,170
Number of cities	845	845	845	845
R^2	0.2540	0.2540	0.4292	0.4292
B. Linguistically moderately close missing immigrants				
Quota exposure × posttreatment	−0.0022*	−0.0033***	−0.0047***	−0.0053***
	(0.0012)	(0.0012)	(0.0015)	(0.0014)
Dependent variable mean	0.1291	0.1244	0.1105	0.0975
Number of observations	2,370,644	2,370,644	565,794	565,794
Number of inventors	52,385	52,385	52,385	52,385
Number of cities	813	813	813	813
R^2	0.2302	0.2302	0.3999	0.3999
C. Linguistically moderately far missing immigrants				
Quota exposure × posttreatment	0.0002	−0.0020	−0.0060*	−0.0073***
	(0.0023)	(0.0022)	(0.0031)	(0.0027)
Dependent variable mean	0.1250	0.1204	0.1060	0.0933
Number of observations	2,018,139	2,018,139	482,816	482,816
Number of inventors	44,749	44,749	44,749	44,749
Number of cities	816	816	816	816
R^2	0.2149	0.2149	0.3850	0.3850
D. Linguistically far missing immigrants				
Quota exposure × posttreatment	0.0042	0.0031	0.0035	0.0022
	(0.0031)	(0.0028)	(0.0054)	(0.0040)
Dependent variable mean	0.1203	0.1157	0.1008	0.0886
Number of observations	965,134	965,134	231,378	231,378
Number of inventors	21,398	21,398	21,398	21,398
Number of cities	813	813	813	813
R^2	0.2494	0.2494	0.3945	0.3945

Note: The dependent variable is patents by incumbent inventors in 1919. The outcome variable is the number of patent applications per year by native-born incumbent inventors who already had at least one patent in 1919. The sample of cities is partitioned into four equally-sized subsamples according to the quartile of linguistic closeness, as measured through the correlation coefficient.

Table 5.6   **How the effect of the quotas on patents varies with linguistic closeness, as measured by the index of similarity**

	Year of patent application			
	1900–1950		1919–29	
	Posttreatment year			
	1922	1924	1922	1924
	(1)	(2)	(3)	(4)
A. Linguistically close missing immigrants				
Quota exposure × posttreatment	−0.0016	−0.0028***	−0.0037**	−0.0049***
	(0.0011)	(0.0010)	(0.0016)	(0.0014)
Dependent variable mean	0.1277	0.1233	0.1084	0.0970
Number of observations	1,892,525	1,892,525	452,132	452,132
Number of inventors	41,902	41,902	41,902	41,902
Number of cities	823	823	823	823
R^2	0.2400	0.2401	0.4147	0.4147
B. Linguistically moderately close missing immigrants				
Quota exposure × posttreatment	−0.0039*	−0.0054**	−0.0066**	−0.0066**
	(0.0020)	(0.0021)	(0.0026)	(0.0029)
Dependent variable mean	0.1253	0.1209	0.1103	0.0971
Number of observations	2,534,367	2,534,367	605,425	605,425
Number of inventors	56,022	56,022	56,022	56,022
Number of cities	823	823	823	823
R^2	0.2175	0.2175	0.3949	0.3949
C. Linguistically moderately far missing immigrants				
Quota exposure × posttreatment	−0.0076**	−0.0085**	−0.0047	−0.0042
	(0.0036)	(0.0034)	(0.0065)	(0.0044)
Dependent variable mean	0.1216	0.1169	0.0990	0.0871
Number of observations	1,436,744	1,436,744	344,294	344,294
Number of inventors	31,986	31,986	31,986	31,986
Number of cities	822	822	822	822
R^2	0.2464	0.2464	0.3978	0.3978
D. Linguistically far missing immigrants				
Quota exposure × posttreatment	0.0099*	0.0119**	0.0082	0.0125**
	(0.0052)	(0.0050)	(0.0071)	(0.0063)
Dependent variable mean	0.1250	0.1196	0.0977	0.0851
Number of observations	707,772	707,772	170,259	170,259
Number of inventors	15,792	15,792	15,792	15,792
Number of cities	819	819	819	819
R^2	0.2391	0.2391	0.3783	0.3783

Note: The dependent variable is patents by incumbent inventors in 1919. The outcome variable is the number of patent applications per year by native-born incumbent inventors who already had at least one patent in 1919. The sample of cities is partitioned into four equally-sized subsamples according to the quartile of linguistic closeness, as measured through the index of similarity.

tion the sample of cities according to linguistic closeness as measured by the index of similarity. Here the results show that the effect of losing immigrants through the quotas on native patenting is positive and significant if the missing immigrants were very linguistically different from the preexisting population. The effect becomes negative and significant when the missing immigrants are moderately linguistically close to the preexisting population; the effect is slightly smaller for those that are very linguistically close.

Figure 5.1 plots the difference between patent applications per year for native inventors in quota-exposed cities and non-quota-exposed cities (above and below the median of quota exposure) over time (before and after the quotas). Each panel of figure 5.1 reports this plot for one of the four groups of cities partitioned according to the linguistic closeness of the missing immigrants with the preexisting population as measured by the correlation coefficient. It is apparent that the largest trend breaks in patent applications at the onset of the quotas are in the moderately close and moderately far cities; the far and close cities exhibit smaller or nonexistent trend breaks in patenting at the time of quota onset.

Figure 5.2 reports the size and confidence intervals of the estimates using the most reliable patent matching (the 1919–1929 data) and 1924 as the first posttreatment year. It is clear that linguistically far missing immigrants produce either small and insignificant or positive and significant effects on native patenting. In contrast, missing immigrants with a moderate linguistic distance from the preexisting population have a large, negative, and significant effect on native patenting. This effect is attenuated for very linguistically close immigrants.

To get a sense of the scale of these effects, we must compare the effect of the quotas on patenting (reported in tables 5.5 and 5.6) with the effect of the quotas on immigrant inflows (reported in tables 5.3 and 5.4). After all, the size of the "first-stage" effects of the quotas on immigrant inflows varied slightly across samples, and this variation could be related to the variation across samples in the effects of the quotas on patenting, which we report in tables 5.5 and 5.6. We first rescale each of the estimated coefficients reported in tables 5.3 and 5.4 by their respective prequota means to obtain the percent declines in new immigrant inflows caused by the quotas in each subsample. We then perform the same rescaling on the effects of the quotas on patenting reported in tables 5.5 and 5.6. Finally, we divide the latter percentages by the former to obtain the ratios reported in table 5.7. The p-values are computed using the Holm-Bonferroni method (Holm 1979).

We report in table 5.7 the resulting estimates for how a 100 percent increase in immigration inflows affects the patenting of incumbent native inventors. In Panel A, we report the results when we measure linguistic closeness through the correlation coefficient, and in Panel B, we report the results when we measure linguistic closeness through the index of similarity. In Panel A, we find that for every increase in immigration inflows of 10 percent,

A   Linguistically Close Cities

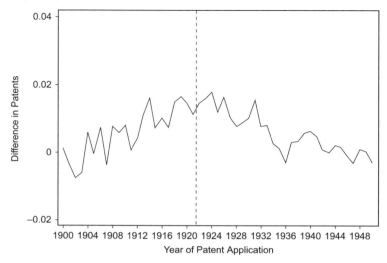

B   Linguistically Moderately Close Cities

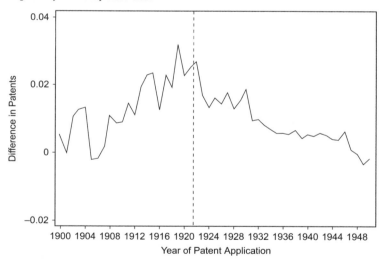

Fig. 5.1   The effect of the quotas on patent applications per year

Note: The figures show the difference in the number of patent applications per year by incumbent inventors between quota exposed cities (those where the quota exposure variable is greater than or equal to the median) and non-quota-exposed cities (those where the variable is below the median). The sample is partitioned into four subsamples according to linguistic closeness between the missing immigrants and the preexisting population, as measured through the correlation coefficient.

C   Linguistically Far Cities

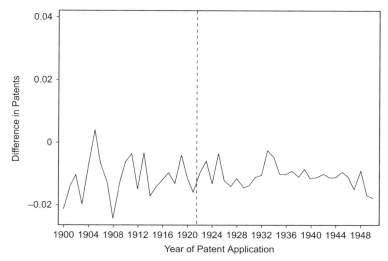

D   Linguistically Moderately Far Cities

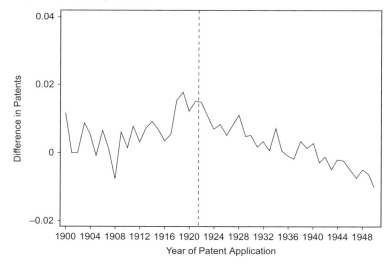

Fig. 5.1   (cont.)

patent applications per year increase by about 1 percent in both moderately linguistically close cities and moderately linguistically far cities. In contrast, there is no significant effect on linguistically far and linguistically close cities. In Panel B, we find that for every increase in immigration inflows of 10 percent, patent applications per year increase by about 1 percent in both moderately linguistically close and linguistically close cities. In contrast, for

A   Correlation Coefficient

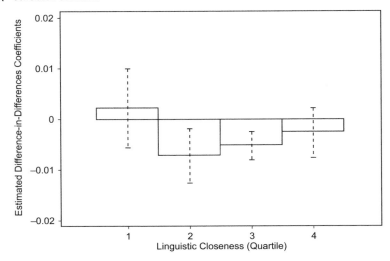

B   Index of Similarity

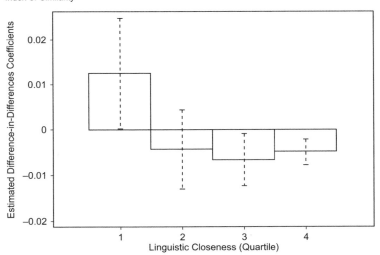

Fig. 5.2   Difference-in-differences coefficients of the effect of the quotas on patent applications per year

Note: Panels (a) and (b) represent the estimated difference-in-differences coefficients in column (4) of table 5.5 and 5.6, respectively. The estimate from the linguistically far cities is located in the first quartile, while the fourth quartile shows the coefficient from the linguistically close cities. The coefficients measure the effect of the quotas on the number of patent applications per year by incumbent inventors (those who had at least one patent by 1919) during the years 1919 through 1929 using 1924 as the first posttreatment year.

Table 5.7   **Effect of immigration inflows on patenting**

	Linguistic closeness			
	Far (1)	Moderately far (2)	Moderately close (3)	Close (4)
	A. Correlation coefficient			
Patent/immigration	−0.0217	0.1057	0.1145	0.0469
p-value	0.5859	0.0083	0.0003	0.2802
	B. Index of similarity			
Patent/immigration	−0.3064	0.0539	0.1095	0.1025
p-value	0.0469	0.3377	0.0227	0.0004

Note: This table shows the effect of quotas on patents relative to its effect on immigration inflows by dividing the estimated coefficients on patents relative to its mean (in column 4 on tables 5.5 and 5.6, respectively) by the estimated coefficients on immigration inflows relative to its mean (in column 4 on tables 5.3 and 5.4, respectively). The *p*-values are computed using Holm-Bonferroni method. The estimated effects are graphically shown on figure 5.3.

linguistically far cities, for every increase in immigration inflows of 10 percent, patent applications per year decrease by 3 percent.

In figure 5.3, we summarize these results, providing graphical evidence of a "U-shaped" curve in the effect of linguistic distance between newcomers and the preexisting population on patent applications.

5.6   Conclusion

In this chapter, we explore the mediating role of language in the effect of immigrants on innovation. We find, as in Doran and Yoon (2019), that low-skilled immigrants affect the innovation of preexisting native inventors. But we further find that the language the immigrants speak matters.

Intuitively, if innovation is the recombination of existing ideas or experiences into new ones (Weitzman 1998), then anything that affects this recombination could affect innovation. Linguistic diversity could affect the number of unique ideas people have to talk about as well as the ability of people to talk about them. The first effect would make linguistic diversity favorable for innovation; the second effect would make linguistic homogeneity favorable for innovation.

It is plausible, therefore, that the optimal amount of linguistic diversity is somewhere in between complete diversity and complete homogeneity. The results we report here are consistent with this hypothesis.

These results are, of course, specific to the low-skilled immigrant workforce prevalent at the time as well as to the state of knowledge and types of inventions common during the period. Future research should determine whether the benefits of new ideas, abilities, and experiences from a linguis-

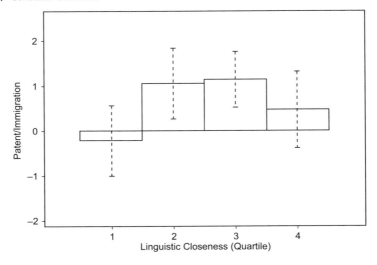

A   Correlation Coefficient

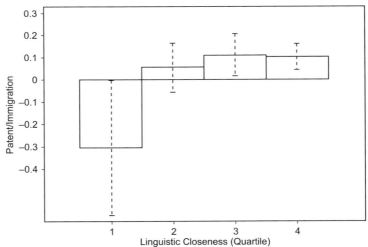

B   Index of Similarity

Fig. 5.3   Effect of immigrant inflows on patent applications

Note: The figure graphically represents the estimated effects reported in table 5.7. We rescale each of the estimated coefficients reported in tables 5.3 and 5.4 by their respective prequota means to obtain the percent declines in new immigrant inflows caused by the quotas in each subsample. We then perform the same rescaling on the effects of the quotas on patenting reported in tables 5.5 and 5.6. Finally, we divide the latter percentages by the former to obtain the ratios reported above. The *p*-values are computed using the Holm-Bonferroni method (Holm 1979).

tically diverse, *highly skilled* immigrant pool outweigh any communication barriers they bring.

References

Abramitzky, R., and L. Boustan. 2017. "Immigration in American Economic History." *Journal of Economic Literature* 55 (4): 1311–14.

Abramitzky, R., L. P. Boustan, and K. Eriksson. 2014. "A Nation of Immigrants: Assimilation and Economic Outcomes in the Age of Mass Migration." *Journal of Political Economy* 122 (3): 467–506.

Acemoglu, D. 2010. "When Does Labor Scarcity Encourage Innovation?" *Journal of Political Economy* 118 (6): 1037–78.

Ager, P., and C. W. Hansen. 2018. "Closing Heaven's Door: Evidence from the 1920s US Immigration Quota Acts." Working Paper.

Alesina, A., and E. L. Ferrara. 2005. "Ethnic Diversity and Economic Performance." *Journal of Economic Literature* 43 (3): 762–800.

Ballatore, R. M., M. Fort, and A. Ichino. 2018. "Tower of Babel in the Classroom: Immigrants and Natives in Italian Schools." *Journal of Labor Economics* 36 (4): 885–921.

Borjas, G. J. 1987. "Self-Selection and the Earnings of Immigrants." *American Economic Review* 77 (4): 531–53.

Borjas, G. J., and K. B. Doran. 2012. "The Collapse of the Soviet Union and the Productivity of American Mathematicians." *Quarterly Journal of Economics* 127 (3): 1143–203.

Chiswick, B. R., and P. W. Miller. 2005. "Linguistic Distance: A Quantitative Measure of the Distance between English and Other Languages." *Journal of Multilingual and Multicultural Development* 26 (1): 1–11.

Doran, K. B., and C. Yoon. 2019. "Immigration and Invention: Evidence from the Quota Acts." University of Notre Dame mimeo.

Duncan, O., and B. Duncan. 1955. "A Methodological Analysis of Segregation Indexes." *American Sociological Review* 20 (2): 210–17.

Greenwood, M. J., and Z. Ward. 2015. "Immigration Quotas, World War I, and Emigrant Flows from the United States in the Early 20th Century." *Explorations in Economic History* 55:76–96.

Holm, S. 1979. "A Simple Sequentially Rejective Multiple Test Procedure." *Scandinavian Journal of Statistics* 6 (2): 65–70.

Kemeny, T. 2017. "Immigrant Diversity and Economic Performance in Cities." *International Regional Science Review* 40 (2): 164–208.

Roy, A. D. 1951. "Some Thoughts on the Distribution of Earnings." *Oxford Economic Papers* 3 (2): 135–46.

Tabellini, M. 2018. "Gifts of the Immigrants, Woes of the Natives: Lessons from the Age of Mass Migration." Harvard Business School Working paper no. 19-005.

US Department of Commerce, Bureau of the Census. 1924, 1929, 1931. *Statistical Abstract of the United States.* Washington, DC: GPO.

Ward, Z. 2017. "Birds of Passage: Return Migration, Self-Selection and Immigration Quotas." *Explorations in Economic History* 64:37–52.

Weitzman, M. L. 1998. "Recombinant Growth." *Quarterly Journal of Economics* 113 (2): 331–60.

Willcox, W. F., ed. 1929. *International Migrations, Volume I: Statistics.* New York: National Bureau of Economic Research.

Immigration and Entrepreneurship

Immigrant Entrepreneurs and Innovation in the US High-Tech Sector

J. David Brown, John S. Earle, Mee Jung Kim, and Kyung Min Lee

6.1 Introduction

How much do immigrants contribute to innovation? Popular accounts of US science, engineering, and high-tech business creation tend to cast immigrants in a starring role, and anecdotes on exceptional immigrants are easy to find, but systematic evidence is rare. A number of studies have examined immigrants as individual inventors, as employees of high-tech firms, and as scientists, engineers, and self-employed (e.g., Wadhwa et al. 2007a and 2007b; Kerr and Lincoln 2010; Hunt 2011).[1]

However, there have been few studies of immigrant entrepreneurs, and

J. David Brown is a senior economist at the Center for Economic Studies, US Census Bureau, and a research fellow at IZA, the Institute of Labor Economics.

John S. Earle is a professor at the Schar School for Policy and Government at George Mason University and a research fellow at IZA, the Institute of Labor Economics.

Mee Jung Kim is a PhD candidate at George Mason University and a Pathways intern at the Center for Economic Studies, US Census Bureau.

Kyung Min Lee is a PhD candidate in public policy at the Schar School for Policy and Government at George Mason University.

We benefited from the comments of Tom Astebro, Ina Ganguli, David Hart, Bill Kerr, Sari Pekkala Kerr, Shulamit Kahn, Megan MacGarvie, Joe Staudt, and participants in two conferences at the NBER. We thank the National Science Foundation (NSF) for support (Grants 1262269 and 1719201 to George Mason University). Any opinions and conclusions expressed herein are ours only and do not necessarily reflect the views of the NSF or the US Census Bureau. All results have been reviewed to ensure that no confidential information is disclosed. The Disclosure Review Board bypass numbers are CBDRB-2018-CDAR-087, DRB-B0017-CED-20181126, and DRB-B0025-CED-20181219. For acknowledgments, sources of research support, and disclosure of the authors' material financial relationships, if any, please see https://www.nber.org/chapters/c14103.ack.

1. Other contributions to these topics include Stephan and Levin (2001), Peri (2007), Hunt and Gauthier-Loiselle (2010), and Kerr (2013).

most of those focus on firm size and growth.[2] Only Hart and Acs (2010) examine innovation measures—research and development (R&D) and patenting—at the firm level using a survey of 1,300 "high-impact" high-tech companies.[3] They report little difference between firms with and without immigrant founders, but they consider a sample of firms already at the right tail of the firm performance distribution. Such data do not permit research to draw any inferences on the relative innovativeness of typical high-tech businesses owned by immigrants and natives, which is the question we address in this chapter.

This chapter aims to contribute to an understanding of the innovation impact of immigrant entrepreneurship in the US high-tech sector using a much larger and richer data set than those heretofore available. We analyze the Annual Survey of Entrepreneurs (ASE), a new database from the US Census Bureau covering about 11,000 owners of 7,400 high-tech employer businesses based on a random sample of all nonfarm businesses. Like the well-known Survey of Business Owners (SBO), the ASE questionnaire contains detailed information on the four largest owners and some characteristics of the businesses, which provide us with control variables for measuring immigrant-native differences conditional on other characteristics, including demographics, human capital, and ownership teams. Unlike the SBO, however, and crucially for this chapter, the ASE includes many innovation measures that form the outcome variables in our study, including reported innovation activities in both products and processes, R&D, trademarks, and patents.[4]

The ASE also contains a number of variables that permit more disaggregated analysis. Data on race/ethnicity permit some examination of immigrants' countries of origin. Data on educational attainment allow us to estimate separately by education group. We are also able to examine immigrant-native differences in the roles played by a number of factors that may be jointly determined with innovation outcomes, including ownership motivations, start-up capital, and choice of industry. For all of these variables, we are interested in both characterizing immigrants relative to native

2. As far as we can determine, the only studies of job creation by immigrant entrepreneurs using broad, representative samples are Fairlie and Lofstrom (2014) and Kerr and Kerr (2017, 2018). Brown et al. (2018) analyze immigrant status among other founder characteristics in a study of high-growth entrepreneurship. Our focus on innovation outcomes is different, but we build on this work and provide some comparisons with our approach in what follows. A few other studies focus on particular industries, regions, or immigrant ethnicities.

3. Saxenian (2002) and Wadhwa et al. (2007a) examine immigrants as owners but do not measure innovation at their firms.

4. The random sampling for the ASE contrasts with the usual approach in "innovation surveys," including the Business Research and Development and Innovation Survey (BRDIS) in the US, where the sample is principally based on firms known or expected to be carrying out R&D.

entrepreneurs and measuring how they influence or mediate immigrant-native entrepreneur differences in innovation performance.

The subject of our study lies at the intersection of several large areas of research. To start with, there is a voluminous literature on the economic effects of immigrants. Most of this research focuses on the consequences of immigration for native worker wages and treats immigrants as a qualitatively similar factor of production so that immigration represents a labor supply shock to a particular region or education-experience group (e.g., Card 1990, 2001; Borjas and Doran 2015; Borjas and Monras 2017; Ottaviano and Peri 2012; Peri 2012, 2015). Other immigration research focuses on the disadvantage faced by immigrants in US labor markets and the extent and pace of immigrant-native convergence in wages, or "assimilation" (Borjas 1985, 2015; Chiswick, Lee, and Miller 2005; Chiswick 2009). Some studies of immigrants consider the possibility that immigrants have certain advantages and document higher rates of science, technology, engineering, and mathematics (STEM) workforce participation, patents, publication citations, and Nobel Prize winners among immigrants (Kerr and Lincoln 2010; Stephan and Levin 2001; Hunt and Gauthier-Loiselle 2010).

Yet much innovation takes place within firms, and our study relates to research on firm-level R&D, patenting, and other aspects of innovation. As is widely recognized, however, R&D and patents both have limitations as measures of innovation, much of which takes place without formal R&D or patenting. Some surveys, including the Community Innovation Surveys (CIS) in Europe and the Business Research and Development and Innovation Survey (BRDIS) in the US, attempt to fill this gap with qualitative questions on product and process innovations (Mairesse and Mohnen 2010). These surveys have documented the incidence of such activities and demonstrated their correlation with productivity (e.g., Griffith et al. 2006; Parisi, Schiantarelli, and Sembenelli 2006; Hall 2011). But the data in these studies are usually based on small samples (e.g., only 5,000 receive the full questionnaire for the BRDIS) that are nonrandomly selected to focus on firms with known R&D activity. Still more important for our purposes, they contain no information on the firm's founders or owners.

Such characteristics have been extensively analyzed in the literature on self-employment determinants, including immigration status (e.g., Fairlie and Lofstrom 2014). But they are seldom measured for owners of firms as distinguished from own-account (employee-less self-employed) workers. And a rich set of owner-founder characteristics has never before been linked to the kind of innovation measures that have become common in firm-level studies.

We find uniformly higher rates of innovation in immigrant-owned firms for 15 of 16 different measures. In most but not all cases, the differences are statistically significant, and in most cases, they survive detailed controls for other demographic and human capital characteristics of the entrepreneurs, as well as the size and family composition of teams. In many cases, they also remain significant in specifications controlling for start-up finance, motivations, and industry. The immigrant-native difference holds for both recent start-ups and older firms and at all levels of the entrepreneur's education. The main exception is owning a copyright or trademark, the most marketing-related activities measured here. Otherwise, the data imply a robust immigrant advantage in innovation.

The rest of the chapter is organized as follows. Section 6.2 describes the data and section 6.3 the methods. Section 6.4 contains results, and section 6.5 concludes.

6.2   Data

We exploit new confidential microdata from the Census Bureau's 2014 ASE. The ASE is an annual survey that supplements the SBO, conducted every five years, providing detailed demographic characteristics on business owners and their motivations to start a business, as well as economic characteristics of their firms. Of particular importance for this chapter, it includes a rich set of innovation measures, which are the main outcome variables in our study.

The ASE sample contains nonfarm businesses with at least one paid employee and receipts of $1,000 or more. Using the Census Business Register (BR) as the sampling frame, the ASE sample is stratified by the 50 most populous Metropolitan Statistical Areas (MSAs), state, and the firm's number of years in business.[5] The ASE sample is randomly selected, except for large companies in each stratum, which are selected with certainty based on volume of sales, payroll, or number of paid employees. The initial 2014 ASE sample was about 290,000 employer firms, and the response rate was 74 percent.

For this chapter, we restrict the full ASE sample to firms in the high-tech sector as defined by the share of STEM employment in the industry.[6] This represents about 5.31 percent of firm-owner observations in the ASE. We also exclude businesses in which no individual owns at least 10 percent of the equity, because detailed owner information is not provided for such businesses. We drop owners who choose the same answers for every motivation question (all very important, all somewhat important, or all not important), because those answering patterns may not reflect the true intensity for each question, as well as firm-owner observations that have missing values for

---

5. See Foster and Norman (2016) for further details about the ASE.

6. We define *high-tech sector* based on the share of STEM employment in the industry using Bureau of Labor Statistics data; for the exact definition, see Goldschlag and Miranda (2016, 58).

any of the variables used in the regressions. Our final sample consists of about 11,000 owners of 7,400 firms. We weight each owner by their ownership equity share, adjusting them to sum up to one within each firm, and we weight each firm by ASE survey weights to make the sample representative for the US economy.

Our main variable of interest is an indicator for whether the owner is an immigrant, defined in the ASE as a noncitizen at birth.[7] As we examine the differences in the propensity to innovate between immigrant and native owners, we control for various other owner and firm characteristics. The owner demographic characteristics consist of gender, age, race and ethnicity, type of education, prior business experience, and veteran status. We also include the relationships among business owners in firms with multiple owners, whether they are couple-owned, noncouple family-owned, or multigenerational. Variable construction is similar to the procedures in Brown et al. (2018).

The ASE asks about nine different motivations for owning the business, including (1) "Best avenue for my ideas/goods/services" (*Ideas*); (2) "Opportunity for greater income/wanted to build wealth" (*Income*); (3) "Couldn't find a job/unable to find employment" (*No Job*); (4) "Wanted to be my own boss" (*Own Boss*); (5) "Working for someone else didn't appeal to me" (*Work for Self*); (6) "Always wanted to start my own business" (*Always Wanted*); (7) "An entrepreneurial friend or family member was a role model" (*Role Model*); (8) "Flexible hours" (*Flexible Hours*); and (9) "Balance work and family" (*Balance Family*). These questions ask how important the reason is: not important, somewhat important, or very important. In the descriptive statistics, we collapse the variables for a particular motivation into a single variable equaling 0 if not important, 1 if somewhat important, and 2 if very important, while in the regressions we include separate dummies for somewhat important and very important for each motivation.

In some specifications, we also use the amount of start-up capital and four-digit North American Industry Classification System (NAICS) industries as controls. The amount of finances used to start or initially acquire the business includes all sources: savings, other assets, and borrowed funds. Finance is expressed as ten categorical variables from less than $5,000 to $3 million or more, as well as "none needed" and "don't know."

Descriptive statistics for owner and firm characteristics are provided in table 6.1. Almost 20 percent of owners of high-tech firms are immigrants, which is higher than the shares of immigrants (defined as born noncitizen) in the general population, at about 13.0 percent; in the adult population, about 15.7 percent; and in self-employment, about 17.9 percent, based

---

7. This definition reflects a change in practice relative to previous surveys such as the SBO, which asked about birthplace (whether in the US). The difference is in people who were born outside the US but as citizens (i.e., because at least one parent was a citizen at the time). We nonetheless retain the conventional labels "immigrant" and "native" in our analysis.

Table 6.1   **Descriptive statistics: demographic characteristics**

Variables	All	Immigrant	Native
Immigrant	19.79	100.00	0.00
Race/ethnicity			
Hispanic	3.59	6.81	2.79
White (non-Hispanic)	80.55	33.58	92.14
Asian Indian (non-Hispanic)	7.93	36.46	0.89
Chinese (non-Hispanic)	2.72	10.38	0.83
Other Asian (non-Hispanic)	2.80	9.52	1.14
Other minority (non-Hispanic)*	2.41	3.25	2.20
Education			
Less than bachelor's degree	23.71	9.55	27.21
Bachelor's degree	43.55	37.20	45.11
Graduate degree	32.74	53.24	27.68
Observations	11,000	2,000	9,000

Note: These are percentages of owners by characteristics from the ASE high-tech sample. Non-Hispanic African Americans are included with "Other minority (non-Hispanic)" because the number of immigrants in this category is too small to disclose.

on our calculations from the 2014 Current Population Survey. The 20 percent of owners within high-tech firms is also higher than the 16 percent of immigrant owners in the full ASE sample that includes all industries and higher than Hart and Acs's (2010) estimate for their "high-impact" sample of high-tech firms, again 16 percent. But it is lower than that reported by Saxenian (2002) for immigrant ownership of high-tech firms in Silicon Valley at 24 percent, Wadhwa et al.'s (2007a, 2007b) estimate of 25 percent, and Kerr and Kerr's (2017) estimate of 24 percent. Each of these sources draws on different types of samples and definitions.

Table 6.1 shows the fraction of the owners in the sample having each characteristic and the fraction for immigrants and the native-born separately. We distinguish Hispanics and among non-Hispanics, whites, Asian Indians, Chinese, other Asians, and others. Among high-tech entrepreneurs, immigrants have a higher share than natives in the Hispanic, Asian Indian, Chinese, and other Asian populations. The largest difference is for Asian Indians, who account for 36 percent of all immigrant owners and only 1 percent of native owners.

Table 6.1 also shows differences in educational attainment. Immigrants are less likely to have only a bachelor's degree, and they are much less likely to have less than a bachelor's degree—only about one-third as likely as natives. But more than half of immigrant owners hold an advanced degree, and they are much more likely than natives—nearly twice as likely—to have graduate education.

Do immigrants differ from natives in their reported motivations for entrepreneurship? Table 6.2 contains the means of the motivation variables on a 0-1-2 scale, as discussed above, for the full sample and for immigrants and

Table 6.2   Descriptive statistics: motivations for owning the business

Variables	All	Immigrant	Native
Idea	1.49	1.51	1.48
Income	1.49	1.46	1.50
No job	0.10	0.14	0.09
Own boss	1.47	1.35	1.50
Work for self	0.90	0.79	0.92
Always wanted to own business	1.18	1.32	1.14
Role model	0.62	0.63	0.62
Flexible hours	1.26	1.21	1.27
Balance work/family	1.28	1.28	1.28
Observations	11,000	2,000	9,000

Note: These are means-of-motivation variables measured on a scale where 0 is not important, 1 is somewhat important, and 2 is very important.

Table 6.3   Descriptive statistics: start-up capital and firm age

Variables	All	Immigrant	Native
Finance			
No capital needed	10.73	9.27	11.09
Capital under 5k	26.35	31.05	25.19
5k to 10k	11.54	12.80	11.22
10k to 25k	14.06	14.98	13.83
25k to 50k	7.77	7.70	7.79
50k to 100k	6.75	5.73	7.00
100k to 250k	5.80	5.14	5.96
250k to 1m	3.50	3.85	3.42
1m to 3m	1.17	1.54	1.08
3m and more	0.50	0.72	0.45
Don't know start-up capital	11.84	7.21	12.98
Firm age			
Young (age <= 5)	39.66	50.50	36.99
Old (age > 5)	60.34	49.50	63.01
Observations	11,000	2,000	9,000

Note: These are the percentages of owners by characteristics from the ASE high-tech sample.

natives separately. Immigrant owners report a higher propensity to cite an inability to find a job as their motivation (although this motivation is uncommon for both groups in this high-tech sample), and a higher share of them say they have always wanted to own the business as a lifelong dream compared to natives. More relevant to innovation, immigrants have a slightly higher propensity to own the business because it is "the best avenue for their ideas, goods, or services." Overall, however, the differences in patterns of motivation appear slight.

Concerning the amount of start-up capital, table 6.3 shows that the

Table 6.4   High-tech industries: definition and composition

High-tech industry	Share of sample	Share of immigrants	Share of natives
Oil & Gas Extraction (2111)	2.29	D	D
Pharmaceutical & Medicine Manufacturing (3254)	0.54	17.63	82.37
Computer & Peripheral Equipment Manufacturing (3341)	0.39	D	D
Communications Equipment Manufacturing (3342)	0.44	D	D
Semiconductor and Other Electronic Component Manufacturing (3344)	1.01	18.41	81.59
Navigational, Measuring, Electromedical, & Control Instruments Manufacturing (3345)	1.38	16.94	83.06
Aerospace Product & Parts Manufacturing (3364)	0.32	D	D
Software Publishers (5112)	1.44	23.25	76.75
Wired Telecommunications Carriers (5171)	0.71	21.00	79.00
Other Telecommunications (5179)	0.94	D	D
Data Processing, Hosting, & Related Services (5182)	2.46	17.67	82.33
Other Information Services (5191)	2.17	17.27	82.73
Architectural, Engineering, & Related Services (5413)	39.07	12.19	87.81
Computer Systems Design & Related Services (5415)	43.67	28.55	71.45
Scientific Research & Development Services (5417)	3.18	23.18	76.82

Note: "D" means suppressed to ensure that no confidential information is disclosed.

immigrant-native differences exhibit a J-shaped relationship such that immigrants are slightly more likely to be in the lowest category of start-up capital and substantially more likely to be in the highest categories. Immigrants are 43 percent more likely than natives to have finances in the range $1–3 million, and for more than $3 million, they are 60 percent more likely.

We also consider firm age as a possible correlate of innovation behavior. Table 6.3 shows that immigrants typically own younger firms (here defined as five years or fewer since first hiring) than do natives. Just over half of the immigrant-owned high-tech firms started up within the previous five years, while 63 percent of the native-owned firms are older than five years.

Nearly three-quarters of the firms in this high-tech sample are in two four-digit NAICS industries: Architectural, Engineering, and Related Services (5413) and Computer Systems Design and Related Services (5415). As shown in table 6.4, immigrant-owned firms are disproportionately located in the latter and underrepresented in the former. No other industry accounts for as much as 3 percent of the sample, and the immigrant-native differences in all these other industries are small and statistically insignificant.[8]

Our outcome variables include detailed innovation, R&D, and intellectual property measures. The ASE asks whether the business conducted 12 different product or process innovation activities in the last three years (2012–14). We create a binary variable for innovation to indicate whether

8. While there are 15 four-digit high-tech industries, some sectors have too few observations for the results to be disclosed.

Table 6.5   **Descriptive statistics: innovation measures**

Variables	All	Immigrant	Native
Innovation activities			
Innovation dummy	69.39	72.01	68.74
Innovation count	3.58	3.89	3.50
Production innovation dummy	56.90	60.55	56.00
Process innovation dummy	60.30	61.61	59.98
R&D activities			
R&D activity (any type)	23.11	28.02	21.90
Work toward patent	13.40	16.98	12.52
Developed prototypes	13.29	17.18	12.34
Applied scientific/technical knowledge	11.16	15.26	10.14
Produced publishable findings	9.68	12.55	8.97
Created generalizable research	11.34	15.73	10.26
Work to discover scientific facts	6.02	9.27	5.22
Work to extend understanding of scientific fact	10.51	14.37	9.56
Intellectual property			
Copyright or trademark	20.03	16.79	20.83
Patent granted or pending	6.60	8.50	6.13
Observations	11,000	2,000	9,000

Note: These are the percentages of owners by innovation measures (except for innovation count) from the ASE high-tech sample.

a firm conducted any product or process innovation in the last three years. We also calculate an innovation count by summing the number of product and process innovation activities. We make binary indicator variables for each type of product and process innovation activities. Product innovations include (1) sold a new good or service that no other business has ever offered before; (2) sold a new good or service that this business has never offered before; (3) improved a good or service's performance by making changes in materials, equipment, software, or other components; (4) developed a new use for a good or service; (5) added a new feature to a good or service; and (6) made it easier for customers to use a good or service. Process innovations include (1) applied a new way of purchasing, accounting, computing, maintenance, inventory control, or other support activity; (2) reduced costs by changing the way a good or service was distributed; (3) upgraded a technique, equipment, or software to significantly improve a good or service; (4) made a significant improvement in a technique or process by increasing automation, decreasing energy consumption, or using better software; (5) decreased production costs by improving the materials, software, or other components; and (6) changed a delivery method to be faster or more reliable.

Table 6.5 shows means of these innovation activities. About 69 percent of firms report they conducted at least one innovation, and the average number of innovation types is 3.6 in our high-tech sample. Although not shown in the table, the most common product innovation is improving a good or service's performance (44.3 percent) and making it easier for customers to use a good or service (41.7 percent); upgrading a technique, equipment, or software to significantly improve a good or service (50.9 percent) is the most frequent process improvement.

The ASE asks business owners whether their business carried out seven different R&D activities in 2014. We create an indicator for whether the business conducted any of these types of R&D. We also construct binary variables for each of the activities separately. We classify the following activities as "Applied R&D": (1) conducted work that might lead to a patent, (2) developed and tested prototypes that were derived from scientific research or technical findings, and (3) applied scientific or technical knowledge in a way that has never been done before. We classify "Basic R&D" as activities that (1) produced findings that could be published in academic journals or presented at scientific conferences; (2) created new scientific research or technical solutions that can be generalized to other situations; (3) conducted work to discover previously unknown scientific facts, structures, or relationships; and (4) conducted work to extend the understanding of scientific facts, relationships, or principles in a way that could be useful to others. In table 6.5, 23.1 percent of firms conducted at least one of these R&D activities in 2014, and the most frequent R&D activity is work that might lead to a patent. In general, the average rate of conducting R&D activities is lower than the innovation activities above.[9]

The last set of outcome variables concerns intellectual property. The ASE asks whether the business owns one or more of each of the following in 2014: copyright, trademark, patent (granted), and patent (pending). We use a dummy variable for owning either a copyright or a trademark and another for ownership of a patent granted or pending. Looking at table 6.5, about 20 percent of firms within the high-tech sector own a copyright or trademark, while less than 5 percent of firms own patents either pending or granted.

A striking result from table 6.5 is the consistently stronger innovation performance of immigrant-owned compared to native-owned firms. Immigrants are more likely to carry out 15 of the 16 measures of innovation. The exceptions are copyrights and trademarks, where native-owned firms have the advantage. Examining the statistical significance of these differences and how they change when other variables are taken into account are the subjects of the next sections.

6.3   Methods

We use the sample of owners and firms to estimate a series of regression models for each firm-level innovation outcome conditional on the owner's immigrant status. To take into account firms with multiple owners, we weight firm-owner observations by ownership shares. Given that the

9. The lower R&D propensity could be partly due to the fact that the R&D questions are about activity in just one year, while the innovation activities are over three years.

ASE is a random sample of employer businesses drawn from the BR, this implies our results are representative of the firm population. We use a linear probability model for binary innovation outcomes and a Poisson regression model for innovation count. Standard errors are clustered at the firm level. Our base specification is

(1) $Y_{ij} = \beta M_{ij} + f(Age_j) + u_{ij}$,

where M_{ij} is an immigrant owner indicator for owner i of firm j. The dependent variables are each type of product innovation, process innovation, R&D activity, and intellectual property. Since businesses are of different ages and innovation may be correlated with firm age, in every specification (including the base), we control for a quadratic function of firm age, $f(Age_j)$. The coefficient on the immigrant owner indicator (β) captures the differences in innovation outcomes, essentially the raw gaps controlling only for firm age, between immigrant and native owners.

The purpose here is simply to describe differences in innovation behavior between immigrant and native owners. Just as in an analysis of gender differences in wages, for example, there is no issue of causality: we do not interpret the results as the impact of turning a random native into an immigrant (just as the interpretation placed on a female coefficient is not the impact of changing a male into a female). But it is also of interest to know whether there are observable differences that might account for the raw gap estimated by equation (1). For this purpose, we estimate another specification with owner characteristic controls as

(2) $Y_{ij} = \beta M_{ij} + f(Age_j) + X_{ij}\gamma + u_{ij}$,

where X_{ij} is a vector of characteristics of owner i of firm j. The vector includes demographic variables (gender, age, and race/ethnicity), proxies for human capital (education, veteran, and prior business), and ownership team variables (size and family relationships). Arguably, these variables are predetermined with respect to innovation behavior. The β estimated from equation (2) is a measure of the innovation gap between native and immigrant owners adjusted for personal characteristics.

In addition, immigrants may differ from natives in ways that are less clearly exogenous and indeed may be jointly determined with innovation: motivations, start-up capital, and industries as shown in the following specification:

(3) $Y_{ij} = \beta M_{ij} + f(Age_j) + X_{ij}\gamma + Q_{ij}\alpha_Q + K_j\alpha_K + S_j\alpha_S + u_{ij}$,

where Q_{ij} is the set of motivation variables, K_j is the set of vectors of the amount of start-up finance categories, and S_j is the set of vectors of four-digit NAICS industry dummies. Most small business owners start their businesses due to nonpecuniary motives with no intention to grow or innovate (Hurst and Pugsley 2011). Given the selection process to come to the US, immigrant owners may have different motivations to own their businesses, which may influence their innovation outcomes. The importance of access to finances for business start-ups is well documented in the literature (e.g., Evans and Jovanovic 1989; Evans and Leighton 1989), and immigrant-owned businesses also tend to have higher start-up capital amounts than those owned by natives (Fairlie 2012). Higher start-up finances among immigrant owners may account for the differences in innovation outcomes between immigrant and native owners. Finally, immigrants may select into specific industries. Immigrants may be more or less likely to own businesses in industries with more innovation activities (e.g., certain parts of the high-tech sector), and this specification controls for this choice, comparing immigrants and natives within industries.

We also examine the heterogeneity of relative innovation performance of immigrant owners along three dimensions: education categories, race/ethnicity, and firm age. The literature on high-skilled immigrants (those with a bachelor's degree or higher) provides evidence that they are more likely to hold patents (e.g., Hunt and Gauthier-Loiselle 2010; Kerr and Lincoln 2010). However, the role of education in immigrant entrepreneurship has been less studied. We therefore examine heterogeneous innovation outcomes by owner education, distinguishing three groups: those with less than a bachelor's degree, those with a bachelor's degree, and those with advanced degrees.

Previous research has also examined immigrants by country of origin. Saxenian (2002) and Wadhwa et al. (2007a, 2007b) report higher shares of Indian and Chinese immigrants (Asian) in high-tech sectors, for example, showing an especially high share for Indians. Although the ASE does not ask for country of origin, we use race/ethnicity to reflect the region of origin. We distinguish Hispanics, and among non-Hispanics, whites, Asian Indians, Chinese, other Asians, and others.

Finally, we investigate whether the relative innovation performance of immigrant owners varies with the age of the firm. Although all specifications control for firm age, it is interesting to ask whether any immigrant advantage in innovation holds only during the early, entrepreneurial phase of a firm's development or also during more mature phases. For this purpose, we permit the immigrant owner coefficient to vary based on whether the firm is five or fewer years old or not.

The specification for heterogeneous immigrant contributions is

$$(4) \qquad Y_{ij} = Z_{ij}M_{ij}\delta + f(Age_j) + X_{ij}\gamma + \varepsilon_{ij},$$

where $Z_{ij}M_{ij}$ are the interaction terms between owner characteristics Z_{ij} (education categories, race/ethnicity, or firm age) and the immigrant indicator M_{ij} for owner i of firm j.

6.4 Results

Tables 6.6 and 6.7 display regression results for each measure of innovation using the three specifications described above: (1) base (no controls

Table 6.6   **Product and process innovation by immigrants**

Variables	Base	+ Demographics	+ Motivations, finance & industry
Innovation activities			
Innovation dummy	2.883	4.669	2.539
	(1.469)	(1.788)	(1.748)
Innovation count	0.090	0.146	0.081
	(0.031)	(0.036)	(0.036)
Product Innovation	3.488	6.438	3.055
	(1.588)	(1.921)	(1.870)
Process innovation	1.632	4.606	2.887
	(1.582)	(1.964)	(1.950)
Observations	11,000	11,000	11,000

Note: Results from LPM estimation of equation (1) at firm age 1. Coefficients and standard errors are multiplied by 100 for ease of reading. All regressions include firm age and age squared. The second column ("+ Demographics") includes demographic variables (gender, age, and race/ethnicity), proxies for human capital (education, veteran, and prior business), and ownership team variables (size and family relationships). The last column includes motivations from table 6.2, start-up finance from table 6.3, and four-digit NAICS industry dummies from table 6.4. Standard errors clustered by firm are in parentheses.

other than firm age), (2) adding demographic controls, and (3) adding motivations, finance, and industry controls. The different types of product and process innovation activities, including the dummy for any activity and the count of the number of activities are in table 6.6. Table 6.7 contains the different types of R&D as well as the intellectual property measures (copyright or trademark and patent granted or pending).

The results show that immigrant-owned firms have higher propensities to conduct product and process innovation as well as R&D activities. The inclusion of demographic controls generally raises the immigrant association with innovation activities, suggesting that immigrant owners tend on average to have other characteristics that are negatively associated with product and process innovation. Demographic controls attenuate the immigrant associations with R&D activities, however.

Differing motivations, levels of start-up capital, and/or choices of industry explain much of the immigrant association with innovation activities but not R&D activities, as evidenced by the significant attenuation of the immigrant coefficients when including those controls in the innovation activity regressions and more modest attenuation or even intensification when adding them to the R&D regressions.[10]

The immigrant effect is positive across all R&D activities, though after

10. In results not shown here, the effect varies considerably across innovation measures. It is especially strong for developing a new use for a good or service. Immigrants have a higher propensity to develop goods or services that no other firm offers but not goods or services that are new only to this firm. The former is a more radical form of innovation. Among process innovations, the immigrant association is insignificant for applying a new way to support

Table 6.7   R&D, copyright, trademark, and patents by immigrants

Variables	Base	+ Demographics	+ Motivations, finance & industry
R&D activity			
R&D activity (any type)	5.580	4.653	3.720
	(1.426)	(1.828)	(1.767)
Work toward patent	3.714	2.886	2.297
	(1.175)	(1.514)	(1.450)
Developed prototypes	4.729	3.885	3.169
	(1.180)	(1.565)	(1.492)
Applied scientific/technical knowledge	4.528	3.698	3.358
	(1.114)	(1.453)	(1.407)
Produced publishable findings	3.342	1.667	1.877
	(1.019)	(1.334)	(1.267)
Created generalizable research	4.772	4.102	3.654
	(1.122)	(1.451)	(1.399)
Work to discover scientific facts	3.749	2.754	3.009
	(0.895)	(1.150)	(1.103)
Work to extend understanding of	4.574	3.062	3.346
scientific facts	(1.084)	(1.405)	(1.341)
Intellectual property			
Copyright or trademark	–3.343	–0.150	–2.201
	(1.199)	(1.592)	(1.555)
Patent granted or pending	2.362	0.035	–0.330
	(0.858)	(1.051)	(1.009)
Observations	11,000	11,000	11,000

Note: Results from LPM estimation of equation (1) at firm age 1. Coefficients and standard errors are multiplied by 100 for ease of reading. All regressions include firm age and age squared. The second column ("+ Demographics") includes demographic variables (gender, age, and race/ethnicity), proxies for human capital (education, veteran, and prior business), and ownership team variables (size and family relationships). The last column includes motivations from table 6.2, start-up finance from table 6.3, and four-digit NAICS industry dummies from table 6.4. Standard errors clustered by firm are in parentheses.

adding controls, it becomes insignificant for producing publishable findings. Immigrant ownership is generally not associated with owning intellectual property, and the association is actually negative and significant in two of the three trademark specifications. The only positive and significant association is with patent pending in the specification without controls.

To investigate whether the immigrant advantage varies with firm age, we permit the immigrant indicator to vary with firm age in two categories: up to five years old and more than five years old. Regression estimates are shown in table 6.8. The propensity to engage in innovation activities is similar for both young and older firms owned by immigrants. The point estimates are

activity and upgrading a technique/equipment/software, while it is quite strong for increasing automation/using better software.

Table 6.8 **Innovation by immigrants: firm age heterogeneity**

Variables	Base	+ Demographics	+ Motivations, finance & industry
Innovation dummy			
Old × Immigrant	4.086	4.630	2.700
	(2.022)	(2.230)	(2.147)
Young × Native	3.982	1.099	1.298
	(1.308)	(1.379)	(1.342)
Young × Immigrant	5.385	4.518	3.530
	(2.032)	(2.393)	(2.341)
Innovation count			
Old × Immigrant	0.127	0.157	0.084
	(0.042)	(0.046)	(0.044)
Young × Native	0.105	0.004	−0.004
	(0.028)	(0.029)	(0.027)
Young × Immigrant	0.164	0.122	0.069
	(0.043)	(0.050)	(0.048)
R&D activity (any type)			
Old × Immigrant	8.592	7.051	5.337
	(1.968)	(2.211)	(2.117)
Young × Native	3.665	3.021	1.924
	(1.195)	(1.250)	(1.207)
Young × Immigrant	6.383	4.899	3.862
	(1.947)	(2.362)	(2.274)
Copyright or trademark			
Old × Immigrant	−2.572	−0.127	−2.165
	(1.719)	(1.965)	(1.938)
Young × Native	−2.186	−3.296	−3.780
	(1.142)	(1.187)	(1.147)
Young × Immigrant	−7.064	−4.577	−6.434
	(1.581)	(1.985)	(1.900)
Patents (granted or pending)			
Old × Immigrant	3.756	1.582	0.490
	(1.252)	(1.302)	(1.246)
Young × Native	0.464	0.848	0.284
	(0.684)	(0.709)	(0.675)
Young × Immigrant	1.336	−0.069	−0.951
	(1.099)	(1.331)	(1.235)
Observations	11,000	11,000	11,000

Note: Results from LPM estimation of equation (1) at firm age 1. Coefficients and standard errors are multiplied by 100 for ease of reading. All regressions include firm age and age squared. The second column ("+ Demographics") includes demographic variables (gender, age, and race/ethnicity), proxies for human capital (education, veteran, and prior business), and ownership team variables (size and family relationships). The last column includes motivations from table 6.2, start-up finance from table 6.3, and four-digit NAICS industry dummies from table 6.4. Standard errors clustered by firm are in parentheses.

Table 6.9a   **Innovation by immigrants: education heterogeneity**

Variables	Base	+ Demographics	+ Motivations, finance & industry
Innovation dummy			
Below BA × Immigrant	6.834	6.655	3.921
	(4.056)	(4.003)	(3.809)
BA × Native	3.273	1.887	0.878
	(1.487)	(1.493)	(1.439)
BA × Immigrant	4.472	6.105	3.225
	(2.456)	(2.664)	(2.556)
Graduate × Native	4.681	4.089	2.181
	(1.664)	(1.684)	(1.639)
Graduate × Immigrant	6.288	7.503	4.405
	(2.155)	(2.468)	(2.428)
Innovation count			
Below BA × Immigrant	0.180	0.186	0.119
	(0.081)	(0.081)	(0.077)
BA × Native	0.119	0.087	0.068
	(0.033)	(0.033)	(0.030)
BA × Immigrant	0.081	0.150	0.070
	(0.053)	(0.058)	(0.056)
Graduate × Native	0.117	0.114	0.087
	(0.036)	(0.036)	(0.034)
Graduate × Immigrant	0.241	0.302	0.218
	(0.045)	(0.051)	(0.049)
Observations	11,000	11,000	11,000

Note: Results from LPM estimation of equation (1) at firm age 1. Coefficients and standard errors are multiplied by 100 for ease of reading. All regressions include firm age and age squared. The second column ("+ Demographics") includes demographic variables (gender, age, and race/ethnicity), proxies for human capital (education, veteran, and prior business), and ownership team variables (size and family relationships). The last column includes motivations from table 6.2, start-up finance from table 6.3, and four-digit NAICS industry dummies from table 6.4. Standard errors clustered by firm are in parentheses.

higher for immigrant-owned older firms for R&D activities and ownership of intellectual property. Among native-owned firms, the propensity to conduct R&D activities is higher for young firms, but for innovation activities, a positive young firm effect disappears once adding controls, and differences are insignificant for intellectual property ownership. Both immigrant-owned firm age categories exhibit higher propensities to engage in innovation and R&D than either native-owned firm age categories across most specifications, while differences are generally insignificant for intellectual property ownership. These results suggest the immigrant advantage is maintained or even increases with firm age.

Regarding variation in the immigrant effect with educational attainment, we specify the equation so that the reference category is natives with less than a bachelor's degree. As shown in table 6.9, the propensity to carry

Table 6.9b	R&D, copyright, trademark, and patents by immigrants: education heterogeneity		

Variables	Base	+ Demographics	+ Motivations, finance & industry
R&D activity (any type)			
Below BA × Immigrant	6.141	5.916	5.498
	(3.662)	(3.762)	(3.747)
BA × Native	4.738	4.037	2.988
	(1.164)	(1.178)	(1.145)
BA × Immigrant	3.350	6.395	4.245
	(2.011)	(2.376)	(2.261)
Graduate × Native	16.89	15.62	11.94
	(1.473)	(1.485)	(1.429)
Graduate × Immigrant	19.86	21.76	17.27
	(2.099)	(2.432)	(2.328)
Copyright or trademark			
Below BA × Immigrant	2.493	3.522	1.435
	(3.337)	(3.398)	(3.241)
BA × Native	5.151	4.248	3.049
	(1.190)	(1.192)	(1.142)
BA × Immigrant	−2.528	2.411	−0.421
	(1.725)	(2.043)	(1.998)
Graduate × Native	10.46	9.201	7.876
	(1.423)	(1.425)	(1.375)
Graduate × Immigrant	4.867	8.811	5.640
	(1.803)	(2.151)	(2.091)
Observations	11,000	11,000	11,000

Note: Results from LPM estimation of equation (1) at firm age 1. Coefficients and standard errors are multiplied by 100 for ease of reading. All regressions include firm age and age squared. The second column ("+ Demographics") includes demographic variables (gender, age, and race/ethnicity), proxies for human capital (education, veteran, and prior business), and ownership team variables (size and family relationships). The last column includes motivations from table 6.2, start-up finance from table 6.3, and four-digit NAICS industry dummies from table 6.4. Standard errors clustered by firm are in parentheses.

out any product or process innovation activity is increasing in education for native-owned firms, but not immigrant-owned firms. For innovation count, there is a higher association with innovation for native-owned firms where the owner has at least a bachelor's degree, but there is little difference between bachelor's and advanced degrees. The coefficients exhibit a U-shape with educational attainment for immigrant-owned businesses. Firms with advanced-degree immigrants have the highest innovation count propensities and those with less-than-bachelor's-degree natives have the lowest. Having a graduate degree is strongly associated with R&D activity for both native- and immigrant-owned firms, and the immigrant effects within the graduate degree category are larger. For copyrights and patents, it is firms with native owners with graduate degrees that distinguish themselves. Across all innova-

Table 6.10a   **Innovation by immigrants: race heterogeneity**

Variables	Base	+ Demographics	+ Motivations, finance & industry
Innovation dummy			
Hispanic × Immigrant	–1.417	–1.955	–1.735
	(5.235)	(5.119)	(4.932)
White × Immigrant	6.816	6.111	4.101
	(2.135)	(2.162)	(2.088)
Asian Indian × Immigrant	0.474	–0.320	–4.872
	(2.394)	(2.478)	(2.488)
Chinese × Immigrant	5.087	4.170	0.628
	(4.126)	(4.053)	(4.047)
Other Asian × Immigrant	–0.819	–1.831	–3.927
	(4.428)	(4.437)	(4.222)
Other Minority × Immigrant	1.046	0.249	–4.786
	(7.565)	(7.353)	(7.141)
Innovation count			
Hispanic × Immigrant	0.031	0.017	0.014
	(0.113)	(0.106)	(0.100)
White × Immigrant	0.217	0.204	0.132
	(0.042)	(0.042)	(0.041)
Asian Indian × Immigrant	0.008	–0.025	–0.172
	(0.052)	(0.053)	(0.051)
Chinese × Immigrant	0.143	0.133	0.024
	(0.088)	(0.084)	(0.081)
Other Asian × Immigrant	–0.079	–0.108	–0.156
	(0.092)	(0.090)	(0.089)
Other Minority × Immigrant	–0.056	–0.072	–0.238
	(0.174)	(0.165)	(0.170)
Observations	11,000	11,000	11,000

Note: Results from LPM estimation of equation (1) at firm age 1. Coefficients and standard errors are multiplied by 100 for ease of reading. All regressions include firm age and age squared. The second column ("+ Demographics") includes demographic variables (gender, age, and race/ethnicity), proxies for human capital (education, veteran, and prior business), and ownership team variables (size and family relationships). The last column includes motivations from table 6.2, start-up finance from table 6.3, and four-digit NAICS industry dummies from table 6.4. Standard errors clustered by firm are in parentheses.

tion measures, the immigrant advantage is generally largest for owners with less than a bachelor's degree.

Finally, we use race and ethnicity to examine differences in the immigrant innovation advantage across the region of origin. Results with white natives as the reference group are shown in table 6.10. Sample sizes get thin, so results are less precisely estimated. One striking result is that firms owned by Asian Indians, despite their high prevalence in the sample, tend to produce less of all types of innovation when full controls are included.

Table 6.10b   **R&D, copyright, trademark, and patents by immigrants: race heterogeneity**

Variables	Base	+ Demographics	+ Motivations, finance & industry
R&D activity (any type)			
Hispanic × Immigrant	1.493	–0.645	1.376
	(4.612)	(4.575)	(4.290)
White × Immigrant	12.99	9.360	8.009
	(2.329)	(2.291)	(2.184)
Asian Indian × Immigrant	–0.457	–4.143	–5.077
	(2.175)	(2.185)	(2.160)
Chinese × Immigrant	13.54	7.047	3.559
	(4.441)	(4.287)	(3.892)
Other Asian × Immigrant	–2.030	–3.537	–5.770
	(3.636)	(3.521)	(3.112)
Other Minority × Immigrant	–0.107	–3.195	–6.906
	(6.737)	(6.292)	(6.233)
Copyright or trademark			
Hispanic × Immigrant	–4.912	–6.061	–5.087
	(3.841)	(3.797)	(3.843)
White × Immigrant	4.280	2.592	–0.095
	(2.097)	(2.064)	(1.975)
Asian Indian × Immigrant	–9.049	–10.02	–11.94
	(1.625)	(1.685)	(1.784)
Chinese × Immigrant	0.486	–2.116	–4.284
	(3.749)	(3.672)	(3.578)
Other Asian × Immigrant	–8.466	–9.400	–9.797
	(2.863)	(2.766)	(2.636)
Other Minority × Immigrant	D	D	D
Observations	11,000	11,000	11,000

Note: Results from LPM estimation of equation (1) at firm age 1. Coefficients and standard errors are multiplied by 100 for ease of reading. All regressions include firm age and age squared. The second column ("+ Demographics") includes demographic variables (gender, age, and race/ethnicity), proxies for human capital (education, veteran, and prior business), and ownership team variables (size and family relationships). The last column includes motivations from table 6.2, start-up finance from table 6.3, and four-digit NAICS industry dummies from table 6.4. Standard errors clustered by firm are in parentheses. "D" means suppressed to ensure that no confidential information is disclosed.

6.5   Conclusion

Much of the research on immigration assumes that natives and immigrants are similar factors in production, in various cases conditional on geographical region, education, and experience. An influx of immigrants is analyzed as a labor supply shock to the region or the skill group. Another large and long-standing body of research focuses on the difficulties immigrants face in adjusting to their new environments, measuring rates of "assimilation," usually defined as the degree of convergence to otherwise similar native workers.

A much smaller literature takes a different approach, treating immigrants as potentially advantaged rather than either similar or disadvantaged relative to natives. Much of this research has focused on individual immigrants in science, the STEM workforce, and entrepreneurship. With some variation, the results suggest disproportionate contributions to some measures of innovation, with immigrants more likely to hold patents, work in STEM fields, achieve high citation indices, and receive Nobel Prizes (Hunt 2011; Kerr 2013; Kahn and MacGarvie 2016). One interpretation of these results is that immigrants self-select from the right tail of the ability distribution and perhaps that the distribution has a fatter right tail than that of natives (Kahn et al. 2017).

Our premise is similar to this literature, asking whether immigrants tend to be more innovative than natives. But our focus is on firms founded and operated by immigrants in comparison to those owned by natives. There has been a lot of "hype" about immigrant entrepreneurs in the US high-tech sector but relatively little evidence on the extent to which they contribute disproportionately to innovation. This chapter provides such evidence, drawing on a large representative sample of high-tech businesses and using detailed information on owner characteristics, motivations, and start-up capital, as well as an extensive set of innovation measures. We focus on the high-tech sector because of its prominence in US growth.

The results suggest higher innovation activities by immigrants for nearly all the innovation measures we are able to analyze. The measures range from detailed product and process innovation, to several forms of R&D, to intellectual property rights associated with innovation, including patents. The only measures where immigrants have notably lower performance compared with natives are for copyrights and trademarks.

Immigrant entrepreneurs tend to be much better educated than their native counterparts in the high-tech sector on average, but the immigrant advantage persists when we control for education and other owner characteristics, and we find an immigrant advantage at all levels of education, again with the exception of copyright or trademark. Immigrant entrepreneurs also tend to operate younger firms, and while we find firm age is negatively correlated with innovation, again the immigrant advantage exists when we control for firm age (as we do in all specifications). Moreover, we find an immigrant advantage in innovation for both younger and older firms.

Future research could expand on these findings by broadening both the population under consideration and the set of outcome variables to be analyzed. A sample including other industries could shed light on the relative innovativeness of immigrant entrepreneurs outside of the high-tech sector. Rather than confining attention to the nativity of individual owners, the analysis could be extended to the possible effects of combining immigrant and native human capital within entrepreneurial teams. Finally, the roles of immigrant entrepreneurs in job creation and productivity growth could be examined in a broader assessment of the contributions of immigrants to innovative entrepreneurship in the US. We hope to report our findings on these issues in the near future.

References

Borjas, George J. 1985. "Assimilation, Changes in Cohort Quality, and the Earnings of Immigrants." *Journal of Labor Economics* 3 (4): 463–89.

Borjas, George J. 2015. "The Slowdown in the Economic Assimilation of Immigrants: Aging and Cohort Effects Revisited Again." *Journal of Human Capital* 9 (4): 483–517.

Borjas, George J., and Kirk B. Doran. 2015. "Cognitive Mobility: Labor Market Responses to Supply Shocks in the Space of Ideas." *Journal of Labor Economics* 33 (1): 109–45.

Borjas, George J., and Joan Monras. 2017. "The Labour Market Consequences of Refugee Supply Shocks." *Economic Policy* 32 (91): 361–413.

Brown, J. David, John S. Earle, Mee Jung Kim, and Kyung Min Lee. 2018. "High-Growth Entrepreneurship." IZA Discussion Papers 11662. Institute for the Study of Labor (IZA).

Card, David. 1990. "The Impact of the Mariel Boatlift on the Miami Labor Market." *ILR Review* 43 (2): 245–57.

Card, David. 2001. "Immigrant Inflows, Native Outflows, and the Local Labor Market Impacts of Higher Immigration." *Journal of Labor Economics* 19 (1): 22–64.

Chiswick, Barry R., Yew Liang Lee, and Paul W. Miller. 2005. "A Longitudinal Analysis of Immigrant Occupational Mobility: A Test of the Immigrant Assimilation Hypothesis." *International Migration Review* 39 (2): 332–53.

Chiswick, Carmel U. 2009. "The Economic Determinants of Ethnic Assimilation." *Journal of Population Economics* 22 (4): 859.

Evans, David S., and Boyan Jovanovic. 1989. "An Estimated Model of Entrepreneurial Choice under Liquidity Constraints." *Journal of Political Economy* 97 (4): 808–27.

Evans, David S., and Linda S. Leighton. 1989. "Some Empirical Aspects of Entrepreneurship." *American Economic Review* 79 (3): 519–35.

Fairlie, Robert W. 2012. "Immigrant Entrepreneurs and Small Business Owners, and Their Access to Financial Capital." *Small Business Administration*, May, 1–46.

Fairlie, Robert W., and Magnus Lofstrom. 2014. "Immigration and Entrepreneurship." In *Handbook of the Economics of International Migration*, vol. 1B, edited by Barry Chiswick and Paul Miller, 877–911. Amsterdam: North Holland.

Foster, Lucia, and Patrice Norman. 2016. "The Annual Survey of Entrepreneurs: An Introduction." CES Discussion Paper 15-40R.

Goldschlag, Nathan, and Javier Miranda. 2016. "Business Dynamics Statistics of High Tech Industries." CES Discussion Paper 16-55.

Griffith, Rachel, Elena Huergo, Jacques Mairesse, and Bettina Peters. 2006. "Innovation and Productivity across Four European Countries." *Oxford Review of Economic Policy* 22 (4): 483–98.

Hall, Bronwyn H. 2011. "Innovation and Productivity." NBER Working Paper no. 17178. Cambridge, MA: National Bureau of Economic Research.

Hart, David M., and Zoltan J. Acs. 2011. "High-Tech Immigrant Entrepreneurship in the United States." *Economic Development Quarterly* 25 (2): 116–29.

Hunt, Jennifer. 2011. "Which Immigrants Are Most Innovative and Entrepreneurial? Distinctions by Entry Visa." *Journal of Labor Economics* 29 (3): 417–57.

Hunt, Jennifer, and Marjolaine Gauthier-Loiselle. 2010. "How Much Does Immigration Boost Innovation?" *American Economic Journal: Macroeconomics* 2 (2): 31–56.

Hurst, Erik, and Benjamin W. Pugsley. 2011. "What Do Small Businesses Do?" *Brookings Papers on Economic Activity*, Fall, 73.

Kahn, Shulamit, Giulia La Mattina, and Megan J. MacGarvie. 2017. "Misfits, Stars, and Immigrant Entrepreneurship." *Small Business Economics* 49 (3): 533–57.

Kahn, Shulamit, and Megan J. MacGarvie. 2016. "How Important Is US Location for Research in Science?" *Review of Economics and Statistics* 98 (2): 397–414.

Kerr, Sari Pekkala, and William R. Kerr. 2018. "Immigrant Entrepreneurship in America: Evidence from the Survey of Business Owners 2007 and 2012." NBER Working Paper no. 24494. Cambridge, MA: National Bureau of Economic Research.

Kerr, William R. 2013. "High-Skilled Immigration, Innovation, and Entrepreneurship: Empirical Approaches and Evidence." NBER Working Paper no. w19377. Cambridge, MA: National Bureau of Economic Research.

Kerr, William R., and Sari Pekkala Kerr. 2017. "Immigrant Entrepreneurs." In *Measuring Entrepreneurial Businesses: Current Knowledge and Challenges*, Studies in Income and Wealth, vol. 75, edited by John Haltiwanger, Erik Hurst, Javier Miranda, and Antoinette Schoar, 187–249. Chicago: University of Chicago Press.

Kerr, William R., and William F. Lincoln. 2010. "The Supply Side of Innovation: H-1B Visa Reforms and US Ethnic Invention." *Journal of Labor Economics* 28 (3): 473–508.

Mairesse, Jacques, and Pierre Mohnen. 2010. "Using Innovation Surveys for Econometric Analysis." In *Handbook of the Economics of Innovation*, vol. 2, 1129–55. Amsterdam: North Holland.

Ottaviano, Gianmarco I. P., and Giovanni Peri. 2012. "Rethinking the Effect of Immigration on Wages." *Journal of the European Economic Association* 10 (1): 152–97.

Parisi, Maria Laura, Fabio Schiantarelli, and Alessandro Sembenelli. 2006. "Productivity, Innovation and R&D: Micro Evidence for Italy." *European Economic Review* 50 (8): 2037–61.

Peri, Giovanni. 2007. "Higher Education, Innovation and Growth." In *Education and Training in Europe*, edited by Giorgio Brunello, Pietro Garibaldi, and Etienne Wasmer, 56–70. Oxford: Oxford University Press.

Peri, Giovanni. 2012. "The Effect of Immigration on Productivity: Evidence from US States." *Review of Economics and Statistics* 94 (1): 348–58.

Peri, Giovanni, Kevin Shih, and Chad Sparber. 2015. "STEM Workers, H-1B Visas, and Productivity in US Cities." *Journal of Labor Economics* 33 (1): 225–55.

Saxenian, AnnaLee. 2002. "Silicon Valley's New Immigrant High-Growth Entrepreneurs." *Economic Development Quarterly* 16 (1): 20–31.

Stephan, Paula E., and Sharon G. Levin. 2001. "Exceptional Contributions to US Science by the Foreign-Born and Foreign-Educated." *Population Research and Policy Review* 20 (1–2): 59–79.

Wadhwa, Vivek, AnnaLee Saxenian, Ben A. Rissing, and Gary Gereffi. 2007a. "America's New Immigrant Entrepreneurs: Part I." Duke Science, Technology and Innovation Paper no. 23. https://ssrn.com/abstract=990152.

Wadhwa, Vivek, Ben Rissing, AnnaLee Saxenian, and Gary Gereffi. 2007b. "Education, Entrepreneurship and Immigration: America's New Immigrant Entrepreneurs, Part II." http://dx.doi.org/10.2139/ssrn.991327.

Immigrant Networking
and Collaboration
Survey Evidence from CIC

Sari Pekkala Kerr and William R. Kerr

7.1 Introduction

High-skilled immigrants are a substantial and growing share of US innovation and entrepreneurship, accounting for about a quarter of US patents and firm starts. While recent research has begun to quantify these broad contributions and measure traits of the types of firms created (e.g., Brown et al. 2018; Kerr and Kerr 2017, 2018), many important factors about the innovation and entrepreneurial processes used by immigrants versus natives and how they interact are less explored.

We examine a particularly important feature—networking and the giving and receiving of advice outside of one's own firm. Individuals working on new concepts, be they embodied in a new growth-oriented firm or a technology being developed in an established company, must acquire and integrate new knowledge. A frequent explanation for the clustering of innovative activity both nationally (e.g., Silicon Valley vs. Bismarck) and locally (e.g., Kendall Square vs. the South Shore in the Boston area) is the information spillovers and knowledge externalities that collocation with other innova-

Sari Pekkala Kerr is a senior research scientist at the Wellesley Centers for Women, Wellesley College.

William R. Kerr is a professor at Harvard Business School and a research associate of the Bank of Finland and of the National Bureau of Economic Research.

We thank our discussant Anne Le Brun, two anonymous referees, and participants at the NBER conference on the Role of Immigrants and Foreign Students in Science, Innovation, and Entrepreneurship for helpful comments. This research was generously supported by the Kauffman Foundation, the National Science Foundation, the Smith Richardson Foundation, and Harvard Business School. William Kerr is a research associate of the Bank of Finland and thanks the bank for hosting him during a portion of this project. For acknowledgments, sources of research support, and disclosure of the authors' material financial relationships, if any, please see https://www.nber.org/chapters/c14107.ack.

tors can provide. Entrepreneurs also cite access to knowledge and beneficial networks as one rationale for joining coworking spaces, incubators and accelerators, and similar facilities, sometimes at a higher rent for the space. The degree to which immigrants and natives differ on these dimensions is unknown but also important for understanding the implications of a rising share of immigrants in our innovative workforce.

We study how immigrants and natives utilize the potential networking opportunities provided by CIC, formerly known as the Cambridge Innovation Center. CIC is widely considered the center of the Boston entrepreneurial ecosystem, with its first facility and headquarters being in Kendall Square adjacent to MIT. Many well-known ventures have emerged from CIC, including Android (purchased by Google), Carbonite, and Hubspot. Start-ups begun at CIC have raised more than $7 billion in venture capital funding and produced thousands of patents since its founding in 2001. To get a sense of this scale, the venture capital raised by CIC firms exceeds the amounts raised in most US states. CIC is also home to the labs and satellite offices of many large companies, with products such as Siri rumored to have been developed there. CIC offers many formal and informal networking opportunities, including the weekly Venture Café, where local entrepreneurs and innovators gather to network and hear talks.

In collaboration with CIC leadership, we surveyed people working at CIC in three locations spread across the Boston area and CIC's first expansion facility in St. Louis, Missouri. A total of 1,334 people participated in the survey (a 24 percent response rate). The survey included extensive questions about the backgrounds of individuals (including education and place of birth), the traits of their firms, their networking attitudes and behaviors both within and outside of CIC, their expectations for their company's future, and their personality traits. CIC leadership was particularly interested in learning about the reasons entrepreneurs chose to locate their firms at CIC and what value CIC was creating for their ventures.

In this chapter, we consider the networking attitudes and behaviors of immigrant entrepreneurs, inventors, and other employees at CIC as contrasted to their native counterparts. There are lengthy literatures on immigrant self-employment and entrepreneurship and on the importance of networking for business outcomes. Yet very little is known about the different ways in which immigrant and native founders access business networks and how they utilize such connections to benefit their ventures. Immigrants operating in a new business environment may show a heightened dependency on the connections available to them through their office location relative to natives more familiar with the local area. CIC provides a unique laboratory to study these questions given our survey's ability to track both formal and informal networking in a detailed manner.

Survey responses show that immigrants value the networking capabilities at CIC more than natives do. This finding (and the others to be described below) are true in the sample averages and also in regressions that condition on person and firm traits and introduce fixed effects for each floor in a CIC building. There is suggestive evidence that immigrants are more likely to locate in CIC for the networking potential, and either way, there is robust evidence that immigrants perceive greater networking benefits and access to other companies as an important contributor to their work derived by locating at CIC.

Networks developed at CIC by immigrants tend to be one person larger than those of natives on average, but these differences are rarely statistically significant. When asked to list the locations of their five most important contacts, immigrant and native entrepreneurs at CIC display mostly a similar reliance on CIC itself. For contacts outside of CIC, immigrant entrepreneurs are substantially more likely to list overseas locations, while native entrepreneurs are overrepresented in terms of contacts elsewhere in the United States.

Looking at networking behavior inside CIC, the largest differences are found in the degree to which immigrants both give advice to and receive advice from people within CIC who work outside of their company. For both of these actions, immigrants report substantially greater rates of information exchange than natives for six surveyed factors: business operations, venture financing, technology, suppliers, people to recruit, and customers. On providing advice, the immigrant differential to natives is highest on business operations and customers and lowest on venture financing. On receiving advice, the differential is highest on venture financing and customers and lowest on suppliers and technology.

Our last set of analyses considers the specific traits of CIC building floors on which the company offices of immigrants and natives are located to see if they interact differently with floor-level environments. The floors within each CIC facility can have a very different feel or purpose: for example, one floor may be more populated with larger, fixed office spaces suitable for established teams, while another floor is a coworking space designed for very small and frequently changing teams or individual entrepreneurs. Conditional on the match of a client's needs to a type of space, the specific floor and office allocation is otherwise based on availability and often has a degree of randomness.

In the building floor analysis, we measure six traits of each floor: inventor percentage, immigrant percentage, average age, female percentage, average firm size, and total number of firms. Controlling for floor fixed effects, we interact these traits with an indicator for whether the respondent is an immigrant to observe whether there is heterogeneity in the immigrant differential due to the various floor characteristics. We do not find evidence that floor traits matter for the strength of the immigrant-native differential with respect to networking. There is some evidence that the greater degree to which immigrants give and receive advice is accentuated on floors that have a high fraction of inventors, but the more important finding is that these floor-level shaping factors are second order to the main effects.

The next section provides a short literature review. Section 7.3 describes CIC and our survey instrument in detail. Section 7.4 presents the main empirical findings, and section 7.5 concludes.

7.2   Literature Review

Entrepreneurs can strongly benefit from collocating with other entrepreneurs, as is evident in Silicon Valley, Boston, North Carolina's Research Triangle, and many other industrial clusters. Extensive literature documents the importance of networking within such clusters and the potential location advantages for entrepreneurs in terms of innovation and discovery, securing financing and other resources, and increasing the performance of their ventures.[1] Katz and Wagner (2014) provide a summary of the more recent concept of the "innovation district" that has become very popular with cities; the authors explain how network considerations are a large part of why such start-up company collocations are proving successful.[2]

Many scholars argue that networks are particularly important at the start-up phase of a business, when good advice and connections to financing are most valuable.[3] Four kinds of social networks are typically discussed in the literature, including family, collegial, transnational, and ethnic networks. One strand of the networking literature has focused on the effect of networking activity on business outcomes and firm performance, and another strand has evaluated the various factors influencing networks' formation and functioning.[4] Explanations for why belonging to a network improves firm performance include the provision of a source of competitive advantage, reduced transaction costs, and enhanced access to knowledge and resources.[5] Given the many potential mechanisms, the importance of networks is likely to vary greatly across heterogeneous firms.

While most of the literature does not differentiate between immigrant

1. For example, see Witt (2007); Elfring and Hulsink (2003, 2007); Powell, Koputt, and Smith-Doerr (1996); Balconi, Breschi, and Lissoni (2004); Breschi and Lissoni (2005, 2009); Glaeser and Kerr (2009); Kerr and Kominers (2015); Greve and Salaff (2003); Sorenson (2005); Aldrich and Reese (1993); Carlino and Kerr (2015); and Aldrich, Rosen, and Woodward (1987).

2. Katz, Vey, and Wagner (2015) further argue that the economic, physical, and networking assets within those districts create the innovation ecosystem that makes them so valuable. Chatterji, Glaeser, and Kerr (2014) discuss the policy environments that support innovation districts.

3. For example, see Davidson and Honig (2003), Aldrich and Zimmer (1986), Kim and Aldrich (2005), Uzzi (1999), Sharir and Lerner (2006), and Weber and Kratzer (2013).

4. For example, see Hoang and Antoncic (2003), Ahuja (2000), Calvó-Armengol et al. (2009), Fershtman and Gandal (2011), Jack (2010), Jack et al. (2010), and Gandal and Stettner (2016).

5. For example, see Dyer and Singh (1998); Lin and Lin (2016); Gulati and Higgins (2003); Zaheer and Bell (2005); Vanhaverbeke et al. (2009); Schott and Jensen (2016); McDonald, Khanna, and Westphal (2017); and Mazzola, Perrone, and Kamuriwo (2016).

and native entrepreneurs, extensive research quantifies that individuals from similar backgrounds tend to network with each other, a phenomenon called "homophily" (e.g., McPherson, Smith-Lovin, and Cook 2001). From the point of view of an immigrant entrepreneur, this may mean that there are fewer obvious network connections available in many foreign locations as compared to a typical native in the same location, and ethnicity has been found to be an important dimension of homophily in entrepreneurial founding teams.[6] Some studies argue that heightened interaction among immigrant networks can explain why immigrant entrepreneurs cluster their businesses in certain locations and industries.[7] Saxenian (2000) describes how Chinese and Indian immigrant networks in Silicon Valley promoted the extensive clustering of Chinese and Indian high-tech entrepreneurs in a small geographic area. Despite the large share of immigrant-owned businesses (e.g., Kerr and Kerr 2018), immigrant entrepreneurs in the US tend to have a smaller network to draw on when seeking financing, mentors, partners, employees, or clients than do typical native-born entrepreneurs (Raijman and Tienda 2000).

A complete literature review on business networks spans many disciplines from economics and sociology to management science and regional analysis.[8] This study contributes in important and novel ways. We provide a rare economics-based view into how immigrant entrepreneurs network and how their networking behavior differs from that of native entrepreneurs. We further compare immigrant entrepreneurs to natives working in the same facility, which is a new empirical approach in this research space. Our CIC sample is both large and focused on companies that tend to be very innovative and growth-oriented, which is difficult to accomplish in many settings. Finally, we complement earlier analyses on the successful ability of immigrant entrepreneurs to network by providing evidence that links the networking behavior to personality traits and other characteristics of the individual and the firm.[9]

6. For example, see Aldrich and Waldinger (1990); Wilson and Martin (1982); Ruef, Aldrich, and Carter (2003); Hegde and Tumlinson (2014); and Gompers, Huang, and Wang (2017).

7. For example, see Light, Bhachu, and Karageorgis (1989); Saxenian (2002); Kalnins and Chung (2006); Chand and Ghorbani (2011); Aliaga-Isla and Riap (2013); Kloosterman, van der Leun, and Rath (1998); Salaff et al. (2003); Kremel (2016); and Kerr and Mandorff (2015). Immigrant clustering for innovation is also observed in Hunt and Gauthier-Loiselle (2010); Kerr and Lincoln (2010); Peri, Shih, and Sparber (2015); and Kerr (2018).

8. Summaries include Branstetter, Gandal, and Kuniesky (2017); Cisi et al. (2016); and Hoang and Antoncic (2003). Recent studies have, for example, focused on the relationship between network structure and behavior (Ballester, Calvó-Armengol, and Zenou 2006; Calvó-Armengol and Jackson 2004; Goyal, Van Der Leij, and Moraga-Gonzalez 2006; Jackson and Yariv 2007; Karlan et al. 2009) as well as the relationship between network structure and business performance (Ahuja 2000; Calvó-Armengol, Patacchini, and Zenou 2009; Fershtman and Gandal 2011; and Gandal and Stettner 2016).

9. See Åstebro et al. (2014) and Kerr, Kerr, and Xu (2018) for reviews of literature.

7.3   CIC and Survey Instrument

7.3.1   CIC History and Operations

CIC was founded in its present format in 2001, known then as the Cambridge Innovation Center. The first facility, known by its address of One Broadway, is in a building adjacent to and owned by MIT. The founders, Tim Rowe and Andy Olmsted, had previously established a "foundry" incubator at the spot. While the foundry model was unsuccessful, Rowe and Olmsted pivoted into what is now often labeled a coworking model, being among the first of its kind.

CIC today offers clients office management services that are flexible in design and month-to-month in duration. CIC rentals include access to "hardware" features such as fully stocked communal kitchens, regular and 3D printing, hardware tool shops, conference rooms, and IT and communications infrastructure. CIC also encourages extensive "software" features for its clients through formal and informal networking opportunities, lectures on topics related to start-ups and innovation, recreational classes like yoga, and proximity to funders, law firms, and other service providers. A complete history of CIC and its present operations are included in the Kerr, Kerr, and Brownell (2017a, 2017b) case studies.

The closest comparison to CIC are coworking spaces like WeWork that have risen to popularity with the "sharing economy."[10] Relative to an operation like WeWork, CIC has both higher-touch services and typically greater price points. The model of CIC also emphasizes a growth in a company's spaces over time (reconfiguring offices during expansions or contractions) and serving a broader population of clients. CIC houses start-ups, single individuals in coworking spaces, not-for-profit organizations, law firms, venture investors, and satellite offices for large corporations. Amazon, Apple, Bayer, Google, PwC and Shell are examples of current and past larger clients. The for-profit CIC is widely recognized as the anchor for Boston's entrepreneurship and innovation ecosystem, with its weekly Venture Café happy hour regularly drawing several hundred participants.

CIC prides itself on housing "more start-ups than anywhere else on the planet." The company now has three locations in the Boston area along with independent entities connected to wet lab spaces and civic meeting spaces. At the One Broadway location, CIC has grown from one floor to its current seven. CIC expanded to St. Louis in 2014, and it has recently opened facilities in Miami, Rotterdam, and Philadelphia. It will open a Providence center in 2019 as part of an aggressive growth plan to reach 50 cities by 2026 (Kerr et al. 2017a, 2017b).

---

10. Related literature on incubators and accelerators includes Aernoudt (2004), Bruneel et al. (2012), Colombo and Delmastro (2002), Gandini (2015), and Grimaldi and Grandi (2005).

   CIC's clients are substantially more innovative and high potential than the average venture in the Boston area. Guzman and Stern (2016, 2017) measure the likely potential of start-ups using digital signals available in their incorporation documents. Ventures registering as C-Corps or in Delaware are more likely to be targeting rapid growth than other companies, and the names of ventures also indicate their aspirations—for example, a venture named "Infinity Global Technologies" is more likely to target growth than one named "Billy's Bicycle Shop." During the 2010–12 period, the ventures registered at CIC had a growth potential score using this technique that was eightfold higher than the average Boston-area firm, and CIC ventures were tenfold more likely to have a patent at the outset or be a Delaware-incorporated firm.[11]

7.3.2   CIC Survey Design

   The scale and diversity of CIC offer a unique platform to study entrepreneurs, inventors, and employees working in innovative enterprises. We conducted a survey in 2017 of clients at four CIC locations, pulling from Cambridge, Boston, and St. Louis. The survey was designed in collaboration with the leadership team at CIC. CIC's client agreement allows them to survey tenants once per year, with responses being voluntary, and this survey served this function. It was launched during spring 2017 and remained open for 13 weeks.

   In an effort to increase participation, CIC sent out one reminder email per location to clients encouraging them to participate. CIC also hosted a pizza lunch at Cambridge's 101 Main Street location, where one researcher handed out fliers, discussed the survey's goals, and had laptops available to fill out the survey. Reminders tended to increase participation for a short while, and CIC leadership made the decision to not send further inquiries and decided when to end the survey.

   Table 7.1 describes the surveyed locations. The survey was sent to 5,645 individuals, of which about 20 percent were identified by the firms as "Heads" to CIC (e.g., for the purposes of directing official correspondence). The average firm has 4.8 people and has been at CIC for 2.8 years, with clients in the longest-running One Broadway and 101 Main Street locations in Cambridge having stayed longer on average. St. Louis houses larger firms on average, reflecting its lower use of individual coworking spaces. Fifty Milk Street, a location in the financial district of Boston, contains the largest share of nonprofit companies, about 19 percent of all clients.

   A total of 1,334 people participated in the survey for a 24 percent response rate. The first survey question required respondents to categorize themselves as an employee, founder and/or CEO, owner, or other (e.g., board member, advisor). Those who designated themselves as an employee received a

---

11. We thank Jorge Guzman for these calculations.

Table 7.1   **Descriptive statistics for CIC locations**

	All	50 Milk	One Broadway	101 Main	St. Louis
Year opened		2014	2001	2012	2014
Individuals	5,645	1,236	2,467	464	1,478
Heads	1,168	346	577	59	186
Nonheads	4,477	890	1,890	405	1,292
Footprint (sq. ft.)	422,177	93,410	155,147	52,465	121,155
Average firm tenure at CIC in years	2.8	2.3	4.4	4.4	1.6
Average firm size at CIC in employees	4.8	3.6	4.6	4.6	7.9
Percent of firms that are nonprofits	10.5	19.1	7.1	7.1	10.0

Note: One Broadway is the original CIC building at the edge of MIT. Boston-area expansions are 101 Main (one block away from One Broadway) and 50 Milk Street (Boston financial district).

shorter set of questions than the other three categories, which were given the same question set. The full survey instrument is included in the appendix (http://www.nber.org/data-appendix/c14107/appendix.pdf).

First, we use the term *entrepreneur* as shorthand to group all nonemployee responses, whether founder, CEO, or owner. Going forward in this analysis, we exclude those reporting their role as "other" for a sample size of 1,222 responses. This latter category is harder to define and frequently captures people with relatively limited day-to-day activities at CIC (e.g., an MIT professor who mostly remains on campus). Second, we use the term *inventor* for those who report having personally filed a patent, and this trait is orthogonal to the entrepreneur-versus-employee distinction. Approximately 31 percent of respondents are entrepreneurs, and 22 percent are inventors.

Our analysis focuses on differences between natives and immigrants, and we define immigrants as those who report that they were born outside of the United States. The overall immigrant share is 26 percent in the sample. This definition includes individuals who arrived in the country as children as well as those who came to the United States later in life to study, work, or directly start a business. The total number of immigrant respondents is 262, with 82 identified as entrepreneurs and 180 as employees. Of the 262 immigrants, 85 are inventors.

Table 7.2 describes survey responses by location. Response rates were between 16 percent and 24 percent across locations. We later learned that some individuals in nonprofit firms felt the survey did not apply to them, which is one reason for the lower response rate at 50 Milk Street. The immigrant share of respondents is approximately one-third for all three Boston facilities and much lower at 5.5 percent in St. Louis. The immigrant share of the CIC sample is about double their 13 percent share of the US population, reflective of their greater role in innovation and entrepreneurship.[12]

12. For example, see Singer (2013), Kerr and Kerr (2017, 2018), and Brown et al. (2018).

Table 7.2   Descriptive statistics on survey responses by facility

	All	50 Milk	One Broadway	101 Main	St. Louis
Number of recipients	5,645	1,236	2,467	464	1,478
Number of respondents	1,222	199	493	86	348
Entrepreneurs	378	55	184	14	114
Employees	844	144	309	72	234
Entrepreneur share	30.9	27.6	37.3	16.3	32.8
Response rate	21.6	16.1	20.0	18.5	23.5
Age					
Percent aged < 25	8.7	11.1	8.5	10.1	7.2
Percent aged 25–34	37.2	37.2	35.5	48.1	36.5
Percent aged 35–44	24.5	30.0	21.2	26.6	25.9
Percent aged 45–54	17.4	13.3	22.5	6.3	14.7
Percent aged > 54	12.3	8.3	12.3	8.9	15.7
Percent immigrant	26.0	33.7	34.8	33.8	5.5
Percent women	40.1	45.3	38.6	42.3	38.7
Percent advanced degree	19.0	8.0	25.8	11.3	17.7

Note: See table 7.1. Some respondents do not designate themselves as being at one of the four facilities.

The shares are also in keeping with their local areas: using the 2014–16 American Community Surveys, the immigrant shares in Boston and St. Louis among employed, college-educated workers aged 20–60 are 18.4 percent and 7.6 percent, respectively; narrowing to those in science, technology, engineering, and mathematics (STEM) fields, the shares increase to 33.5 percent and 17.8 percent, respectively. The overall CIC sample is about 60 percent male, 61 percent between the ages of 25 and 44, and 19 percent holders of advanced degrees.

7.3.3   Survey Responses and Sample Comparisons

Table 7.3 provides detailed demographics and backgrounds for the whole sample and also splits by immigrant versus native respondents. In some cases, the overall average will not exactly match the weighted average of the two groups due to individual respondents choosing to not report specific variables. Differences do emerge immediately, with natives being slightly more likely to be entrepreneurs at CIC companies and immigrants almost twice as likely to be inventors.

In terms of demographics, natives are more likely to be female, white, at either extreme of the age distribution, a bachelor's or master's degree holder, and with degrees in business and economics. They also are slightly more likely to have prior industry experience but less likely to have previous start-up experience as either an employee or a founder. In comparison, immigrants tend to be clustered between ages 25 and 54, are more likely to have a doctorate and to have studied in STEM fields, and also more likely

Table 7.3   Descriptive statistics for immigrants versus natives

	All	Natives	Immigrants
Respondents	1,222	744	262
Percent of sample		74.0	26.0
Role and background			
Entrepreneur	30.9	33.2	31.3
Employee	69.1	66.8	68.7
Inventor	21.5	17.5	32.9
Female	40.2	42.0	35.1
Age			
Under 25	8.7	9.7	5.8
25–34	37.2	36.3	40.3
35–44	24.5	23.3	26.7
45–54	17.4	16.5	20.2
Over 55	12.3	14.2	7.0
Race and ethnicity			
Asian	12.8	5.7	33.5
African American	3.5	4.6	0.8
Hispanic/Latino	5.5	3.0	13.1
White	73.5	83.8	48.5
Other responses	3.8	3.8	4.2
Education			
BA/MA	75.3	76.4	70.9
PhD	19.0	17.4	24.5
Other	5.7	6.2	4.6
Field of Education			
STEM	36.0	31.3	49.8
Business or economics	29.3	31.0	24.9
Other	34.6	37.7	25.3
Experience			
Prior work in industry	62.6	62.8	61.8
Prior work in a startup	47.9	45.3	53.8
Prior entrepreneur	32.3	31.0	36.3

Note: Some respondents do not designate themselves as being immigrants or natives. Entrepreneurs are defined as those who identify their position as Founder, CEO or Owner. Inventors are defined as those who report having personally filed for a patent.

to have previous start-up experience, especially as an employee. Using the National Survey of College Graduates, Hunt (2011) links the higher rates of immigrant inventiveness especially to their fields of study and educational attainment.

CIC itself does not collect similar demographic information on its client population, but CIC's leadership believes that our survey respondent demographics reflect the overall population of their facilities very well. Some greater insight does exist for the gender dimension. A 2015 CIC study found that 28 percent of company heads were women, which is roughly on par with the 24 percent among our respondent entrepreneurs. Similarly, a 5 percent random sample of CIC clients in 2017 showed that 35 percent of all CIC-based company employees were women, which closely compares to the 40 percent share in our sample. To put things into a broader context, other comparison points for women's leadership include 5.4 percent of Fortune 500 CEOs, 24 percent of congressional representatives, and 12 percent of executive officer positions in the top 15 Silicon Valley firms.[13]

Conditional on starting the survey, response rates were high for most questions. Questions regarding experiences at CIC and demographics had response rates of over 80 percent, while questions regarding personality had response rates of over 75 percent. Questions with the lowest response rates included those related to patents associated with the firm and interest in future CIC events. We believe that response rates for patenting activity of the firm were lower because the question lacked a "do not know" option. These fields are not used in the present study.

7.4   Survey Results

7.4.1   Measuring Networking Attitudes and Behaviors

We next describe how the survey captured attitudes toward networking and the importance of networking opportunities in the choice to locate the company within CIC. Table 7.4 provides the survey questions used to calculate the values for most of the variables analyzed below, and the appendix (http://www.nber.org/data-appendix/c14107/appendix.pdf) has the full survey instruments for additional reference. Figures 7.1–7.3 display the response patterns by immigrant status. We group questions into three sets; these sets rely on questions from different parts of the survey and are not necessarily sequentially presented in this chapter.

We group the first set of questions around the respondents' self-reported perceptions of CIC's networking benefits. Respondents were asked to rate aspects of CIC in terms of their importance to the decision to locate the company there, with value one (1) being "not very important" and value five (5) being "very important." A related question asked respondents how being located at CIC actually helped their business "better network among other businesses," on a scale from "not at all" (1) to "very much" (5). Similar five-point scales were used to gauge the purposefulness of individuals' networking; to measure perceptions of how CIC helped them access companies at CIC, within the vicinity of CIC, or in the greater Boston or St. Louis area; and to measure whether respondents see a premium in CIC value-added compared to costs and over other competitors' offerings. In all cases, the raw average for the immigrant respondents exceeds that of the

---

13. For example, see Zarya (2016), Brown (2017), and Bell and White (2014). See also Desilver (2018).

Table 7.4   Networking baselines for immigrants versus natives

	All	Natives	Immigrants
Respondents	1,222	744	262
Located in CIC for networking opportunities?	3.63	3.62	3.79
Does CIC networking environment help your business?	3.67	3.65	3.76
How purposeful are you in building your business network?	2.85	2.80	3.03
CIC is important because of access to other companies within CIC	3.26	3.22	3.36
. . . within the vicinity of CIC	3.40	3.34	3.57
. . . in the greater Boston / St. Louis area	3.63	3.57	3.78
CIC's value outweighs the cost to tenants?	3.67	3.66	3.72
CIC offers more valuable connections than other co-working facilities?	3.78	3.77	3.86
Person count: people in other CIC firms who could benefit your business in the next six months?	4.53	4.45	4.89
Person count: people in other CIC firms whose name you would remember in six months?	5.91	5.89	6.13
Measure of unique locations a respondent listed for where they network	2.90	2.92	2.90
Frequency of advice (1–4)			
Provide advice: business operations	2.02	1.97	2.17
Provide advice: venture financing	1.69	1.64	1.81
Provide advice: technology	2.05	1.99	2.23
Provide advice: suppliers	1.69	1.64	1.81
Provide advice: people to recruit	1.87	1.83	1.98
Provide advice: customers	1.87	1.82	2.01
Receive advice: business operations	1.89	1.83	2.06
Receive advice: venture financing	1.66	1.58	1.84
Receive advice: technology	1.98	1.94	2.10
Receive advice: suppliers	1.68	1.64	1.79
Receive advice: people to recruit	1.80	1.76	1.89
Receive advice: customers	1.83	1.77	2.00

Note: See table 7.3.

natives. Immigrants are more likely to consider networking opportunities an important factor in choosing to locate at CIC and to report having benefited from CIC in this regard.

A second group of questions uses survey responses to infer information on the types of networks possessed by individuals. Respondents were asked to estimate the number of people at CIC (outside of the employees/investors of their own company) that they know well enough to believe that these people could be of benefit to their business over the next six months. Again, the scale had five options ranging from "none" to "over 20." Similarly, respondents estimated how many people at CIC they knew well enough to believe they would remember the respondents' names in six months if they left CIC today. The response options were the same as in the previous

A   Importance of CIC Networking

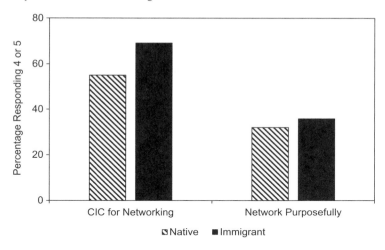

B   Location of Most Important Connections

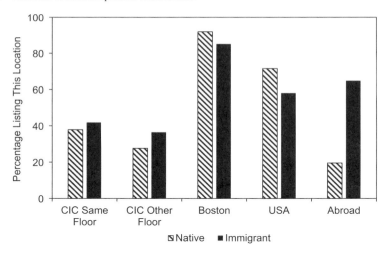

Fig. 7.1   Networking importance, location, and advice

question. For analysis, we converted the binned values into the midpoints of their range, except for the bottom/top category: "none" coded as zero, "1–4 persons" coded as three, "5–10 persons" coded as eight, "11–20 persons" coded as 15, and "more than 20 persons" coded as 20. Immigrants report knowing more of both types of individuals at CIC, especially those who are likely to be beneficial to their business (4.9 versus 4.5). Figure 7.3 plots the cross-sectional pattern of networks by time in CIC. For all respondents who

C   Providing Advice at CIC by Topic

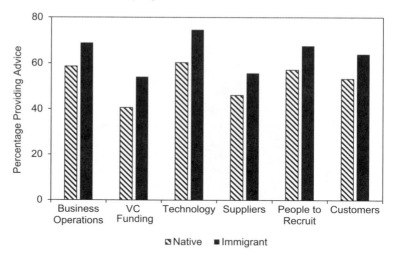

D   Receiving Advice at CIC by Topic

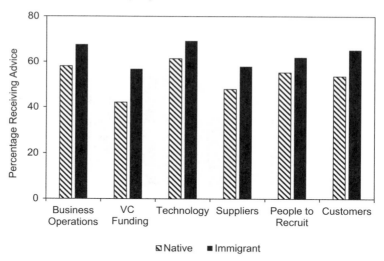

Fig. 7.1   (cont.)

answered that they knew at least one such person, we further asked whether these connections were made before or after joining CIC.

We constructed another measure of networking through the responses of individuals regarding where exactly they networked at CIC. This question was asked of people indicating that CIC helped their business network at a level of three or higher on a five-point scale. Respondents could choose one

A   CIC is Important because of Access to Companies...

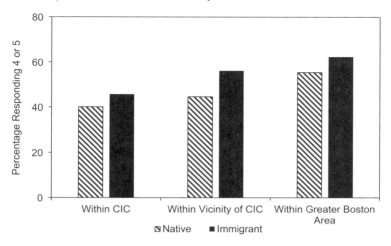

B   To What Extent Do You Agree with the Following about CIC?

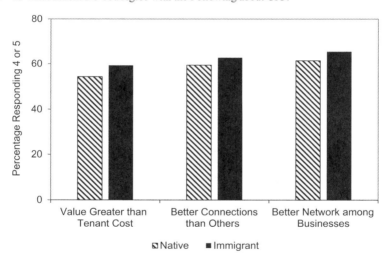

Fig. 7.2   CIC importance and number of beneficial contacts

or more of the following possibilities: (a) Informally: Conversations or introductions at Venture Café; (b) Informally: Conversations or introductions in a CIC kitchen; (c) Other public spaces at CIC; (d) Other informal channels; (e) Purposefully seek out meetings with firms located inside CIC (ask via email, phone, LinkedIn, . . .); (f) Purposefully seek out meetings with firms located nearby / outside CIC (ask via email, phone, LinkedIn, . . .); (g) Other CIC-based firms purposefully ask to meet with me; and (h) Other. When we

C   Number of People Who Could Benefit Your Business over Next 6 Months

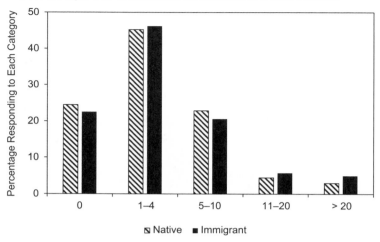

D   Number of People Whose Name You Would Remember in 6 Months

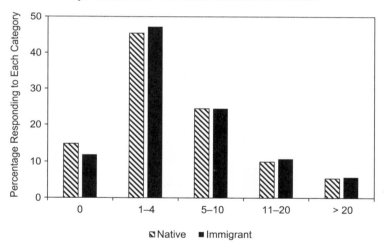

Fig. 7.2   **(cont.)**

tallied the number of boxes checked, immigrants and natives showed very similar values of about 2.9 unique network locations.

At the very end of the survey, we asked the entrepreneurs a rather detailed question about the locations of their most important contacts (based on Nanda and Khanna 2010): "Please think of 5 people not directly connected with your company with whom you have had important conversations related to your business in the last 6 months. These may be family members, friends, former colleagues, instructors, or other persons with whom you dis-

A   Number of People Whose Name You Would Remember in 6 Months
    (Full Sample)

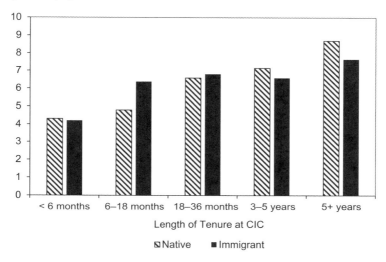

B   Number of People Who Could Benefit Your Business over Next 6 Months
    (Full Sample)

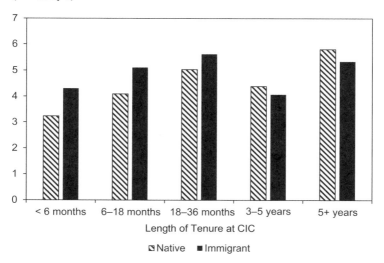

Fig. 7.3   Beneficial contacts by tenure at CIC

C Number of People Whose Name You Would Remember in 6 Months
(Sample without Pre-existing Network)

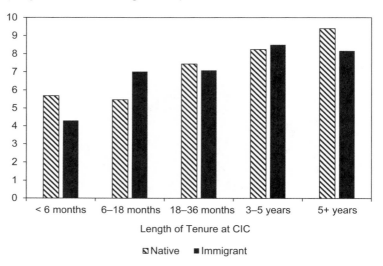

D Number of People Who Could Benefit Your Business over next 6 Months
(Sample without Pre-existing Network)

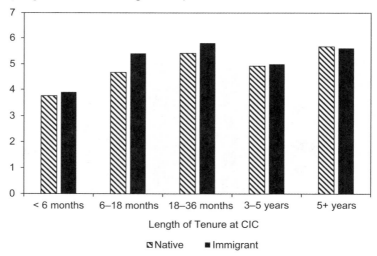

Fig. 7.3 **(cont.)**

cussed aspects of your business (e.g., strategy, business development, market conditions, financing) but NOT employees, investors, or clients that have a direct stake in the company. Where are these external colleagues located?" The respondent had five options: the same floor at CIC, another floor at CIC, within the Boston (or St. Louis) area, within the United States, and overseas. Natives were significantly more likely to have their most important connections either in the greater Boston (or St. Louis) area or elsewhere in the United States, while immigrants were much more likely to have these important connections abroad.

A third set of questions asked respondents about the frequency at which they either provided or received advice on various aspects of running their business to/from "people outside of your company at CIC." The frequency options ranged from "never" (1) to "weekly" (4). Six topic categories were considered: business operations, venture financing, technology, suppliers, people to recruit, and customers. Immigrants report substantially higher rates of both providing and receiving advice on all topics.

The full survey asks many more questions about growth expectations, company financing history, personality traits of individuals and their attitudes toward risk, and so on. Participants were also incentivized to complete the survey with a reward that was designed to also capture an element of their risk attitudes by presenting them with a choice between a sure prize and a lottery of known probabilities. These questions are studied in other papers (e.g., Kerr, Kerr, and Dalton 2019).

7.4.2   Analytical Results

Tables 7.5–7.9 analyze these survey responses with least-squares regressions. Each row corresponds to a survey question, and we report eight results per question across the columns. In all cases, we only report the coefficient and standard error on an indicator variable for the respondent being an immigrant. Regressions are unweighted and report robust standard errors, and estimations that cluster standard errors at the firm level deliver very similar results. Columns 1–4 report results where we leave the dependent variable in its raw form, while Columns 5–8 consider transformations of the dependent variable to have a binary form of low versus high responses (given unit value). For each question, we describe the scale of the baseline values and their transformation.

The four columns in each set repeat a pattern. Our initial estimation controls for person-level covariates and building fixed effects. Person-level covariates include controls for gender, age, race, educational attainment, full- versus part-time status, prior industry experience, prior start-up experience, and prior patenting history. Covariates are introduced using indicators for value ranges; item nonresponse was grouped into an "unknown" category. The second estimation incorporates fixed effects for individual CIC floors within buildings. Across the four buildings, there are a total of

20 floors in our sample. The third estimation adds an additional firm-level control for the number of the firm's employees working at CIC. The last analysis excludes St. Louis to focus just on Boston given the substantial differences between the two cities in terms of immigrant share and other features. At the right-hand side of each table, we report the observation counts in total and for Boston only.

Table 7.5 considers the perceptions of networking at CIC by immigrants versus natives. The perceptions of respondents have several attractive properties: they capture the benefits and costs known by respondents but unobservable to the researcher or CIC leadership, they measure the saliency of an effect that is otherwise difficult to judge, and (for the purposes of CIC) they are what ultimately matters for the company's location choice at CIC. The downsides of these perceptions are the mirror images of the advantages, most notably that respondents may have an inaccurate understanding of their true networking behavior or that they may engage in "cheap talk."

The variables reported in table 7.5 are measured on a five-point scale ranging from "strongly disagree" (1) to "strongly agree" (5) or comparable wording. For the binary analysis, we group scores of four or five into the high bin that is given a unit value. The first row presents some indication that immigrants may locate their businesses at CIC for better networking opportunities, and this pattern is most evident in the binary analysis. Either way, immigrants in the second row show substantially higher perceptions of CIC helping their businesses via networking than do natives. The differential is on the order of 10 percent of the baseline average of 3.67 in table 7.4. Immigrants show a similarly higher purposefulness in building their networks.

When respondents articulate the location of the other companies that CIC specifically helps them access, a modest edge is given to other companies located within CIC, although an important immigrant differential is also observed for accessing other local non-CIC firms. As the baseline value in table 7.4 is rising from 3.26 for companies within CIC to 3.63 for nonvicinity companies in the greater Boston/St. Louis area, the relative effect for immigrants of CIC-based connections is higher than initially evident in table 7.5. These results are robust in both the baseline and binary analyses. Finally, immigrants are somewhat more likely to consider CIC benefits as outweighing the costs and/or what other local coworking spaces could provide, but these results are not precisely measured.

Table 7.6 turns to measures we can construct of actual networking behavior at CIC. This is a useful complement to the perceptions of networking, given the pros and cons noted above. The first metrics consider the person counts within a respondent's CIC network outside of the respondent's own company. These person count questions allowed for five ranges from "none" to "more than 20." Baseline estimations use the midpoints of these ranges, as described earlier, with 0 for the smallest and 20 for the largest category. The binary analysis combines responses with eleven or more persons as the high category.

Table 7.5 Impact of CIC on perceived networking activity for immigrants versus natives

Question	Baseline values For immigrant indicator				Binary analysis For immigrant indicator				Sample size	
	(1)	(2)	(3)	(4)	(5)	(6)	(7)	(8)	Full	Boston only
Located in CIC for networking opportunities?	0.101 (0.191)	0.068 (0.180)	0.135 (0.186)	0.169 (0.189)	0.144* (0.074)	0.131* (0.071)	0.160** (0.074)	0.182** (0.082)	326	222
Does CIC's networking environment help your business?	0.331*** (0.108)	0.339*** (0.108)	0.341*** (0.109)	0.338*** (0.116)	0.130*** (0.040)	0.129*** (0.040)	0.130*** (0.041)	0.125*** (0.044)	985	698
How purposeful are you in building your business network?	0.292*** (0.098)	0.303*** (0.099)	0.323*** (0.100)	0.291*** (0.105)	0.050 (0.039)	0.043 (0.039)	0.054 (0.039)	0.045 (0.041)	1,003	712
CIC is important because of access to other companies within CIC	0.281*** (0.090)	0.288*** (0.091)	0.298*** (0.093)	0.280*** (0.099)	0.095** (0.039)	0.096** (0.039)	0.095** (0.040)	0.083** (0.042)	994	707
. . . within the vicinity of CIC	0.208** (0.097)	0.222** (0.098)	0.223** (0.098)	0.193* (0.105)	0.106*** (0.041)	0.106** (0.041)	0.100** (0.042)	0.082* (0.044)	992	705
. . . in the greater Boston / St. Louis area	0.233** (0.096)	0.219** (0.098)	0.214** (0.098)	0.214** (0.098)	0.081* (0.043)	0.073* (0.043)	0.071 (0.044)	0.071 (0.044)	706	706
CIC's value outweighs the cost to tenants	0.151* (0.081)	0.122 (0.082)	0.120 (0.083)	0.098 (0.087)	0.089** (0.041)	0.068 (0.041)	0.062 (0.042)	0.050 (0.045)	986	700
CIC offers more valuable connections than other coworking facilities	0.131 (0.081)	0.120 (0.081)	0.122 (0.082)	0.110 (0.088)	0.044 (0.040)	0.041 (0.040)	0.039 (0.041)	0.031 (0.044)	981	695
Person-level covariates	x	x	x	x	x	x	x	x		
Building fixed effects	x	x	x	x	x	x	x	x		
Floor fixed effects		x	x	x		x	x	x		
Firm-level covariates			x	x			x	x		
Boston only				x				x		

Note: Baseline responses were on a 1 to 5 scale with 1 = strongly disagree and 5 = strongly agree. Binary analysis bins responses with 0 = 1, 2, or 3 and 1 = 4 or 5. Person-level covariates include controls for gender, age, race, educational attainment, prior industry experience, prior startup experience, full-time vs. part-time status, and patenting history. Firm level covariates include firm size. Covariates are introduced using indicators for value ranges; non-response was grouped into an "unknown" category. Regressions report robust standard errors and are unweighted.

Table 7.6   Impact of CIC on measured networking activity for immigrants versus natives

Question	Baseline values *For immigrant indicator*				Binary analysis *For immigrant indicator*				Sample size	
	(1)	(2)	(3)	(4)	(5)	(6)	(7)	(8)	*Full*	*Boston only*
Person count: People in other CIC firms who could benefit your business in the next six months	0.664* (0.392)	0.538 (0.402)	0.672* (0.400)	0.497 (0.417)	0.034 (0.024)	0.023 (0.025)	0.029 (0.025)	0.012 (0.026)	1,004	714
Person count: People in other CIC firms whose name you would remember in six months	0.371 (0.427)	0.118 (0.431)	0.303 (0.431)	0.170 (0.458)	0.014 (0.030)	-0.001 (0.030)	0.009 (0.030)	0.000 (0.032)	1,003	712
Person count: Sum of the two responses	0.996 (0.740)	0.626 (0.752)	0.951 (0.747)	0.640 (0.778)	0.022 (0.021)	0.012 (0.022)	0.022 (0.021)	0.008 (0.022)	1,005	714
Measure of unique locations a respondent listed for where they network	0.037 (0.150)	-0.007 (0.155)	0.036 (0.153)	-0.023 (0.168)	-0.014 (0.026)	-0.025 (0.028)	-0.021 (0.028)	-0.037 (0.029)	791	539
Person-level covariates	x	x	x	x	x	x	x	x		
Building fixed effects	x	x	x	x	x	x	x	x		
Floor fixed effects		x	x	x		x	x	x		
Firm-level covariates			x	x			x	x		
Boston only				x				x		

Note: See table 7.5. Person count questions allowed for five ranges from none to more than 20. Baseline estimations use the midpoints of ranges and 20 for the largest category; binary analysis bins responses with $0 = 10$ or fewer and $1 = 11$ or more. Respondents indicated across eight options where they networked, and the metric used in the analyses is the sum of these checked options.

Immigrants report on average a 0.6 person larger professional network at CIC compared to a baseline average of 4.5 persons. This difference is about twice as large as the second form of the question that was designed to elicit familiarity with those around a respondent (baseline average of 5.9 persons). While we do not know the overlaps of these two groups, we also report a regression that sums the two counts. Across all these outcomes, there is some modest evidence that CIC enables a larger professional network for immigrants than it does for natives, perhaps with a total network advantage of 0.5–1.0 person. But these results are not precisely measured and should be treated with caution. By contrast, and reflecting the identical raw responses in table 7.4, we observe no difference between immigrants and natives in terms of the count of locations or the types of networking employed.

In general, the differential in immigrant perceptions of CIC networking advantages in table 7.5 appears a bit more robust than the actual network effects in table 7.6. Two factors, however, should be noted. One is that the relative magnitudes of the point estimates in table 7.6 are substantial for the professional network—on the order of 10 percent to 20 percent of the effect—and comparable to perception differences. Second, the counterfactual for network size is hard to define. It could have been that absent CIC's networking potential, the professional networks of immigrants would have been substantially smaller than those of natives, yet we are only able to measure these differences conditional on being inside of CIC.

Table 7.7 considers immigrant differences using the additional networking questions that were asked of entrepreneurs only. These leaders were first asked to rate the importance of the five most significant people they met at CIC for their businesses. Immigrants suggest that these five contacts are marginally more important, but the differences are far from statistically significant.

Second, we analyze differences in the top five contacts that entrepreneurs have by counting up the number of contacts mentioned in each location. This count can range from zero to five for any one location, and for the binary analysis, we group three or more contacts into the high category. Table 7.7 first analyzes the five options as asked in the survey, and then an additional analysis is provided that groups the same floor and another floor responses at CIC into a single outcome. There are substantial differences in the locations of top entrepreneur contacts, with immigrant entrepreneurs pointing significantly more to overseas contacts versus those in the local area surrounding CIC. Network reliance on CIC itself is comparable for the two groups.

Tables 7.8 and 7.9 turn to our third set of questions on the giving and receiving of advice across six broad topics: business operations, venture financing, technology, suppliers, people to recruit, and customers. Table 7.4 noted that immigrants reported substantially higher rates of exchanging

Table 7.7   **Founder networks for immigrant versus natives**

Question	Baseline values For immigrant indicator				Binary analysis For immigrant indicator				Sample size	
	(1)	(2)	(3)	(4)	(5)	(6)	(7)	(8)	Full	Boston only
Think of the 5 most important people you met at CIC specifically. How important were they for your business?	0.043 (0.150)	0.030 (0.149)	0.061 (0.150)	0.079 (0.170)	0.026 (0.076)	0.030 (0.078)	0.045 (0.079)	0.047 (0.086)	311	210
How many of these top five contacts are located on the same floor as you?	0.012 (0.118)	0.023 (0.122)	0.064 (0.128)	0.131 (0.145)	-0.000 (0.023)	0.001 (0.024)	0.005 (0.026)	0.024 (0.030)	309	209
. . . on another floor at CIC?	0.037 (0.117)	0.037 (0.120)	0.036 (0.116)	0.074 (0.122)	-0.003 (0.022)	0.002 (0.022)	-0.007 (0.019)	-0.012 (0.022)	309	209
. . . within the Boston / St. Louis area?	-0.423** (0.193)	-0.429** (0.196)	-0.389* (0.203)	-0.244 (0.220)	-0.078 (0.072)	-0.078 (0.075)	-0.074 (0.079)	-0.106 (0.087)	309	209
. . . within the United States?	-0.356* (0.188)	-0.314* (0.190)	-0.380* (0.193)	-0.526** (0.216)	-0.040 (0.059)	-0.016 (0.059)	-0.021 (0.061)	-0.066 (0.066)	309	209
. . . overseas?	0.748*** (0.127)	0.695*** (0.129)	0.686*** (0.133)	0.573*** (0.148)	0.083** (0.037)	0.075** (0.035)	0.074** (0.034)	0.066** (0.038)	309	209
Measure for networking on same floor or another floor at CIC	0.049 (0.166)	0.060 (0.166)	0.100 (0.172)	0.205 (0.187)	-0.029 (0.043)	-0.032 (0.045)	-0.022 (0.045)	0.028 (0.048)	309	209
Person-level covariates	x	x	x	x	x	x	x	x		
Building fixed effects	x	x	x	x	x	x	x	x		
Floor fixed effects		x	x	x		x	x	x		
Firm-level covariates			x	x			x	x		
Boston only				x				x		

Note: See table 7.5. Baseline responses for first two questions were on a 1 to 5 scale with 1 = strongly disagree, 5 = strongly agree. Binary analysis bins responses with 0 = 1, 2, or 3 and 1 = 4 or 5. Lists of important contacts by location were transformed into count variables ranging from zero to five. Binary analysis bins responses with 0 = 2 or fewer mentions and 1 = 3 or more mentions.

Table 7.8 Providing advice at CIC for immigrants versus natives

Question: How often do you provide advice on the following topics to people outside of your company at CIC?	Baseline values — For immigrant indicator				Binary analysis — For immigrant indicator				Sample size	
	(1)	(2)	(3)	(4)	(5)	(6)	(7)	(8)	Full	Boston only
Business operations	0.260***	0.269***	0.296***	0.238***	0.123***	0.129***	0.143***	0.123***	994	706
	(0.081)	(0.081)	(0.079)	(0.084)	(0.038)	(0.038)	(0.037)	(0.040)		
Venture funding	0.176**	0.175**	0.194***	0.118	0.117***	0.120***	0.125***	0.094**	987	702
	(0.070)	(0.071)	(0.070)	(0.072)	(0.039)	(0.039)	(0.039)	(0.041)		
Technology	0.201***	0.178**	0.188**	0.160**	0.113***	0.110***	0.116***	0.113***	994	706
	(0.076)	(0.077)	(0.077)	(0.081)	(0.036)	(0.036)	(0.036)	(0.039)		
Suppliers	0.185***	0.184**	0.190***	0.160**	0.102**	0.099**	0.104**	0.082*	984	699
	(0.070)	(0.073)	(0.072)	(0.073)	(0.041)	(0.041)	(0.041)	(0.044)		
People to recruit	0.214***	0.233***	0.250***	0.195***	0.120***	0.125***	0.131***	0.098**	992	704
	(0.070)	(0.071)	(0.070)	(0.073)	(0.039)	(0.039)	(0.039)	(0.042)		
Customers	0.282***	0.285***	0.312***	0.235***	0.139***	0.140***	0.147***	0.108**	988	700
	(0.077)	(0.078)	(0.077)	(0.081)	(0.040)	(0.040)	(0.040)	(0.043)		
Person-level covariates	x				x					
Building fixed effects	x	x			x	x				
Floor fixed effects		x	x			x	x			
Firm-level covariates			x	x			x	x		
Boston only				x				x		

Note: See table 7.5. Baseline responses are on a 1 to 4 scale with 1 = never, 2 = infrequently, 3 = monthly, and 4 = weekly. Binary analysis bins 0 = never vs. 1 = any other selection.

Table 7.9   Receiving advice at CIC for immigrants versus natives

Question: How often do you receive advice on the following topics from people outside of your company at CIC?	Baseline values *For immigrant indicator*				Binary analysis *For immigrant indicator*				Sample size	
	(1)	(2)	(3)	(4)	(5)	(6)	(7)	(8)	*Full*	*Boston only*
Business operations	0.252***	0.256***	0.278***	0.237***	0.095**	0.098**	0.109***	0.090**	990	701
	(0.073)	(0.074)	(0.073)	(0.077)	(0.039)	(0.039)	(0.039)	(0.043)		
Venture funding	0.257***	0.276***	0.293***	0.264***	0.133***	0.149***	0.158***	0.151***	990	701
	(0.068)	(0.069)	(0.069)	(0.070)	(0.040)	(0.040)	(0.040)	(0.043)		
Technology	0.178**	0.187*	0.212***	0.194**	0.079**	0.088**	0.101**	0.099**	988	702
	(0.077)	(0.080)	(0.080)	(0.086)	(0.039)	(0.040)	(0.041)	(0.045)		
Suppliers	0.165**	0.169**	0.185***	0.154**	0.104**	0.110***	0.120***	0.100**	989	700
	(0.067)	(0.068)	(0.068)	(0.070)	(0.041)	(0.041)	(0.041)	(0.045)		
People to recruit	0.144**	0.160**	0.173**	0.132*	0.067*	0.080*	0.086**	0.062	986	698
	(0.070)	(0.071)	(0.071)	(0.074)	(0.041)	(0.041)	(0.042)	(0.045)		
Customers	0.274***	0.281***	0.310***	0.265***	0.128***	0.126***	0.139***	0.103**	989	702
	(0.074)	(0.075)	(0.075)	(0.078)	(0.040)	(0.041)	(0.041)	(0.045)		
Person-level covariates	x				x					
Building fixed effects	x	x			x	x				
Floor fixed effects		x	x			x	x			
Firm-level covariates			x	x			x	x		
Boston only				x				x		

Note: See table 7.5. Baseline responses are on a 1 to 4 scale with 1 = never, 2 = infrequently, 3 = monthly, and 4 = weekly. Binary analysis bins 0 = never vs. 1 = any other selection.

advice on all these dimensions. Baseline responses are on a four-point scale from "never" (1) to "weekly" (4). The binary analysis bins responses other than "never" into the high category.

Tables 7.8 and 7.9 confirm that these differences are robust to controlling for the other traits of individuals, companies, and the floors on which respondents work. As the average baseline value for most of these variables is on the order of 1.8 in table 7.4, these quantified differences are often 10 percent or greater. On providing advice, the immigrant differential to natives is highest on business operations and customers and lowest on venture financing. On receiving advice, the differential is highest on venture financing and customers and lowest on suppliers and technology. But these differences are small relative to the larger context of high rates of giving and receiving advice.

We have conducted a number of robustness checks on these analyses. We condensed our regression tables by only showing Boston-specific results for the full specification with person- and firm-level covariates, and the comparability carries through on other regression variants too. Adding St. Louis to the sample tends to raise slightly the immigrant differential, indicating a modestly greater immigrant reliance in St. Louis on CIC networking than in Boston.

We introduce person- and firm-level controls via indicator variables for ranges, and we kept missing values via an unknown category to maintain consistent sample sizes across columns. Our results are robust across these design choices, which is not surprising given the raw effects evident in table 7.4 alongside the substantial coefficients observed in regression analyses.

In terms of additional covariates, we also find very similar results when including the binary response by a respondent if the network was preknown before coming to CIC. We have also run analyses where we control for the tenure of an individual at CIC. These analyses are quantitatively similar in aggregate, with effects growing or shrinking modestly on some outcomes. There is sufficient risk for overcontrolling with these variables (e.g., we do not know what fraction of a respondent's network is preknown before locating at CIC) that we have left them out of the baseline results reported here.

7.4.3   Extended Analysis

Our last set of analyses is not formally reported but qualitatively described. These analyses consider traits of CIC floors on which immigrants and natives are located to see if they interact differently with floor-level environments. The floors within a CIC facility have different feels or purposes: for example, one floor may be more populated with larger, fixed office spaces suitable for established teams, while another floor is a coworking space designed for very small teams or individual entrepreneurs. Some of these floor-level differences are intentional, while others are due to legacy layouts of buildings. Conditional on the match of a client's needs to a type of space, allocation to a specific office is otherwise based on availability and often has some randomness.

We measure six traits of each floor: inventor percentage, immigrant percentage, average age, female percentage, average firm size, and total number of firms. The measures are derived from respondent data for floors. We control for floor fixed effects, which captures the main effects of these variables, and we interact these floor-level traits with whether a respondent is an immigrant to observe whether there is heterogeneity in the immigrant differential due to various floor characteristics. We restrict this analysis to floors where 15 or more people responded to the survey. We further drop St. Louis due to some limitations on our floor information for this facility and its overall very different immigrant background.

The most important finding from these analyses are null results for interactions—that is, the immigrant differential captured in this chapter mostly operates independently of the floor environment. As important, we specifically find evidence that the differential for immigrant networking and giving and receiving advice does not depend on the immigrant being on a floor with many other immigrants. Thus while we do not observe the immigrant and native components of a respondent's network, we have reason to believe the networks are not strongly segmented in CIC. There is some evidence that the greater degree to which immigrants give and receive advice is accentuated on floors that have a high fraction of inventors, but the more important finding is that these floor-level shaping factors are second order to the main effects. We conclude that floor traits do not shape the strength of the immigrant differential with respect to networking.

7.5   Conclusion

Networking and the giving and receiving of advice are important for entrepreneurship and innovation. Our analysis of CIC finds that immigrants take more advantage of networking opportunities at CIC, especially around the exchange of advice. This effect is quite robust, holding in the raw data and tightly controlled specifications, and it does not appear to be mediated very much by floor-level traits. We are not able to assess whether this generates long-term performance advantages for immigrants, but it at least leads them to value CIC to a greater extent than natives do.

Looking forward, we hope other researchers continue to examine differences in behaviors of immigrants within entrepreneurship and innovation compared to natives. It is now well established that immigrants are a large and growing component of the US science and engineering workforce, and they have comparable overall quality on many dimensions to natives engaged in the field. But there remains much to explore about how their preferences and interactions shape the communities of which they are becoming an ever-larger share.

References

Aernoudt, R. 2004. "Incubators: Tool for Entrepreneurship?" *Small Business Economics* 23:127–35.

Ahuja, G. 2000. "Collaboration Networks, Structural Holes, and Innovation: A Longitudinal Study." *Administrative Science Quarterly* 45 (3): 425–55.

Aldrich, H. E., and P. R. Reese. 1993. "Does Networking Pay Off? A Panel Study of Entrepreneurs in the Research Triangle in Churchill, N.C." In *Frontiers of Entrepreneurship Research*, edited by S. Birley, J. Doutriaux, E. J. Gatewood, F. S. Hoy, and W. E. Wetzel, 325–39. Wellesley, MA: Babson College.

Aldrich, H. E., B. Rosen, and W. Woodward. 1987. "Impact of Social Networks on Business Foundings and Profit: A Longitudinal Study." In *Frontiers of Entrepreneurship Research*, edited by N. S. Churchill, J. Hornaday, O. J. Krasner, and K. Vespter, 154–68. Wellesley, MA: Center for Entrepreneurial Studies.

Aldrich, H. E., and R. Waldinger. 1990. "Ethnicity and Entrepreneurship." *Annual Review of Sociology* 16 (1): 111–35.

Aldrich, H. E., and C. Zimmer. 1986. "Entrepreneurship through Social Networks." In *Population Perspectives on Organizations*, edited by H. Aldrich, 13–28. Uppsala: Acta Universitatis Upsaliensis.

Aliaga-Isla, R., and A. Riap. 2013. "Systematic Review of Immigrant Entrepreneurship Literature: Previous Findings and Ways Forward." *Entrepreneurship and Regional Development* 25 (9–10): 819–44.

Åstebro, T., H. Herz, R. Nanda, and R. A. Weber. 2014. "Seeking the Roots of Entrepreneurship: Insights from Behavioral Economics." *Journal of Economic Perspectives* 28 (3): 49–70.

Balconi, M., S. Breschi, and F. Lissoni. 2004. "Networks of Inventors and the Location of Academic Research: An Exploration of Italian Data." *Research Policy* 33 (1): 127–45.

Ballester C., A. Calvó-Armengol, and Y. Zenou. 2006. "Who's Who in Networks. Wanted: The Key Player." *Econometrica* 74 (5): 1403–17.

Bell, D. A., and S. S. White. 2014. *Gender Diversity in Silicon Valley: A Comparison of Silicon Valley Public Companies and Large Public Companies*. Fenwick and West LLP.

Branstetter L., N. Gandal, and N. Kuniesky. 2017. "Network-Mediated Knowledge Spillovers: A Cross-country Comparative Analysis of Information Security Innovations." NBER Working Paper no. 23808. Cambridge, MA: National Bureau of Economic Research.

Breschi, S., and F. Lissoni. 2005. "Cross-Firm Inventors and Social Networks: Localised Knowledge Spillovers Revisited." *Annales d'Économie et de Statistique* 79/80:189–209.

Breschi, S., and F. Lissoni. 2009. "Mobility of Inventors and Networks of Collaboration: An Anatomy of Localised Knowledge Flows." *Journal of Economic Geography* 9 (4): 439–68.

Brown, A. 2017. "Despite Gains, Women Remain Underrepresented among U.S. Political and Business Leaders." Pew Research Center, March 20. http://www.pewresearch

.org/fact-tank/2017/03/20/despite-gains-women-remain-underrepresented-among
-u-s-political-and-business-leaders/.

Brown, J. D., J. S. Earle, M. J. Kim, and K.-M. Lee. 2018. "Immigrant Entrepreneurs, Job Creation, and Innovation." Census Bureau Working Paper. Washington, DC.

Bruneel, J., T. Ratinho, B. Clarysse, and A. Groen. 2012. "The Evolution of Business Incubators: Comparing Demand and Supply of Business Incubation Services across Difference Incubator Generations." *Technovation* 32:110–21.

Calvó-Armengol, A., and M. O. Jackson. 2004. "The Effects of Social Networks on Employment and Inequality." *American Economic Review* 94 (3): 426–54.

Calvó-Armengol, A., E. Patacchini, and Y. Zenou. 2009. "Peer Effects and Social Networks in Education." *Review of Economic Studies* 76 (4): 1239–67.

Carlino, G., and W. R. Kerr. 2015. "Agglomeration and Innovation." In *Handbook of Regional and Urban Economics*, vol. 5, edited by G. Duranton, J. V. Henderson, and W. C. Strange, 349–404. Amsterdam: Elsevier.

Chand, M., and M. Ghorbani. 2011. "National Culture, Networks and Ethnic Entrepreneurship: A Comparison of the Indian and Chinese Immigrants in the US." *International Business Review* 20 (6): 593–606.

Chatterji, A., E. L. Glaeser, and W. R. Kerr. 2014. "Clusters of Entrepreneurship and Innovation." In *Innovation Policy and the Economy*, vol. 14, edited by J. Lerner and S. Stern, 129–66. Chicago: University of Chicago Press.

Cisi, M., F. Devicienti, A. Manello, and D. Vannoni. 2016. "Network Agreements and Firms' Economic Performance: New Empirical Evidence from Italian SMEs." Working paper 039. Department of Economics and Statistics, University of Torino.

Colombo, M. G., and M. Delmastro. 2002. "How Effective are Technology Incubators? Evidence from Italy." *Research Policy* 31:1103–22.

Davidson, P., and B. Honig. 2003. "The Role of Social and Human Capital among Nascent Entrepreneurs." *Journal of Business Venturing* 18 (3): 301–31.

Desilver, D. 2018. "A Record Number of Women Will Be Serving in the New Congress." Pew Research. December 18. http://www.pewresearch.org/fact-tank/2018/12/18/record-number-women-in-congress/.

Dyer, J. H., and H. Singh. 1998. "The Relational View: Cooperative Strategy and Sources of Interorganizational Competitive Advantage." *Academy of Management Review* 23 (4): 660–79.

Elfring, T., and W. Hulsink. 2003. "Networks in Entrepreneurship: The Case of High-Technology Firms." *Small Business Economics* 21:409–22.

Elfring, T., and W. Hulsink. 2007. "Networking by Entrepreneurs: Patterns of Tie-Formation in Emerging Organizations." *Organization Studies* 28:1849–66.

Fershtman, C., and N. Gandal. 2011. "Direct and Indirect Knowledge Spillovers: The 'Social Network' of Open-Source Projects." *RAND Journal of Economics* 42 (1): 70–91.

Gandal, N., and U. Stettner. 2016. "Network Dynamics and Knowledge Transfer in Virtual Organizations." *International Journal of Industrial Organization* 48:270–90.

Gandini, A. 2015. "The Rise of Coworking Spaces: A Literature Review." *ephemera* 15 (1): 193–205.

Glaeser, E. L., and W. R. Kerr. 2009. "Local Industrial Conditions and Entrepreneurship: How Much of the Spatial Distribution Can We Explain?" *Journal of Economics and Management Strategy* 18 (3): 623–63.

Gompers, P. A., K. Huang, and S. Q. Wang. 2017. "Homophily in Entrepreneurial Team Formation." Harvard Business School Working Paper no. 17-104.

Goyal, S., M. J. Van Der Leij, and J. L. Moraga-Gonzalez. 2006. "Economics: An Emerging Small World." *Journal of Political Economy* 114 (2): 403–12.

Greve, A., and J. W. Salaff. 2003. "Social Networks and Entrepreneurship." *Entrepreneurship: Theory and Practice* 28 (1): 1–22.

Grimaldi, R., and A. Grandi. 2005. "Business Incubators and New Venture Creation: An Assessment of Incubating Models." *Technovation* 25:111–21.

Gulati, R., and M. Higgins. 2003. "Which Ties Matter When? The Contingent Effects of Interorganizational Partnerships on IPO Success." *Strategic Management Journal* 24 (2): 127–44.

Guzman, J., and S. Stern. 2016. "The State of American Entrepreneurship? New Estimates of the Quantity and Quality of Entrepreneurship for 15 US States, 1988–2014." NBER Working Paper no. 22095. Cambridge, MA: National Bureau of Economic Research.

Guzman, J., and S. Stern. 2017. "Nowcasting and Placecasting Entrepreneurial Quality and Performance." In *Measuring Entrepreneurial Businesses: Current Knowledge and Challenges*, Studies in Income and Wealth, vol. 75, edited by J. Haltiwanger, E. Hurst, J. Miranda, and A. Schoar, 63–109. Chicago: University of Chicago Press.

Hegde, D., and J. Tumlinson. 2014. "Does Social Proximity Enhance Business Relationships? Theory and Evidence from Ethnicity's Role in US Venture Capital." *Management Science* 60 (9): 2355–80.

Hoang, H., and B. Antoncic. 2003. "Network-Based Research in Entrepreneurship: A Critical Review." *Journal of Business Venturing* 18 (2): 165–87.

Hunt, J. 2011. "Which Immigrants Are Most Innovative and Entrepreneurial? Distinctions by Entry Visa." *Journal of Labor Economics* 29 (3): 417–57.

Hunt, J., and M. Gauthier-Loiselle. 2010. "How Much Does Immigration Boost Innovation?" *American Economic Journal: Macroeconomics* 2 (2): 31–56.

Jack, S. 2010. "Approaches to Studying Networks: Implications and Outcomes." *Journal of Business Venturing* 25:120–37.

Jack, S., S. Moult, A. R. Anderson, and S. Dodd. 2010. "An Entrepreneurial Network Evolving: Patterns of Change." *International Small Business Journal: Researching Entrepreneurship* 28 (4): 315–37.

Jackson, M., and L. Yariv. 2007. "Diffusion of Behavior and Equilibrium Properties in Network Games." *American Economic Review* 97 (2): 92–98.

Kalnins, A., and W. Chung. 2006. "Social Capital, Geography, and Survival: Gujarati Immigrant Entrepreneurs in the U.S. Lodging Industry." *Management Science* 52 (2): 233–47.

Karlan, D., M. Mobius, T. Rosenblat, and A. Szeidl. 2009. "Trust and Social Collateral." *Quarterly Journal of Economics* 124 (3): 1307–61.

Katz, B., J. S. Vey, and J. Wagner. 2015. "One Year After: Observations on the Rise of Innovation Districts." Report, Metropolitan Policy Program, Brookings Institute.

Katz, B., and J. Wagner. 2014. "The Rise of Innovation Districts: A New Geography of Innovation in America." Report, Metropolitan Policy Program, Brookings Institute.

Kerr, S. P., and W. R. Kerr. 2017. "Immigrant Entrepreneurship." In *Measuring Entrepreneurial Businesses: Current Knowledge and Challenges*, Studies in Income and Wealth, vol. 75, edited by J. Haltiwanger, E. Hurst, J. Miranda, and A. Schoar, 187–249. Chicago: University of Chicago Press.

Kerr, S. P., and W. R. Kerr. 2018. "Immigrant Entrepreneurship in America: Evidence from the Survey of Business Owners 2007 and 2012." NBER Working Paper no. 24494. Cambridge, MA: National Bureau of Economic Research.

Kerr, S. P., W. R. Kerr, and M. Dalton. 2019. "Risk Attitudes and Personality Traits of Entrepreneurs and Venture Team Members." *Proceedings of the National Academy of Sciences of the United States of America* 116 (36): 17712–16.

Kerr, S. P., W. R. Kerr, and T. Xu. 2018. "Personality Traits of Entrepreneurs: A Review of Recent Literature." *Foundation and Trends in Entrepreneurship* 14 (3): 279–356.

Kerr, W. R. 2018. *The Gift of Global Talent: How Migration Shapes Business, Economy & Society*. Palo Alto, CA: Stanford University Press.

Kerr, W. R., S. Kerr, and A. Brownell. 2017a. "CIC: Catalyzing Entrepreneurial Ecosystems (A)." HBS No. N-817-126. Cambridge, MA: Harvard Business School.

Kerr, W. R., S. Kerr, and A. Brownell. 2017b. "CIC: Catalyzing Entrepreneurial Ecosystems (B)." HBS No. N-817-127. Cambridge, MA: Harvard Business School.

Kerr, W. R., and S. D. Kominers. 2015. "Agglomerative Forces and Cluster Shapes." *Review of Economics and Statistics* 97 (4): 877–99.

Kerr, W. R., and W. F. Lincoln. 2010. "The Supply Side of Innovation: H-1B Visa Reforms and U.S. Ethnic Invention." *Journal of Labor Economics* 28 (3): 473–508.

Kerr, W. R., and M. Mandorff. 2015. "Social Networks, Ethnicity, and Entrepreneurship." NBER Working Paper no. 21597. Cambridge, MA: National Bureau of Economic Research.

Kim, P. H., and H. E. Aldrich. 2005. "Social Capital and Entrepreneurship." *Foundations and Trends in Entrepreneurship* 1 (2): 55–104.

Kloosterman, R., J. van der Leun, and J. Rath. 1998. "Across the Border: Immigrants' Economic Opportunities, Social Capital and Informal Business Activities." *Journal of Ethnic and Migration Studies* 24 (2): 249–68.

Kremel, A. 2016. "Fulfilling the Need of Business Advisory Services among Swedish Immigrant Entrepreneurs." *Journal of Entrepreneurship and Public Policy* 5 (3): 343–64.

Light, I., P. Bhachu, and S. Karageorgis. 1989. "Migration Networks and Immigrant Entrepreneurship." In *Immigration and Entrepreneurship: Culture, Capital, and Ethnic Networks*, edited by I. Hubert and P. Bhachu, 25–50. New Brunswick, NJ: Transaction.

Lin, F.-J., and Y.-H. Lin. 2016. "The Effect of Network Relationship on the Performance of SMEs." *Journal of Business Research* 69 (5): 1780–84.

Mazzola, E., G. Perrone, and D. S. Kamuriwo. 2016. "Network Positions and the Probability of Being Acquired: An Empirical Analysis in the Biopharmaceutical Industry." *British Journal of Management* 27 (3): 516–33.

McDonald, M. L., P. Khanna, and J. D. Westphal. 2017. "Getting Them to Think Outside the Circle: Corporate Governance, CEOs' External Advice Networks, and Firm Performance." *Academy of Management Journal* 51 (3): 452–75.

McPherson, M., L. Smith-Lovin, and J. M. Cook. 2001. "Birds of a Feather: Homophily in Social Networks." *Annual Review of Sociology* 27 (1): 415–44.

Nanda, R., and T. Khanna. 2014. "Diasporas and Domestic Entrepreneurs: Evidence from the Indian Software Industry." *Journal of Economics and Management Strategy* 19 (4): 991–1012.

Peri, G., K. Shih, and C. Sparber. 2015. "STEM Workers, H-1B Visas and Productivity in US Cities." *Journal of Labor Economics* 33 (3): S225–S255.

Powell, W., K. Koput, and L. Smith-Doerr. 1996. "Interorganizational Collaboration and the Locus of Innovation: Networks in Learning in Biotechnology." *Administrative Science Quarterly* 41 (1): 116–45.

Raijman, R., and M. Tienda. 2000. "Immigrant Pathways to Business Ownership: A Comparative Ethnic Perspective." *International Migration Review* 34:682–706.

Ruef, M., H. E. Aldrich, and N. Carter. 2003. "The Structure of Founding Teams:

Homophily, Strong Ties, and Isolation among U.S. Entrepreneurs." *American Sociological Review* 68 (2): 195–222.

Salaff, J. W., A. Greve, W. Siu-Lun, and L. X. L. Ping. 2003. "Ethnic Entrepreneurship, Social Networks, and the Enclave." In *Approaching Transnationalisms*, edited by B. S. A. Yeoh, M. W. Charney, and T. C. Kiong, 61–82. Boston, MA: Springer.

Saxenian, A. 2000. "Silicon Valley's New Immigrant Entrepreneurs." San Francisco: Public Policy Institute of California.

Saxenian, A. 2002. "Silicon Valley's New Immigrant High-Growth Entrepreneurs." *Economic Development Quarterly* 16 (1): 20–31.

Schott, T., and K. Jensen. 2016. "Firms' Innovation Benefiting from Networking and Institutional Support: A Global Analysis of National and Firm Effects." *Research Policy* 45 (6): 1233–46.

Sharir, M., and M. Lerner. 2006. "Gauging the Success of Social Ventures Initiated by Individual Social Entrepreneurs." *Journal of World Business* 41 (1): 6–20.

Singer, A. 2013. "Contemporary Immigrant Gateways in Historical Perspective." *Daedalus, the Journal of the American Academy of Arts and Sciences* 142 (3): 76–91.

Sorenson, O. 2005. "Social Networks and Industrial Geography." In *Entrepreneurships, the New Economy and Public Policy*, edited by U. Cantner, E. Dinopoulos, and R. F. Lanzillotti, 55–69. Berlin: Springer.

Uzzi, B. 1999. "Embeddedness in the Making of Financial Capital: How Social Relations and Networks Benefit Firms Seeking Financing." *American Sociological Review* 64 (4): 481–505.

Vanhaverbeke, W., V. Gilsing, B. Beerkens, and G. Duysters. 2009. "The Role of Alliance Network Redundancy in the Creation of Core and Non-core Technologies: A Local Action Approach." *Journal of Management Studies* 46 (2): 215–44.

Weber, C., and J. Kratzer. 2013. "Social Entrepreneurship, Social Networks and Social Value Creation: A Quantitative Analysis among Social Entrepreneurs." *International Journal of Entrepreneurial Venturing* 5 (3): 217–39.

Wilson, K., and W. A. Martin. 1982. "Ethnic Enclaves: A Comparison of the Cuban and Black Economies in Miami." *American Journal of Sociology* 88:135–60.

Witt, P. 2007. "Entrepreneurs' Networks and the Success of Start-Ups." *Entrepreneurship and Regional Development* 16 (5): 391–412.

Zaheer, A., and G. Bell. 2005. "Benefiting from Network Position: Firm Capabilities, Structural Holes, and Performance." *Strategic Management Journal* 26 (9): 809–25.

Zarya, V. 2016. "Female Fortune 500 CEOs Are Poised to Break This Record in 2017." *Fortune*, December 22. http://fortune.com/2016/12/22/female-fortune-500-ceos-2017.

Are Foreign STEM PhDs More Entrepreneurial?
Entrepreneurial Characteristics, Preferences, and Employment Outcomes of Native and Foreign Science and Engineering PhD Students

Michael Roach, Henry Sauermann, and John Skrentny

8.1 Introduction

A large body of literature shows that immigrant and foreign workers are more likely than US natives to become entrepreneurs (Borjas 1986; Fairlie 2008; Hunt 2011; Fairlie and Lofstrom 2015; Kahn, La Mattina, and Mac-Garvie 2017). Recent studies have also shown that immigrants play key roles as founders and early employees in technology firms (Hart and Acs 2011) and in entrepreneurial clusters such as Silicon Valley (Saxenian 1994). Although this pattern is well documented, the underlying reasons why immigrants are more entrepreneurial remain an important area of investigation. Some researchers argue that labor market factors such as discrimination (Oreopoulos 2011) or language requirements (Hunt 2011) constrain opportunities for career advancement in existing firms, making entrepreneurship more attractive than wage employment. Moreover, the availability of immi-

Michael Roach is the J. Thomas and Nancy W. Clark Assistant Professor of Entrepreneurship at Cornell University.

Henry Sauermann is associate professor of strategy and holder of the POK Pühringer PS Chair in Entrepreneurship at ESMT Berlin (European School of Management and Technology).

John Skrentny is professor of sociology at the University of California, San Diego.

We thank the organizers of the NBER conference on the Role of Immigrants and Foreign Students in Science, Innovation and Entrepreneurship as well as Ben Rissing and Stephan Yale-Loehr for helpful comments. We are indebted to Megan MacGarvie and Shulamit Kahn for their guidance on the development of this chapter. Roach and Sauermann appreciate support from the National Science Foundation (SciSIP Award 1262270) and the Ewing Marion Kauffman Foundation Junior Faculty Fellowship. Any opinions, findings, conclusions, and recommendations are those of the authors and do not reflect the view of the funding agencies. For acknowledgments, sources of research support, and disclosure of the authors' material financial relationships, if any, please see https://www.nber.org/chapters/c14101.ack.

grant networks (Saxenian 2002) or coethnic financing (Bengtsson and Hsu 2015) may encourage or facilitate immigrants' moves to entrepreneurship. Others contend that immigrants differ from natives in individual character-istics and preferences such as risk tolerance (Blume-Kohout 2016) or that they may self-select into science, technology, engineering, and mathematics (STEM) fields that provide greater exposure to entrepreneurial opportuni-ties (Hunt 2011).

Although considerable research effort has been directed toward under-standing founding activity among immigrants, little attention has been paid to foreign workers who join start-ups as employees rather than as founders. Such entrepreneurial employees are particularly important in technology-intensive ventures (Baron, Hannan, and Burton 2001; Roach and Sauer-mann 2015; Kim 2018), where foreign PhDs constitute a significant and par-ticularly productive part of the science and engineering workforce (Stephan and Levin 2007; National Science Board 2014). As such, it is important to understand differences between native and foreign PhD students with respect to individual attributes such as risk preferences or entrepreneurial aspirations, as well as whether such individual characteristics might explain differences between native and foreign PhDs in their likelihood to take employment in technology-based start-ups.

We provide initial comparative evidence on entrepreneurial preferences and outcomes of native and foreign science and engineering doctorates using survey data from more than 5,600 STEM PhD students at 39 US research universities. These students were observed during graduate educa-tion and then again after transition into their first-time employment, includ-ing becoming founders. As such, the data allow us to compare foreign and native PhD students or start-up employees with respect to their ex-ante entrepreneurial career preferences as well as their ex-post employment.

We report three key findings. First, foreign PhD students differ from their native peers with respect to characteristics and preferences typically associ-ated with entrepreneurship. Specifically, foreign PhD students are more risk tolerant, have greater preferences for autonomy, and are more interested in commercialization activities than are native PhD students. Second, foreign PhD students are more likely than natives to have intentions of becom-ing founders or joining a start-up as employees, suggesting that they might become important entrepreneurial actors and human capital for technology start-ups. Third, however, foreign PhDs are less likely than native PhDs to either become founders or join start-ups as employees after graduation and instead are more likely to work in established firms. Given the stronger entrepreneurial interests of foreign PhDs prior to entering the private sector, these differences in employment outcomes are unlikely to reflect differences in career preferences and instead point to possible labor market factors that may constrain entrepreneurial activity and start-up employment.

8.2 Data

Our empirical analysis utilizes the Science and Engineering PhD Panel Survey (SEPPS), a national longitudinal survey of 5,669 science and engineering PhD students from 39 top-tier US research universities. To obtain the initial sample, we identified US research universities with doctoral programs in science and engineering fields by consulting the National Science Foundation's reports on earned doctorates (National Science Foundation 2009). Our selection of universities was based primarily on program size while also ensuring variation in private/public status and geographic region. The 39 universities in our sample produced roughly 40 percent of the graduating PhDs in science and engineering fields in 2009.

We collected roughly 30,000 email addresses from department websites and invited individuals to participate in the online survey using a four-contact strategy (one invitation, three reminders). For departments that did not list students' email addresses, we contacted department administrators to request that they forward a survey link to their graduate students. Overall, 88 percent of our responses were obtained directly from respondents, and 12 percent were obtained through administrators. The initial contact for all respondents occurred over a two-week period in February 2010, and all responses were collected within an eight-week window. Adjusting for 6.3 percent undeliverable emails, the direct survey approach achieved an adjusted response rate of 30 percent.[1] Respondents were surveyed again in 2013 and 2016 with an average response rate of 73 percent of the initial 2010 sample. Given our interest in career preferences prior to entering the workforce, we use the most recent survey prior to graduation.

We distinguish between foreign and native PhD students through a survey question that asked whether the respondent was a US citizen during graduate school. PhD students who were US citizens were classified as *native*, while non-US citizens were classified as *foreign*. Approximately 34.3 percent of our sample are foreign PhD students. To examine for potential response bias, we benchmarked our sample to the NSF Survey of Earned Doctorates (SED), where the share of foreign-born science and engineering PhDs graduating in 2012 was 40.2 percent (National Science Foundation 2017).[2] Whereas the SED includes all doctorate-granting universities, our sample is drawn from top-tier R1 universities, where the share of foreign-born PhDs may differ. Given that PhD students at top research universities likely differ in their preferences, ability, and employment opportunities, our results may

1. See Sauermann and Roach (2013) for details on the survey methodology, sample, and response rate.
2. Authors' calculations based on data table 17 for science and engineering fields and graduation years corresponding to the survey used in this study: https://ncses.nsf.gov/pubs/nsf19301/assets/data/tables/sed17-sr-tab017.xlsx.

not be generalizable to all PhD students from US universities. Among the foreign PhD students in our sample, approximately 24.0 percent are from China and 15.7 percent are from India.[3] The share of foreign PhD students is highest in computer science (54.1 percent) and engineering (43.0 percent) and lowest in the life sciences (23.4 percent). Our statistical analyses control for 18 detailed fields of study to account for heterogeneity in the nature of research, norms regarding career paths, and other unobserved factors.

8.3   Results

Building on prior work on predictors of entrepreneurship, we first examine differences between foreign and native PhD students with respect to individual characteristics such as ability and risk tolerance in section 8.3.1. We then study differences in founder intentions and preferences for joining start-up employment in section 8.3.2. In section 8.3.3, we examine foreign PhD students' intentions to remain in the US after graduation. We then compare foreign and native PhDs with respect to their postgraduation outcomes as founders, start-up employees, or established firm employees and explore the extent to which these outcomes may be explained by ex-ante career preferences in section 8.3.4.

8.3.1   Comparing Entrepreneurial Characteristics of Native and Foreign PhD Students

The entrepreneurship literature has examined a range of individual characteristics as predictors of entrepreneurial behaviors and founder transitions (Shane, Locke, and Collins 2003; Astebro, Chen, and Thompson 2011; Kerr, Kerr, and Xu 2017). Recent work suggests that these characteristics may also explain career preferences to join start-ups as an employee (Roach and Sauermann 2015). Our survey allows us to compare foreign and native PhD students with respect to a number of characteristics commonly associated with entrepreneurship, including preferences for specific job attributes such as autonomy and commercialization and individual characteristics such as risk tolerance and ability. Table 8.1 reports mean values for these variables for native and foreign PhD students.

Risk Tolerance. We obtain a proxy for risk tolerance by using a lottery-type question (Charness, Gneezy, and Imas 2013). More specifically, we asked respondents to choose between one of two gambles on a 10-point scale that ranged from "strongly prefer a 100% chance to win $1,000" to "strongly prefer a 50% chance to win $2,000." Higher values reflect a greater willing-

---

3. Foreign PhD students were asked for their nationality in the survey. Approximately 4 percent of respondents did not report their citizenship or nationality. We used LinkedIn data on the country of their undergraduate degree as an indicator of their nationality where possible to fill in missing data.

ness to choose a riskier outcome with a higher potential payoff, which we interpret as a greater tolerance for risk.

Importance of Autonomy and Income. We measure respondents' preferences for autonomy and financial income by asking them to rate the importance of these job attributes, among other job attributes, on a five-point scale from "not at all important" to "extremely important." To measure autonomy, we asked about the importance of "freedom to choose research projects," and to measure income, we asked about the importance of "financial pay (e.g., salary, bonuses)."

Interest in Work Activities. We measure individuals' interest in different work activities on a five-point scale that ranged from "extremely uninteresting" to "extremely interesting." The set of activities included "commercializing research results into products and services" (interest in commercialization), "management or administration" (interest in management), "research that contributes fundamental insights or theories (basic research)" (interest in basic research), and "research that creates knowledge to solve practical problems (applied research)" (interest in applied research).

Ability. We employ two different measures to proxy for ability. First, we use the academic reputation of a PhD student's university department based on the National Research Council's rankings (National Research Council 2010).[4] Although these are department-level research rankings rather than individual-level measures of ability, department quality is observable to prospective employers and is likely an important factor in hiring decisions. Moreover, it is likely that highly ranked departments are more selective in admitting and training PhD students such that department quality is likely correlated with individual ability as well. Second, we obtain a subjective individual-level measure of ability by asking respondents to rate their own (research) ability relative to their peers using a slider scale that ranged from 1 to 10. Although this measure likely captures both true ability and overconfidence (Camerer and Lovallo 1999), we expect that individuals' perceptions of their own ability influence their job search behaviors, their confidence during job interviews, and their own expectations of success, especially in entrepreneurship (Roach and Sauermann 2015; Lazear 2016).

Table 8.1 reports summary statistics for these variables for native PhD students, all foreign PhD students combined, and separately for foreign PhD students from China, India, and Western countries (Western Europe, Canada, and Australia). The table also reports potentially important control variables taken from the survey, including gender and marital status. In addition, to control for social factors that may shape entrepreneurial prefer-

---

4. NRC rankings are not available for some departments in our sample. In such cases, we used the university average for the broader field of study. For example, if the ranking of the department of electrical engineering for a given university was unavailable, we used the average of all engineering departments at the same university.

Table 8.1 Summary statistics comparing native and foreign PhD preferences and characteristics

Variable	Native (n = 3,880)		All foreign (n = 1,792)		China (n = 447)		India (n = 295)		Western (n = 175)	
	Mean	Std. dev.	Mean	Std. dev.	Mean	Std. dev.	Mean	Std. dev.	Mean	Std. dev.
Risk tolerance	1.88	2.29	2.54	3.00	2.92	3.29	2.68	3.21	1.85	2.18
Importance of autonomy	3.94	0.85	4.06	0.75	3.88	0.73	4.21	0.63	4.07	0.83
Importance of income	3.94	0.74	4.08	0.65	4.09	0.60	4.09	0.68	3.89	0.70
Interest in basic research	3.93	0.98	3.84	0.99	3.43	1.06	4.06	0.85	4.05	0.93
Interest in applied research	4.34	0.68	4.35	0.65	4.25	0.61	4.45	0.61	4.37	0.75
Interest in commercialization	3.27	1.11	3.69	1.02	3.91	0.84	3.78	1.06	3.30	1.17
Interest in management	2.83	1.18	3.03	1.11	3.41	0.95	2.91	1.16	2.62	1.20
Self-assessed ability	6.17	1.66	6.66	1.64	6.79	1.59	6.80	1.55	6.40	1.66
Lab academic norms	4.23	0.77	4.05	0.77	4.05	0.71	4.10	0.77	4.11	0.82
Lab entrepreneurial norms	3.23	0.72	3.40	0.69	3.51	0.68	3.47	0.70	3.23	0.72
Founder role model	0.10	0.30	0.13	0.33	0.12	0.33	0.11	0.31	0.12	0.33
Male	0.58	0.49	0.70	0.46	0.71	0.45	0.75	0.43	0.71	0.46
Married	0.51	0.50	0.55	0.50	0.51	0.50	0.63	0.48	0.55	0.50

Table 8.2a   **Differences in preferences and characteristics between foreign and native PhD students**

	All foreign (n = 1,792)		China (n = 447)		India (n = 295)		Western (n = 175)	
Risk tolerance	0.59***	(0.08)	1.02***	(0.14)	0.75***	(0.20)	−0.04	(0.14)
Importance of autonomy	0.13***	(0.02)	−0.04	(0.05)	0.27***	(0.03)	0.12	(0.08)
Importance of income	0.13***	(0.02)	0.14***	(0.03)	0.14**	(0.05)	−0.05	(0.06)
Interest in basic research	−0.03	(0.03)	−0.42***	(0.05)	0.27***	(0.04)	0.11	(0.08)
Interest in applied research	−0.03*	(0.02)	−0.13***	(0.03)	0.02	(0.03)	0.03	(0.06)
Interest in commercialization	0.33***	(0.04)	0.55***	(0.05)	0.31***	(0.08)	0.06	(0.09)
Interest in management	0.21***	(0.04)	0.58***	(0.05)	0.04	(0.09)	−0.14	(0.08)
National Research Council ranking of university dept.	−0.06	(0.03)	−0.13**	(0.04)	−0.09	(0.05)	0.02	(0.04)
Self-assessed ability	0.54***	(0.05)	0.68***	(0.06)	0.68***	(0.07)	0.30*	(0.12)

Note: OLS coefficients regressing preferences and characteristics onto foreign nationality controlling for degree field and university fixed effects (n = 5,669). Robust standard errors clustered on university reported in parentheses; *** $p < 0.001$, ** $p < 0.01$, * $p < 0.05$.

ences during graduate school, we include founder role models, measured as a binary variable according to whether or not the PhD advisor had founded a start-up, and lab norms that encourage working in start-ups, measured on a five-point scale that ranged from "strongly discouraged" to "strongly encouraged" (Roach and Sauermann 2015; Roach 2017).

To account for potential systematic differences across degree fields and universities, we estimate differences in the above individual characteristics using OLS to regress individual preferences and characteristics onto a foreign PhD student categorical variable (foreign is 1, native is 0) while controlling for degree field and university fixed effects. Tables 8.2a and 8.2b show the key coefficients. The first set of results in table 8.2a shows significant differences between foreign and native PhD students even after controlling for detailed degree field (17 science and engineering fields) and university fixed effects (39 universities), while the next three sets of regressions distinguish different groups of foreign PhD students (e.g., Chinese, Indian, Western), with native PhD students as the omitted category. Table 8.2b shows differences between foreign and native PhDs students by major degree field controlling for detailed degree field and university fixed effects. Standard errors are clustered by university.

Focusing first on the results comparing all foreign PhD students to natives, we find that the risk tolerance of foreign PhD students is significantly higher than that of natives (0.59 points higher than the native PhD mean of 1.88). Foreign PhD students also report greater importance of autonomy and income, as well as a higher interest in commercialization activities. We also find that foreign PhD students have a higher self-assessed ability. More detailed regressions that break out certain nationalities show that PhD students from Western countries do not differ much from native

Table 8.2b   Differences in preferences and characteristics between foreign and native PhD students by degree field

	Life sciences (n = 1,979)		Chemistry (n = 644)		Physics (n = 846)		Engineering (n = 1,612)		Comp. sci. (n = 645)	
Risk tolerance	0.63***	(0.14)	0.79**	(0.23)	0.64**	(0.19)	0.52**	(0.18)	0.32	(0.22)
Importance of autonomy	0.15**	(0.04)	0.16*	(0.07)	0.15*	(0.07)	0.11*	(0.05)	-0.01	(0.06)
Importance of income	0.12**	(0.04)	0.14	(0.08)	0.09	(0.05)	0.12***	(0.03)	0.23**	(0.07)
Interest in basic research	-0.13	(0.07)	-0.06	(0.12)	0.15*	(0.07)	0.08	(0.06)	-0.20**	(0.06)
Interest in applied research	0.01	(0.04)	0.02	(0.05)	-0.02	(0.06)	-0.09**	(0.03)	-0.03	(0.06)
Interest in commercialization	0.49***	(0.07)	0.48***	(0.11)	0.31***	(0.09)	0.14**	(0.05)	0.35***	(0.08)
Interest in management	0.14*	(0.07)	0.41**	(0.15)	0.27***	(0.07)	0.12	(0.06)	0.34**	(0.11)
National Research Council ranking of university dept.	-0.08	(0.05)	0.04	(0.07)	-0.08	(0.06)	-0.14*	(0.06)	-0.04	(0.02)
Self-assessed ability	0.44***	(0.08)	0.72***	(0.14)	0.66***	(0.13)	0.47***	(0.10)	0.49***	(0.11)

Note: OLS coefficients regressing preferences and characteristics onto PhD student nationality (native or foreign) by degree field controlling for degree field and university fixed effects (n = 5,669). Robust standard errors clustered on university reported in parentheses; *** $p < 0.001$, ** $p < 0.01$, * $p < 0.05$.

PhD students, while large differences emerge between native and PhD students from China and India.

Table 8.2b provides additional detail by showing differences between foreign and native PhD students for the broad fields of the life sciences, chemistry, physics, engineering, and computer sciences. Although coefficients vary in magnitude, the overall patterns are consistent across fields. Taken together, we find significant differences between native and foreign PhD students with respect to a number of individual characteristics, including factors commonly associated with entrepreneurship, most notably tolerance for risk, interest in commercialization, and self-assessed ability. Our analyses also suggest the need to go beyond aggregate considerations to distinguish foreign individuals coming from different cultural backgrounds.

8.3.2   Entrepreneurial Career Preferences during Graduate School

To examine how native and foreign PhD students differ in their entrepreneurial career preferences, we asked respondents while in graduate school about the attractiveness of different career paths after graduation as well as their own expectations of becoming founders in the US. To measure founder intentions, we asked, "How likely are you to start your own company?" on a five-point Likert scale ranging from "Definitely will not" (1) to "Definitely will" (5). We code *founder intentions* as 1 for respondents who reported that they "definitely will" (5) start their own company and 0 otherwise. To measure preferences for joining a start-up as an employee, we asked respondents, "Putting job availability aside, how attractive or unattractive do you personally find each of the following careers?," where careers included "start-up job with an emphasis on research or development" and "established firm job with an emphasis on research or development." Respondents rated each career independently using a five-point scale ranging from "extremely unattractive" (1) to "neither attractive nor unattractive" (3) to "extremely attractive" (5). We code *joiner preferences* as 1 for respondents who reported that a start-up job was "attractive" (4) or "extremely attractive" (5) but did not express a founder intention and 0 otherwise. We note that this measure captures joiner preferences in an absolute sense rather than relative to other careers. As such, a joiner preference does not necessarily imply that other careers were rated as less attractive, nor that joining a start-up was respondents' most preferred career (see Roach and Sauermann 2018). Rather, this measure captures individuals with a predisposition toward working in a start-up.

Table 8.3a compares shares of PhD students with founder intentions and joiner preferences among foreign and native PhD students. Overall, a higher share of foreign PhD students reports entrepreneurial preferences relative to native PhD students. Approximately 21 percent of foreign PhD students express founder intentions during graduate school compared to about 10 percent of native PhD students. Similarly, 49 percent of foreign

Table 8.3a   **Share of PhD students with entrepreneurial career preferences by nationality**

	Native (n = 3,880)	All foreign (n = 1,792)	China (n = 447)	India (n = 295)	Western (n = 175)
Founder interest	10.3%	20.7%	24.1%	25.4%	13.1%
Joiner interest	41.7%	49.1%	50.6%	50.8%	48.3%
Total entrepreneurial interests	52.0%	69.7%	74.7%	76.2%	61.4%

Table 8.3b   **Share of PhD students with entrepreneurial career preferences by degree field**

	Life sciences (n = 1,979)		Chemistry (n = 644)		Physics (n = 846)		Engineering (n = 1,612)		Comp. sci. (n = 645)	
	Native	Foreign	Native	Foreign	Native	Foreign	Native	Foreign	Native	Foreign
Founder interest	6.6%	13.7%	6.7%	19.2%	7.4%	9.8%	16.4%	26.1%	20.2%	27.9%
Joiner interest	38.2%	50.0%	46.0%	56.9%	39.8%	55.8%	46.6%	46.5%	43.4%	45.1%
Total entrepreneur-ial interests	44.8%	63.7%	52.7%	76.1%	47.1%	65.6%	63.0%	72.7%	63.6%	73.0%

PhD students express a preference for joining a start-up as an employee compared to approximately 42 percent of native PhD students. When analyzing nationalities separately, we see that roughly one-quarter of Chinese and Indian PhD students have founder intentions and roughly half have joiner preferences. A slightly higher share of foreign PhD students from Western countries have entrepreneurial interests compared to natives, but Western PhD students are still less entrepreneurial than Chinese and Indian PhD students with respect to their founder intentions. Comparisons by field in table 8.3b show that significantly higher founder intentions of foreign students hold across all fields with the exception of physics, while stronger joiner intentions are observed in life sciences, chemistry, and physics but not engineering or computer science.

We again estimate a series of regression analyses to account for systematic differences across fields and universities. The dependent variable is a categorical measure indicating whether an individual has a founder interest, a joiner preference, or a preference to work either in an established firm or in academia and not in entrepreneurship.[5] Table 8.4 reports multinomial logistic regression results with established firm career preference (and no entrepreneurial preference) as the reference category for the dependent variable (relative risk ratios reported; values less than 1 indicate a negative relationship).

Model 1 reports the baseline results controlling for demographic charac-

5. For individuals who have no founder interest and have no preference for joining a startup, we compared the ratings of attractiveness of working in an established firm or in a faculty position to assign them to the respective categories.

Table 8.4 Founder intentions and joiner career preferences during graduate school

Method												
						Multinomial logit						
Dependent variable / Model	Founder (1a)	Joiner (1b)	Academia (1c)	Founder (2a)	Joiner (2b)	Academia (2c)	Founder (3a)	Joiner (3b)	Academia (3c)	Founder (4a)	Joiner (4b)	Academia (4c)
Foreign PhD	2.88***	1.95***	1.13	1.96***	1.70***	1.21						
	(0.39)	(0.19)	(0.12)	(0.24)	(0.16)	(0.15)						
Chinese							3.06***	1.83***	0.72	1.81***	1.61***	1.01
							(0.46)	(0.24)	(0.13)	(0.27)	(0.23)	(0.22)
Indian							4.45***	2.89***	1.41	2.77***	2.30***	1.23
							(1.08)	(0.69)	(0.42)	(0.71)	(0.54)	(0.32)
Western							1.64	1.64*	1.19	1.53	1.61*	1.07
							(0.50)	(0.34)	(0.24)	(0.50)	(0.34)	(0.27)
Other foreign							2.69***	1.88***	1.24	1.93***	1.64***	1.32*
							(0.52)	(0.23)	(0.16)	(0.35)	(0.20)	(0.19)
Risk tolerance				1.10***	1.02	0.97				1.09***	1.02	0.97
				(0.03)	(0.02)	(0.02)				(0.03)	(0.02)	(0.02)
Importance of autonomy				1.91***	1.33***	1.73***				1.91***	1.33***	1.73***
				(0.14)	(0.06)	(0.11)				(0.14)	(0.06)	(0.11)
Importance of income				0.85	0.94	0.63***				0.84	0.94	0.62***
				(0.07)	(0.06)	(0.05)				(0.07)	(0.06)	(0.05)
Interest in basic research				1.11*	1.26***	1.27***				1.11	1.25***	1.27***
				(0.06)	(0.05)	(0.08)				(0.06)	(0.05)	(0.08)
Interest in applied research				0.89	0.98	0.59***				0.89	0.98	0.59***
				(0.10)	(0.08)	(0.05)				(0.10)	(0.08)	(0.05)
Interest in commercialization				2.59***	1.51***	0.68***				2.58***	1.51***	0.68***
				(0.19)	(0.08)	(0.03)				(0.18)	(0.08)	(0.03)
Interest in management				1.33***	1.03	0.99				1.33***	1.03	0.99
				(0.08)	(0.03)	(0.04)				(0.07)	(0.03)	(0.04)

(continued)

Table 8.4 (continued)

| | Multinomial logit | | | | | | | | | | | |
| Method | | | | | | | | | | | | |
Dependent variable Model	Founder (1a)	Joiner (1b)	Academia (1c)	Founder (2a)	Joiner (2b)	Academia (2c)	Founder (3a)	Joiner (3b)	Academia (3c)	Founder (4a)	Joiner (4b)	Academia (4c)
National Research Council ranking of university dept.				1.14 (0.08)	0.97 (0.05)	1.00 (0.07)				1.14 (0.08)	0.97 (0.05)	1.00 (0.07)
Self-assessed ability				1.18*** (0.05)	1.04 (0.03)	1.04 (0.03)				1.18*** (0.05)	1.04 (0.03)	1.04 (0.03)
Lab entrepreneurial norms				1.19*** (0.07)	1.23*** (0.07)	1.03 (0.06)				1.19*** (0.07)	1.23*** (0.07)	1.03 (0.06)
Founder role model				1.45** (0.18)	0.90 (0.09)	0.94 (0.11)				1.46** (0.18)	0.91 (0.09)	0.94 (0.11)
Male	4.44*** (0.57)	2.20*** (0.17)	1.45*** (0.11)	4.10*** (0.59)	2.11*** (0.16)	1.36*** (0.12)	4.46*** (0.58)	2.21*** (0.17)	1.46*** (0.11)	4.11*** (0.60)	2.12*** (0.16)	1.37*** (0.12)
Married	1.12 (0.13)	1.11 (0.08)	1.12 (0.10)	1.13 (0.14)	1.07 (0.08)	0.95 (0.10)	1.12 (0.13)	1.11 (0.08)	1.11 (0.10)	1.12 (0.14)	1.06 (0.08)	0.95 (0.10)
Children	1.06 (0.21)	1.16 (0.20)	1.25 (0.24)	0.96 (0.21)	1.10 (0.20)	1.29 (0.29)	1.08 (0.21)	1.18 (0.20)	1.25 (0.24)	0.97 (0.21)	1.12 (0.20)	1.28 (0.28)
Field of study fixed effects	Y	Y	Y	Y	Y	Y	Y	Y	Y	Y	Y	Y
University fixed effects	Y	Y	Y	Y	Y	Y	Y	Y	Y	Y	Y	Y
Observations		5,707			5,707			5,707			5,707	
Log-likelihood		−6,801.28			−5,975.60			−6,788.24			−5,971.73	

Note: Coefficients reported as relative risk ratios. The dependent variable consists of four categories: *founder interest* ("definitely will" start own company), *joiner interest* (attracted to start-up employment but not likely to start own company), *academia interest* (not attracted to start-up employment but attracted to academic employment), and the reference group *established firm interest* (not attracted to start-up employment but attracted to established firm employment). In all specifications, native PhD students are the omitted category; coefficient estimates for foreign PhD students together and by nationality are relative to native PhD students. Robust standard errors clustered on university reported in parentheses; *** $p < 0.001$, ** $p < 0.01$, * $p < 0.05$.

teristics, field, and university. Foreign PhD students have an almost three times higher odds of expressing a founder intention than native PhD students relative to an established firm preference (Model 1a) and almost twice the odds of native PhD students to have a joiner preference (Model 1b). These differences persist even when ability and preferences for specific job characteristics are included, although including these variables does lead to a significant reduction in the estimated differences, indicating that they may partly explain why foreign students have stronger entrepreneurial interests (Model 2). Model 3 distinguishes between different nationalities and shows that Chinese and Indians are significantly more likely than native PhD students to have founder intentions (Model 3a) and joiner preferences (Model 3b). PhD students from Western countries do not differ from natives in their founder intentions and are only slightly more likely to have joiner preferences (Model 3b).

Taken together, foreign PhD students report stronger founder intentions as well as preferences for working in a start-up environment than do native PhD students. To some extent, these differences appear to reflect differences in individual characteristics such as risk tolerance, an interest in commercialization, and subjective ability. One potential explanation is that those individuals who come to the US as graduate students are less risk averse and of higher ability than the average person in their home country, resulting in higher levels of such characteristics among foreign PhD students. There may also be selection effects among natives prior to entering the PhD such that US citizens who have strong entrepreneurial interests choose to engage in entrepreneurship early on rather than pursuing a PhD. It is again notable that differences in entrepreneurial interests are more pronounced between natives and foreign PhD students from China and India than between natives and foreign PhD students from Western countries. The latter observation is consistent with recent findings by Hunt (2011) and Kahn et al. (2017), who find that Asian PhD students exhibit a greater interest in entrepreneurship than do European PhD students, who tend to show preferences similar to US natives.

8.3.3   Intentions to Stay

Before turning our attention to employment outcomes, it is important to consider whether foreign PhD students plan to stay in the US. Indeed, the extent to which foreign PhD students with founder intentions or joiner preferences intend to stay and work in the US has important implications for US immigration policies to retain STEM PhD students from US universities (Kahn and MacGarvie 2018).

To gain insights into foreign PhD students' intentions to stay in the US after graduation, we asked them during graduate school, "After completing your current PhD degree and any postdocs, which of the following best describes your future plans?," where the options were to stay in the US permanently, work in the US for a few years before returning to their home

Table 8.5a   **Foreign PhD students' intentions to stay in the US by nationality**

	Founder interest (n = 274)	Joiner interest (n = 682)	All foreign (n = 1,358)	China (n = 447)	India (n = 295)	Western (n = 175)
Stay in the US permanently	41.6%	42.8%	42.2%	17.4%	48.4%	37.9%
Work in US before returning home	37.6%	40.1%	37.2%	54.1%	35.8%	38.6%
Return home after graduation	17.8%	11.9%	15.3%	24.3%	8.8%	15.7%
Move to another country	0.7%	0.9%	0.8%	0.0%	2.3%	2.1%
Don't know yet	2.2%	4.4%	4.6%	4.2%	4.7%	5.7%

Table 8.5b   **Foreign PhD students' intentions to stay in the US by degree field**

	Life Sciences (n = 336)	Chemistry (n = 114)	Physics (n = 195)	Engineering (n = 463)	Comp. sci. (n = 260)
Stay in the US permanently	47.9%	36.8%	38.0%	38.9%	48.1%
Work in US before returning home	33.9%	43.9%	35.9%	39.1%	35.8%
Return home after graduation	13.7%	13.2%	16.4%	17.9%	11.9%
Move to another country	0.3%	1.8%	1.0%	0.7%	1.2%
Don't know yet	4.2%	4.4%	8.7%	3.5%	3.1%

country, return to their home country immediately after graduation, move to some other country, or don't know yet. Table 8.5a reports the share of foreign PhD students' future plans by founder and joiner interests, as well as by nationality. Roughly 80 percent of foreign PhD students with either founder or joiner preferences intend to work in the US at least temporarily after graduation, indicating that entrepreneurially oriented individuals would like to stay and work in the US after graduation. Across nationalities, approximately 70 percent to 80 percent of foreign PhD students have intentions of working in the US at least temporarily, although there are larger differences across nationality in the share who intend to stay in the US permanently and those who intend to eventually return to their home countries. Table 8.5b reports stay intentions by degree field, where again roughly 80 percent of foreign PhDs intend to stay in the US permanently or temporarily after graduation. These shares are consistent with observed aggregate stay rates for science and engineering doctorates in the US, although the observed stay rates by nationality vary (Finn 2012; Kahn and MacGarvie 2018).

Table 8.6a   **Current status of PhDs 1–5 years after graduation by nationality**

	Native (n = 3,250)	All foreign (n = 1,504)	China (n = 387)	India (n = 264)	Western (n = 148)
Founder	2.0%	1.9%	2.8%	1.1%	3.4%
Start-up employment	5.3%	3.6%	2.8%	4.9%	5.4%
Established firm employment	29.1%	38.6%	50.4%	48.5%	29.1%
Other industry	14.6%	11.6%	9.6%	9.9%	23.0%
Academia	27.5%	28.5%	20.9%	22.0%	21.6%
Postdoc	12.8%	9.8%	9.8%	6.8%	8.1%
Other nonprofit	8.8%	6.0%	3.6%	6.8%	9.5%

Table 8.6b   **Current status of PhDs 1–5 years after graduation by degree field**

	Life sciences (n = 1,565)		Chemistry (n = 549)		Physics (n = 678)		Engineering (n = 1,296)		Comp. sci. (n = 583)	
	Native	Foreign	Native	Foreign	Native	Foreign	Native	Foreign	Native	Foreign
Founder	1.2%	1.5%	0.7%	0.8%	0.8%	0.0%	4.4%	1.9%	2.2%	3.8%
Start-up employment	3.7%	2.7%	5.7%	4.7%	5.4%	3.6%	6.3%	3.5%	10.0%	4.5%
Established firm employment	14.7%	14.9%	34.0%	37.5%	29.7%	22.3%	40.7%	48.7%	51.9%	57.5%
Other industry	19.0%	15.8%	15.4%	11.7%	12.8%	16.1%	12.7%	9.7%	2.6%	7.7%
Academia	34.3%	36.9%	25.9%	31.3%	27.2%	35.8%	18.1%	24.5%	24.4%	19.8%
Postdoc	18.1%	17.3%	9.7%	7.8%	15.5%	17.6%	7.8%	6.4%	4.1%	3.8%
Other nonprofit	9.0%	11.0%	8.6%	6.3%	8.7%	4.7%	10.1%	5.2%	4.8%	2.9%

8.3.4 Postgraduation Entrepreneurial Outcomes: Founding or Joining Start-Ups

We now turn our attention to the ex-post career outcomes of PhDs after graduation. To obtain comprehensive data on employment outcomes, we supplemented the survey with hand-curated career profile data from LinkedIn and Google searches. Using both survey and online search data, we identified postgraduate outcomes for 83.6 percent of first-wave respondents. Tables 8.6a and 8.6b report on the current status of our respondents approximately one to five years after graduation. Specific employment outcomes are for those respondents working in the US only (82.6 percent of foreign PhDs); foreign PhDs who are working outside the US or whose current status was undetermined are not included. Note that 34.7 percent of PhDs in our sample have done a postdoc, with a slightly higher share of native PhDs (36.5 percent) compared to foreign PhDs (31.0 percent). However, individuals who transitioned to academia or industry after having done a postdoc are classified based on the current position in subsequent analyses so that the postdoc classification only refers to PhDs who were last observed as still being in a postdoc position.

To identify whether PhDs were employed in a start-up or an established firm, we rely on survey and LinkedIn data on employer age and number of employees at the time an individual started working at the company. We code start-ups (i.e., young and small) as any employer that is five years or younger and has 100 or fewer employees at the time the employee joined the company. All other employers are coded as "established" firms, including fast-growing entrepreneurial ventures that had more than 100 employees at the time the PhD joined the company (e.g., Uber) and corporate spinoffs that are typically young and large (e.g., Google Life Sciences spinoff Verily).

Approximately 65 percent of Chinese and Indian PhDs are employed in the US private sector, with the vast majority in industrial research and development (R&D) positions in established firms or start-ups. Just over 60 percent of Western PhDs are employed in the private sector, and over one-quarter of these are in other industry careers such as consulting, finance, and patent law. For comparison, roughly 50 percent of native PhDs are employed in the US private sector. Table 8.6b shows that the share of PhDs working in industry varies greatly by field—from 65 percent to 70 percent in engineering and computer science to 35 percent in the life sciences—but the shares of foreign and native PhDs within field are roughly comparable.

We now explore whether foreign and native PhDs differ in their propensity to become founders or to take positions in start-ups after graduation, focusing on the 2,318 PhDs who entered employment in US industrial R&D occupations between 2010 and 2016. To identify R&D occupations, we rely on survey responses regarding work activities (e.g., basic research, development) as well as LinkedIn data on job titles (e.g., research scientist, software engineer). We exclude from our sample individuals employed in consulting, finance, and non-R&D occupations. In addition, we exclude self-employed PhDs and retain only founders of technology companies who are the CEO, CTO, or CSO of their companies. In this industry-only sample, 4.6 percent of foreign PhDs were founders and 7.4 percent worked in start-ups, compared to 6.3 percent of native PhDs who were founders and 14.3 percent who worked in start-ups, indicating that foreign graduates were less likely to become founders and to join start-ups as employees.

To examine these differences more systematically, we estimate multinomial logistic regressions where the dependent variable is whether a PhD was a founder or a start-up employee versus an established firm employee (omitted category of the dependent variable). Table 8.7 shows the results, reporting relative risk ratios (values below 1 indicate a negative relationship). The baseline Model 1 shows that foreign PhDs are significantly less likely than natives to join a start-up and are also somewhat less likely to found their own firms (though sample size for founders is small, leading to imprecise estimates). These differences become even more pronounced once we control

Table 8.7   Multinomial logistic regressions of entrepreneurial outcomes

Method								
	Multinomial logit							
Dependent variable	Founder	Start-up employment	Founder	Start-up employment	Founder	Start-up employment	Founder	Start-up employment
Model	(1a)	(1b)	(2a)	(2b)	(3a)	(3b)	(4a)	(4b)
Foreign PhD	0.76	0.51***	0.59*	0.48***				
	(0.19)	(0.08)	(0.15)	(0.07)				
Chinese					0.67	0.31**	0.48*	0.28**
					(0.25)	(0.12)	(0.18)	(0.11)
Indian					0.34*	0.48	0.25***	0.44*
					(0.15)	(0.18)	(0.10)	(0.17)
Western					1.70	0.74	1.66	0.73
					(0.65)	(0.22)	(0.64)	(0.22)
Other foreign					0.58	0.57**	0.46*	0.54***
					(0.19)	(0.11)	(0.16)	(0.10)
Founder interest			7.81***	1.98**			8.35***	2.02**
			(2.30)	(0.44)			(2.47)	(0.44)
Joiner interest			1.51	1.67**			1.53	1.67***
			(0.47)	(0.27)			(0.48)	(0.26)
Male	1.45	1.04	1.08	0.94	1.44	1.06	1.07	0.96
	(0.37)	(0.14)	(0.30)	(0.14)	(0.37)	(0.15)	(0.30)	(0.14)
Married	1.23	1.11	1.16	1.09	1.27	1.09	1.20	1.08
	(0.24)	(0.16)	(0.24)	(0.16)	(0.25)	(0.16)	(0.24)	(0.16)
Children	1.19	0.87	1.24	0.86	1.20	0.86	1.25	0.84
	(0.26)	(0.20)	(0.28)	(0.20)	(0.26)	(0.21)	(0.28)	(0.21)
Constant	0.03***	0.14***	0.02***	0.09***	0.03***	0.14***	0.02***	0.09***
	(0.02)	(0.05)	(0.01)	(0.04)	(0.02)	(0.05)	(0.01)	(0.04)
Field of study fixed effects	Y	Y	Y	Y	Y	Y	Y	Y
Year started job fixed effects	Y	Y	Y	Y	Y	Y	Y	Y
Observations	2,422		2,422		2,422		2,422	
Log-likelihood	−1,282.42		−1,241.65		−1,278.67		−1,236.12	

Note: Coefficients reported as relative risk ratios relative to established firm employment. In all specifications, native PhDs are the omitted category; coefficient estimates for foreign PhDs together and by nationality are relative to native PhDs. Robust standard errors clustered on university reported in parentheses; *** $p < 0.001$, ** $p < 0.01$, * $p < 0.05$.

for foreign students' ex-ante entrepreneurial career preferences (Model 2). The seemingly inconsistent finding that foreign PhDs have a greater interest in entrepreneurship during graduate school but lower rates of participation in entrepreneurship after graduation is illustrated in figure 8.1. Further analyses distinguishing foreign nationalities show that these patterns are driven largely by Chinese and Indian PhDs, while Western PhDs show entrepreneurial outcomes similar to those of native PhDs.

8.4   Discussion

Foreign PhDs are a large share of the most specialized and advanced STEM workers in the US and may be a particularly important source of human capital for entrepreneurial firms. Although there has been considerable research comparing immigrants and natives with respect to founding activities, less is known about how foreign-born and natives might differ in their characteristics prior to engaging in entrepreneurship. Moreover, and of particular concern for the career paths of STEM PhDs, little attention has been paid to employment in start-ups. Using panel data from 5,660 US PhD graduates, we find that foreign PhD students are more interested in founding or joining start-ups than are natives prior to graduation but are significantly less likely to become founders or to enter start-up employment in their first industry job after graduation.

This apparent inconsistency between ex-ante entrepreneurial preferences and ex-post outcomes suggests that foreign PhDs may face certain constraints in their ability to participate in entrepreneurship that US citizens do not. For example, foreign PhDs with founder intentions may be required to seek employment in large, established firms rather than start their own companies in order to obtain temporary or permanent work visas.[6] As such, immigration policies that enable foreign PhDs to become entrepreneurs may facilitate higher rates of foreign PhDs starting potentially high-growth technology companies. Regarding working in a start-up, start-ups may be less likely to sponsor work visas than established firms, or PhDs may believe that established firms provide a better pathway to either temporary (e.g., H-1B) or permanent work visas (National Academies Press 2007; Roach and Skrentny 2019).

Our chapter also speaks to the results in chapter 2 in this volume by

6. We should note that for new graduates, the F-1 Optional Practical Training work authorization enables foreign doctorates to work on their own company for up to three years with the STEM extension. During this time, foreign founders could self-petition for a permanent resident visa through a National Interest Waiver, or they could be sponsored by the start-up for a temporary or permanent visa. The latter option is only available if the venture secures funding and establishes an independent board of directors with discretion over the founder's employment within the venture. Thus, while there are pathways for new graduates to become founders, they entail significant risk and commitment of resources and also may impair the venture's ability to secure funding or attract key employees.

A Entrepreneurial Preferences

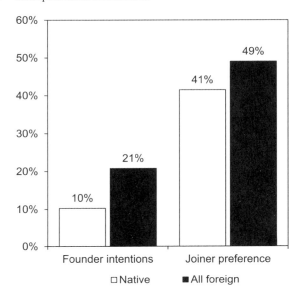

B Entrepreneurial Outcomes

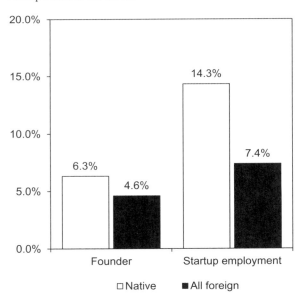

Fig. 8.1   Entrepreneurial preferences and outcomes of native and foreign PhDs

Ganguli and Gaulé. Both chapters, for example, consider career and location preferences of native and foreign PhDs; however, Ganguli and Gaulé focus primarily on differences between foreign and native PhDs with respect to academic career preferences, while we focus on differences in entrepreneurial career preferences. In addition, both chapters point to visa policies as a potential mechanism to explain differences between native and foreign PhDs. In their case, visa policies may shape career preferences, whereas our results suggest that visa policies may shape career outcomes, conditional on preferences. Future research can productively examine how students' beliefs regarding visa policies interact with preferences for locations and for different career paths in academia (such as research or teaching, as emphasized by Ganguli and Gaulé's research [chapter 2]) and in industry (such as established firms or start-ups, as emphasized here).

Although this research takes a novel approach toward understanding STEM PhD career paths by measuring both ex-ante entrepreneurial career preferences and ex-post employment outcomes, future work could fruitfully investigate more deeply the job search and transition processes. Our results suggest that such work should also be sensitive to potential differences between different groups of foreign workers—for example, those from China, India, or Western countries. These individuals may differ not only in their career preferences but also in the labor market constraints they face, such as country-specific quotas for work permits (Amuedo-Dorantes and Furtado 2018; Kahn and MacGarvie 2018).

While this chapter emphasizes the supply-side perspective of individual workers, the observed patterns may also have important implications for firms that often compete for highly skilled human capital. Both individuals' career preferences and institutional constraints are likely to shape the supply of labor to different types of firms and thus may affect firms' ability to grow and innovate. Of course, the patterns we observed will also be shaped by labor market demand. Although the demand side remained only implicit in our study, future work that integrates both supply- and demand-side perspectives may be particularly promising.

Given our limited understanding of the mechanisms underlying our results, we do not yet have a sufficient empirical basis for concrete policy recommendations. However, our results reinforce the notion that foreign science and engineering PhDs are an important potential source of STEM human capital (Stephan and Levin 2007; National Science Board 2014). At the same time, our findings that foreign graduates with entrepreneurial preferences appear to be more constrained from pursuing such careers suggest that the allocation of this human capital may not be optimal. As such, our study provides urgency to research and policy discussions related to retaining and supporting high-skilled foreign-born who come to the US for graduate school. Given the strong entrepreneurial interest of foreign PhDs, foreign graduates may also deserve closer attention in efforts to encourage the commercialization of university research through entrepreneurial spinouts.

References

Amuedo-Dorantes, C., and D. Furtado. 2019. "Settling for Academia? H-1B Visas and the Career Choices of International Students in the United States." *Journal of Human Resources* 53 (2): 401–29.

Astebro, T., J. Chen, and P. Thompson. 2011. "Stars and Misfits: Self-Employment and Labor Market Frictions." *Management Science* 57 (11): 1999–2017.

Baron, J. N., M. T. Hannan, and M. D. Burton. 2001. "Labor Pains: Change in Organizational Models and Employee Turnover in Young, High-Tech Firms." *American Journal of Sociology* 106 (4): 960–1012.

Bengtsson, O., and D. H. Hsu. 2015. "Ethnic Matching in the U.S. Venture Capital Market." *Journal of Business Venturing* 30:338–54.

Blume-Kohout, M. E. 2016. "Why Are Some Foreign-Born Workers More Entrepreneurial Than Others?" *Journal of Technology Transfer* 41 (6): 1327–53.

Borjas, G. J. 1986. "The Self-Employment Experience of Immigrants." *Journal of Human Resources* 21 (4): 485–506.

Camerer, C., and D. Lovallo. 1999. "Overconfidence and Excess Entry: An Experimental Approach." *American Economic Review* 89 (1): 306–18.

Charness, G., U. Gneezy, and A. Imas. 2013. "Experimental Methods: Eliciting Risk Preferences." *Journal of Economic Behavior and Organization* 87:43–51.

Fairlie, R. W. 2008. *Estimating the Contribution of Immigrant Business Owners to the U.S. Economy.* Washington, DC: US Small Business Administration, Office of Advocacy.

Fairlie, R. W., and M. Lofstrom. 2015. "Immigration and Entrepreneurship." CESIFO Working Paper no. 5298.

Finn, M. G. 2012. *Stay Rates of Foreign Doctorate Recipients from U.S. Universities.* Oak Ridge, TN: Oak Ridge Institute for Science and Education (ORISE).

Ganguli, I., and P. Gaulé. 2019. "Will the US Keep the Best and the Brightest (as Postdocs)? Career and Location Preferences of Foreign STEM PhDs." In *The Role of Immigrants and Foreign Students in US Science, Innovation, and Entrepreneurship,* edited by I. Ganguli, S. Kahn, and M. MacGarvie, 49–69. Chicago: University of Chicago Press.

Hart, D. M., and Z. J. Acs. 2011. "High-Tech Immigrant Entrepreneurship in the United States." *Economic Development Quarterly* 25 (2): 116–29.

Hunt, J. 2011. "Which Immigrants Are Most Innovative and Entrepreneurial? Distinctions by Entry Visa." *Journal of Labor Economics* 29 (3): 417–57.

Kahn, S., G. La Mattina, and M. J. MacGarvie. 2017. "'Misfits,' 'Stars,' and Immigrant Entrepreneurship." *Small Business Economics* 49 (3): 533–57.

Kahn, S., and M. MacGarvie. 2018. "The Impact of Permanent Residency Delays for STEM PhDs: Who Leaves and Why." NBER Working Paper no. 25175. Cambridge, MA: National Bureau of Economic Research.

Kerr, S. P., W. R. Kerr, and T. Xu. 2017. "Personality Traits of Entrepreneurs: A Review of Recent Literature." Harvard Business School Working Paper no. 18-047.

Kim, D. 2018. "Is There a Startup Wage Premium? Evidence from MIT Graduates." *Research Policy* 47 (3): 637–49.

Lazear, E. P. 2016. "Overconfidence and Occupational Choice." NBER Working Paper no. 21921. Cambridge, MA: National Bureau of Economic Research.

National Academies Press. 2007. *Rising above the Gathering Storm: Energizing and Employing America for a Brighter Economic Future*. Washington, DC: National Academies Press.

National Research Council. 2010. *A Data-Based Assessment of Research-Doctorate Programs in the United States*. Washington, DC: National Academies Press.

National Science Board. 2014. *Science and Engineering Indicators 2014*. Arlington, VA: National Science Foundation.

National Science Foundation. 2009. *Survey of Earned Doctorates*. Arlington, VA: National Science Foundation.

National Science Foundation. 2017. *Survey of Earned Doctorates*. Arlington, VA: National Science Foundation.

Oreopoulos, P. 2011. "Why Do Skilled Immigrants Struggle in the Labor Market? A Field Experiment with Thirteen Thousand Resumes." *American Economic Journal: Economic Policy* 3 (4): 148–71.

Roach, M. 2017. "Encouraging Entrepreneurship in University Labs: Research Activities, Research Outputs, and Early Doctorate Careers." *PLoS ONE* 12 (2): e0170444.

Roach, M., and H. Sauermann. 2015. "Founder or Joiner? The Role of Preferences and Context in Shaping Different Entrepreneurial Interests." *Management Science* 61 (9): 2160–84.

Roach, M., and H. Sauermann. 2018. "Who Joins a Startup? Ability, Preferences, and Entrepreneurial Human Capital." Working Paper.

Roach, M., and J. Skrentny. 2019. "Why Foreign STEM PhDs Are Unlikely to Work for US Technology Startups." *Proceedings of the National Academy of Sciences of the United States of America* 116 (34): 16805–10.

Sauermann, H. and M. Roach. 2013. "Increasing Web Survey Response Rates in Innovation Research: An Experimental Study of Static and Dynamic Contact Design Features." *Research Policy* 42 (1): 273–86.

Saxenian, A. 1994. *Regional Advantage: Culture and Competition in Silicon Valley and Route 128*. Cambridge, MA: Harvard University Press.

Saxenian, A. 2002. "Silicon Valley's New Immigrant High-Growth Entrepreneurs." *Economic Development Quarterly* 16 (1): 20–31.

Shane, S., E. A. Locke, and C. J. Collins. 2003. "Entrepreneurial Motivation." *Human Resource Management Review* 13:257–79.

Stephan, P., and S. Levin. 2007. *Foreign Scholars in US Science: Contributions and Costs*. Madison: University of Wisconsin Press.

Contributors

Stefano Breschi
Department of Management and
    Technology
Università L. Bocconi
Via Sarfatti 25
20136 Milan, Italy

J. David Brown
Center for Economic Studies
US Census Bureau
4600 Silver Hill Road
Washington, DC 20233

Kirk Doran
Department of Economics
University of Notre Dame
3048 Jenkins Nanovic Hall
Notre Dame, IN 46556

John S. Earle
Schar School of Policy and
    Government
George Mason University
3351 Fairfax Drive, MS 3B1
Arlington, VA 22201

Patrick Gaulé
Department of Economics
University of Bath
Claverton Down
Bath BA2 7AY United Kingdom

Ina Ganguli
Department of Economics
University of Massachusetts, Amherst
412 N. Pleasant Street
Amherst, MA 01002

Shulamit Kahn
Questrom School of Business
Boston University
595 Commonwealth Avenue
Boston, MA 02215

William R. Kerr
Harvard Business School
Rock Center 212
Soldiers Field
Boston, MA 02163

Sari Pekkala Kerr
Wellesley Centers for Women (WCW)
Wellesley College
106 Central Street
Wellesley, MA 02481

Gaurav Khanna
School of Global Policy and Strategy
University of California, San Diego
RBC #1416
9500 Gilman Dr. #0519
La Jolla, CA 92093-0519

Mee Jung Kim
Schar School of Policy and
    Government
George Mason University
3351 Fairfax Drive
Arlington, VA 22201

Kyung Min Lee
Schar School of Policy and
    Government
George Mason University
3351 Fairfax Drive
Arlington, VA 22201

Munseob Lee
School of Global Policy and Strategy
University of California, San Diego
RBC #1302
9500 Gilman Dr. #0519
La Jolla, CA 92093-0519

Francesco Lissoni
GREThA UMR CNRS 5113
Université de Bordeaux
avenue Léon Duguit
33608 Pessac cedex, France

Megan MacGarvie
Questrom School of Business
Boston University
595 Commonwealth Avenue
Boston, MA 02215

Anna Maria Mayda
School of Foreign Service and
    Department of Economics
Georgetown University
Washington, DC 20057

Ernest Miguelez
GREThA UMR CNRS 5113
Université de Bordeaux
avenue Léon Duguit
33608 Pessac, France

Francesc Ortega
Department of Economics
Queens College CUNY
300A Powdermaker Hall
65-30 Kissena Blvd.
Queens, New York 11367

Giovanni Peri
Department of Economics
University of California, Davis
One Shields Avenue
Davis, CA 95616

Michael Roach
Charles H. Dyson School of Applied
Economics and Management
Warren Hall
Cornell University
Ithaca, NY 14853-6201

Henry Sauermann
ESMT Berlin
Schlossplatz 1
10178 Berlin, Germany

Kevin Shih
Department of Economics
Queens College CUNY
65-30 Kissena Blvd.
Queens, NY 11367

John Skrentny
Department of Sociology 0533
University of California, San Diego
9500 Gilman Dr.
La Jolla, CA 92093-0533

Chad Sparber
Department of Economics
Colgate University
13 Oak Drive
Hamilton, NY 13346

Chungeun Yoon
Department of Economics
University of Notre Dame
3060 Jenkins Nanovic Hall
Notre Dame, IN 46556

Author Index

Subject Index